BALTIC
APPROACHES

TO MARK THE ENTRY INTO SERVICE OF
M.V. 'HEBRIDEAN SPIRIT'
THIS BOOK IS PRESENTED TO

George Wright Esq

WITH THE COMPLIMENTS OF
THE DIRECTORS OF ALTNAMARA SHIPPING PLC

AND COMES WITH ALL GOOD WISHES
FROM THE AUTHOR

ENDPAPERS Carta Marina *by Olaus Magnus, Italy, 1539*
(kind permission of Uppsala University Library)

BALTIC APPROACHES

PETER UNWIN

WITH MAPS AND ILLUSTRATIONS BY
ALAN WOOLLETT

MICHAEL RUSSELL

For Monica

The right of Peter Unwin to be identified
as the author of this work
has been asserted by him in accordance with
the Copyright, Designs and Patents Act, 1988

Extract from *Venusberg* by Anthony Powell
(Duckworth, 1932) reprinted by kind permission
of David Higham Associates Ltd, London

First published in Great Britain 1996
by Michael Russell (Publishing) Ltd
Wilby Hall, Wilby, Norwich NR16 2JP

Reprinted with corrections 2001

Typeset in Sabon by The Typesetting Bureau
Allen House, East Borough, Wimborne, Dorset
Printed and bound in Great Britain
by Biddles Ltd, Guildford and King's Lynn

Indexed by Andrew & Jackie Best

ISBN 0 85955 228 4

Contents

Acknowledgements

I am indebted to a number of people for help with different stages of the writing of this book.

First, the exploration phase. In Denmark Hugh Arbuthnott and Klaus Carsten Pedersen, in Sweden Mats Karlsson and Bo Jerlstrom, in Germany Hans Joachim and Ingrid Seeler, in Lithuania Michael Peart, in Latvia Richard Ralph and in Finland Nicholas Thorne all gave me welcome guidance.

Second, the writing. David Kirby, Michael Branch, Adrian Higham, Angela Lambert, Anthony Howard and Rudi Thorning-Petersen all worked their way carefully and helpfully through an over-long first draft. And Torsten Örn and Riivo Sinijarv gave me generous encouragement when I moved on to a second.

Bob O'Hara came to the rescue at a critical point and saved me from the twin problems of technological change and computer illiteracy. Alan Woollett drew the pictures and maps, and Fiona Greenwood provided the lettering for the latter. And Andrew Best and his wife Jackie sustained me throughout a final burst of re-writing, editing, indexing and delivery to the publisher.

I am grateful to them all.

Maps

Preface

This book is about the Baltic Sea and the countries that surround and define it. It is not an academic treatise nor a travelogue; still less is it a guidebook. Its aim is to provide one outsider's impressions of a neglected area: its geographical and historical significance, what it looks like, the way it is changing today and what its destiny may be tomorrow. These impressions spring from my own travel around the Baltic, from eclectic reading, and from a long period of brooding about the area which goes back to the years I spent in Copenhagen, looking out on the Sound that separates Denmark from Sweden and which at the same time links the Baltic to the oceans and the world.

I have two principal audiences in mind. First, all those who know little of the Baltic but sense uneasily that they should know more. Millions of Americans have Scandinavian, north German and Baltic roots. For the British it is not some distant sea: it is only 500 miles from London at its nearest and 1,300 at St Petersburg. You can fly from Heathrow to Stockholm, halfway up the Baltic, in not much more than two hours. Nor is the region unimportant. In war and peace it has mattered to Britain right through our history, as it has mattered to our continental neighbours. Now, as it comes together again after half a century of division, it matters again.

All the Baltic countries have their special significance. Four of them are members of the European Union, and four more hope to join. Three are members of NATO and, again, others wish to be. Germany, a Baltic power as well as a western and central European one, is by any measure central to almost everything Europe wants to achieve. In weakness or strength, Russia could yet spell danger in the eastern Baltic. The Scandinavian countries are important markets and at the same time emotionally and psychologically closer to the British than most other European countries. Poland and the three Baltic states still have the power to pluck at our heart-strings, and if Russia were to turn against any of them, each could become a flash-point of trouble.

Secondly, this book is intended for those who live around the Baltic, in Scandinavia, in Germany and in the countries further east. There are 50 million of them, many fluent in English to a degree which puts some of us native speakers to shame. They understand the region in a way the outsider cannot. But perhaps they know too much about the Baltic, or about their own bits of it, just as the outsider knows too little. They see the Baltic through nation-tinted spectacles – a Dane's eye view, or a German's; a Latvian's, or a Swede's. This book offers an overview of the whole region, and a stranger's overview at that.

To those who know the Baltic and to those who want to know more, I offer a portrait of an area that in the last few years has acquired a new vitality. The cold war divided it, breaking the human and commercial links that for a millennium made it a channel for contact between East and West. Now the cold war is history and the peoples of the Baltic are discovering a new togetherness. They share a desire for prosperity in the European Union or as close to it as they can get, internationally-guaranteed security, and national and personal freedom to be themselves. But they want something else, too: a clearer, more concrete expression of the things northern Europe has in common. Go there today and you find natural beauty, a sense of space that most of the rest of Europe has forgotten, and innumerable relics of a proud and sometimes bitter past. You encounter also a hubbub of talk about the revived meaning of the Baltic and of the factors that bind together the peoples who live around its shores. Northern Europe today is an exciting place, and an excited one. In the last decade it has come alive.

June 1996   PETER UNWIN

I

Approaches

In the 1980s I lived for three years in Copenhagen. My job was to
explain my own country to my hosts, and my hosts to the government
that paid me to represent Britain in Denmark. The first task was easy,
for the Danes had relatively few misapprehensions about Britain. The
second should have been no harder; Denmark seemed at first sight the
most transparent of national societies. But closer examination revealed
paradoxes as inexplicable as any I had encountered as a diplomat in
Hungary, Germany, the United States and Japan.

In search of enlightenment I turned to Denmark's long and complicated history. I learnt a lot about the attitudes I encountered in my
daily work in Copenhagen, but my search in its turn produced new
problems. At their heart was the existential question: how had Denmark persisted over the centuries as a nation state, exposed as she
was to all the winds that blew from Scandinavia on the one hand and
Germany on the other?

I found the answer in geography. Denmark lies exposed to Germany and Scandinavia, but at the same time she has always commanded the entrances to the Baltic. Shipping dues had made her kings
rich. Her strategic importance to NATO depended on her position as
the stopper in the neck of the Baltic bottle. The Baltic, I realised, held
the key to understanding Denmark.

Copenhagen is one of the most enchanting of European cities. A
day's exploration offers many delights: the serpentine spire of the
seventeenth-century stock exchange, a delectable quadrilateral of
royal palaces around a peaceful square, a fortress with its own
windmill behind grassy ramparts, and a great brick battleship of a
city hall. By the time I lived there the stretch of water that divides the
city in two had lost most of its shipping, but canals probe inwards
towards the city centre, ice-black in winter, sparkling when the sun
shines. They are a constant reminder that Copenhagen was a port
before it was a capital, and a port that owed its wealth to its position
at the narrow entrance to the Baltic.

Along the coast, the Baltic asserts itself again. Incoming aircraft make their final approach to Kastrup airport over the Sound that separates Denmark from Sweden, and every time I returned to Copenhagen I resolved to find a way to explore the desolate island of Saltholm which we overflew half a minute before we landed. North of the city the old road to Hamlet's castle at Helsingør follows the shore, unfolding changing views over the water. In the summer the coast road, the Strandvej, offers ready pleasures: sparkling sea, yacht harbours, a stand of trees silhouetted against the water. On a bitter winter's day its delights are less obvious: black with cold it might be, the ice heaped up in broken waves along the shore-line, but I could always rely on the view of the Sound from the Strandvej to lift the gloom of the northern winter.

Summer or winter, the Sound offers an unbroken procession of ships moving southwards into the Baltic and north towards the oceans. I watched them once from the terrace of a friend's house in Sletten, looking out towards the island of Ven which lies in the middle of the fairway. I tried half-heartedly to focus Bo's telescope on a south-bound container ship and asked idly where she was bound. 'Gdynia,' he said, with that crystal confidence that betrays deep ignorance, and then, yielding to truthfulness and humility, '. . . or Rostock, or Stockholm, or Leningrad.'

We speculated about Baltic cities, the obvious ones that Bo had mentioned and other, more fanciful or romantic destinations. The Polish city of Gdansk was backed by a thousand years of Danzig's Baltic commerce. Karlskrona was the Swedish Navy's main base, where rumour had it that Russian submarines still lurked among the skerries. Helsinki and Tallinn faced one another across the Gulf of Finland, the one open to any tourist who could afford Nordic prices, the other the inaccessible capital of a nation which seemed permanently extinguished within the Soviet Union. Visby, on the island of Gotland, was a port that commerce had forgotten, yet in its medieval glory days it had been a trading city as important as Bruges or London.

I knew that traders with the west had built a port at Hedeby near Schleswig in northern Germany before the time of the Vikings, and that the Vikings themselves had sailed up the Gulf of Finland bound for Novgorod and Constantinople. I had seen in Lübeck the city from which German merchants set out to trade with the east and in doing so created the Hanseatic League. The Teutonic Knights, who brought the Cross and slavery to the heathen Prussians, were shadowy figures. I had university memories of Gustavus Adolfus and Wallenstein fighting for control of the Baltic, and of Peter the Great opening his window on the world at St Petersburg. I vaguely remembered Hitler's attack on Poland when I was seven years of age and Stalin's extinction of the three Baltic republics when I was eight. I had adult memories of anti-Communist riots in Gdynia and strikes in Gdansk. And only yesterday, when I was living in Budapest in the early 1980s, the Poles took over where the Hungarians had left off twenty-five years earlier, generating a movement around an electrician in Gdansk's Lenin Shipyard that was to set Poland free.

When Bo and I discussed Baltic destinations I was in a curmudgeonly frame of mind. I had thirty years of diplomacy behind me, and Lord Salisbury's words rang like tinnitus in my ears:

> A diplomatist's glory is the most ephemeral of all forms of that transient reward . . . there is nothing dramatic in the success of a diplomatist. His victories are made up of a series of microscopic advantages; of a judicious suggestion here, of an opportune civility there, of a wise concession at one moment and a farsighted persistence at another; of sleepless tact, immovable calmness, and patience that no folly, no provocation, no blunders can shake.

I felt that, for the time being at least, I had had enough of human beings, and of the tact, calmness and patience people demanded of me. I wanted geography instead.

Places have always fascinated me, from Quebec on its rock to the Okavanga in Botswana; Dürnstein on the Danube to Blanchlands in the heart of the west Durham moors. I looked forward to the time when I would have an opportunity to turn away from people and back to places. And as I studied the names on Bo's map of the Baltic they assumed a particular attraction. They reminded me just how unfamiliar the region was to people like me. Danes such as Bo might fly to Stockholm or Helsinki about their Scandinavian affairs, but for Englishmen these were unlikely destinations. Western businessmen spent more time in Warsaw or Poznan than in Gdansk or Gdynia. Most of the German Baltic coast was a forbidding part of an unwelcoming Communist country, and Latvia, Lithuania and Estonia were no more than Soviet provinces. All these places were for their different reasons as unknown to tourists as they were to businessmen. Scandinavia cost holidaymakers too much. The southern Baltic offered them too little. The eastern Baltic was closed to all except the most persistent.

In any case the whole thrust of British interest over the centuries had pointed to the south and west. From the high Middle Ages onwards, France was for the British their principal rival, simultaneously the object of suspicion and admiration. The Grand Tour led through France to the Mediterranean and the warm south. The great maritime break-out took the British westwards to the Americas, south to the Cape and round the Cape to the Orient. Thomas Cook chose the Nile for his first foreign excursion, and sickly Englishwomen went to the Riviera or Amalfi to recuperate or die. Much later, when I launched myself into this book and was talking about the Baltic to anyone who would listen, a retired British diplomat told me that his father, a naval officer who knew the wider world, had taken him as a boy in the 1930s to play on a Baltic beach at Warnemünde. But the Baltic was no real holiday destination for the English before the war, any more than it now rivals the Mediterranean or Disneyland. The Baltic, I could see, might confront a British explorer with historical resonance, but with profound unfamiliarity as well.

Yet when I embarked upon the haphazard reading that underpins this book, I began to discover the inevitable exceptions to the rule. British visitors to the area added up over the centuries to a diverting group of people, whose traces we will uncover at various stages of our journey around northern Europe's inland sea. For instance, in 1153 Nicholas Breakspear was appointed papal legate in Scandinavia. His mission was a short one, for a year later he was recalled to Rome to become, as Adrian IV, the only English pope. Another twelfth-century English cleric, Henry of Uppsala, brought the Cross to Finland and remains to this day its patron saint.

Two centuries later an English nobleman, Henry of Derby, whom Chaucer took as the model for his Knight in *The Canterbury Tales* and who in time became King Henry IV, rode out with the Teutonic Knights to subjugate the Lithuanians. Three hundred years after that, Samuel Pepys briefly visited the Baltic at the very beginning of his career, and his diaries show that he kept his naval administrator's eye on its affairs ever afterwards. Nelson made his famous mark in the Baltic, when in 1801 he destroyed the Danish fleet at Copenhagen. An expeditionary force in which Arthur Wellesley, later Duke of Wellington, commanded a brigade, bombarded the city itself six years later, and throughout my time in Copenhagen I never ceased to be astonished by the magnanimity of Danish historical opinion about them both.

Other British admirals besides Nelson have sailed in Baltic waters. One was Sir Charles Napier, whose pathological timidity in the Gulf of Finland during the Crimean War so incensed his officers. Another was Sir Walter Cowan, a holder of the Victoria Cross who displayed equally pathological aggressiveness against Bolsheviks and Germans alike in the Baltic states' struggle for independence at the end of the First World War. The adventures in that same war of Arthur Ransome, as courageous as any naval fire-eater, sit oddly on the shoulders of the author of *Swallows and Amazons*.

And it was on a floundering Baltic steamer that Anthony Powell in his novel *Venusberg* staged one of the most effective seduction scenes in English literature. The young English journalist Lushington has been warned that the Baltic may be rough. He has not been warned of the wiles of an Austrian lady with a roving eye whom he encounters in the company of two lubricious Baltic barons. On deck after dinner, she asks him:

'Which of the two Counts shares your cabin?'
'Neither of them. I have a cabin to myself. On the port side.'
'Which side is that? I don't know what that means.'
'There. That side.'
'They say that the sea rolls less on that side. That is the best side to have a cabin.'
'Which side is yours?'
'It is on the other side. At the far end of the passage. But do you find that it rolls much on your side?'
'Not so much as you might think. I am lucky to have a cabin to myself. Don't you agree?'
'Does it roll there more than it is rolling now ? What do you think?'
'I don't know. I think it does.'
'It rolls very badly on the side I am on too.'
'You share a cabin with your friend, of course?'
'Yes.'
They did not speak for some minutes. The wind was increasing

and had begun to blow shrilly through the rigging, which creaked and strained insistently. The lights were still on in the smoke saloon. The two Counts would talk for some time yet. He said:

'Would you like to come down to my cabin and see if the boat rolls as much on that side as the side that you are on?'

'Yes,' she said. 'It would interest me to see.'

I stayed for another eighteen months in Copenhagen, and business and pleasure took me a little deeper into the Baltic. I flew to Bornholm, the exquisite little Danish island that lies far away to the east between the southern cape of Sweden and the Polish coast. At the last minute a British minister cancelled a long-planned visit to Denmark, leaving me with an unexpected four clear days. We drove across southern Sweden to Kalmar on the east coast, where the Scandinavian monarchies once made an ill-fated attempt at unity. From there we went on to discover another Baltic island, Öland, and came back by way of Karlskrona and the southern cape of Sweden. In Bornholm and in the enchanting manor houses of the old Danish provinces of Sweden, in Kalmar Castle and among Öland's early historical remains, we found evidence of the Baltic's eloquent past. I began to realise how much there was to discover in this northern world.

Beyond Bornholm and Öland lay other Baltic islands, like the Åland archipelago in the mouth of the Gulf of Bothnia, ancient Gotland and – most mysterious of all – the islands of Estonia. Beyond Kalmar were the cities of the eastern Baltic, deployed in a great swirling question mark from Stockholm through Turku and Helsinki to St Petersburg, and from there through Tallinn and Riga to Kaliningrad and on to Gdansk. To capture an impression of that Baltic world, which I imagined was unalterably set in amber, seemed challenge enough to get the most curmudgeonly of retired public servants out of bed in the morning.

I left Copenhagen at the end of 1988, and spent the next four years travelling to places that could not have been further from the Baltic. During that time Europe was miraculously transformed. I was in Kenya when the last Soviet troops left Afghanistan; and in Barbados when the Queen accepted an invitation to visit the Soviet Union. Between visits to India and Canada, I went back to Budapest for the reburial in state of Imre Nagy, finding a society whose every attitude had changed in the short years since I had lived there. I was in Rome for an agricultural conference when television suddenly showed us ecstatic crowds dancing on the Berlin wall. Change became irreversible. Soviet troops began to withdraw from positions in central Europe which they had occupied for almost two generations. Germany was reunited. Even within the Soviet Union, Moscow's grip weakened, until Communism collapsed and the Union itself disintegrated.

The Baltic world was engulfed in this avalanche of change. With reunification the Federal Republic of Germany tripled her coastline overnight and assumed responsibility for the wilderness that Communism left behind in the east German Baltic ports. Poland achieved real freedom for the first time since 1939. The failed coup in Moscow in 1991 gave Estonia, Latvia and Lithuania the chance to recover the independence they had lost in 1940. With Communism gone there was no longer an obligation to commemorate Lenin's name, and Leningrad became St Petersburg again.

North of the Baltic and in Denmark, change was less dramatic but as fundamental. In 1990 I asked a Danish minister who was visiting London why Danish policy towards Europe was so much more open than it had been when, only two years earlier, it had been my job to tell London where it was heading. 'The prospect of German reunification' was his answer; and the need to help anchor Germany in the old institutions was his meaning. By the end of that year Denmark and Scandinavia were reaching out to the Baltic republics and to Poland, with a political boldness unthinkable a year earlier.

At the same time the collapse of the Soviet Union meant for Finland the loss of markets on her doorstep. She suddenly found herself looking economic hardship in the eye. So did Sweden, where the Scandinavian economic and social model was overreaching itself just as Communism had done, so much more spectacularly, across the water. But with change in the Soviet Union, Finland and Sweden obtained almost overnight a freedom of diplomatic manoeuvre that Moscow, with its insistence on every jot and tittle of their neutrality throughout the cold war, had denied them. The days of making do on the fringes of the European Community were over. They found themselves free to open the bargaining for full membership.

So the countries of the Baltic awoke to the knock of opportunity. They were free at home, free to commit themselves in Europe, and free to build new links with one another. The confrontation that had kept the area divided for half a century faded away. Analysts turned their backs on security problems and military threats and instead wrote about trade, investment and co-operation. I revised the lectures I used to offer to unwary audiences, to talk no longer about life in Denmark or the adventures of the English in the north, but about change in the Baltic, now a sea of hope.

Yet not all the Baltic's difficulties had miraculously faded away. Change elsewhere in Europe threw a harsher light upon its remaining problems. In central Europe, Soviet power withdrew. Garrisons removed themselves from Germany, Hungary, Poland and Czechoslovakia. In northern Europe they remained where they had always been, on the Finnish frontier, around St Petersburg and in Kaliningrad. It took protracted negotiation to extricate them from Estonia and Latvia in 1994, and Russian nationalists continued to talk about both, and about Finland and Lithuania, as Russia's 'near abroad'.

It was true that the eastern Baltic was not like Bosnia or Kosovo or the southern republics of what had been the Soviet Union. But it was one of the few places on earth where a bruised and humiliated Russia confronted the old West face to face. The Russian military looked out from St Petersburg and Kaliningrad onto a sea which ten years earlier they had dominated. Russians saw western ideas and values advancing towards St Petersburg, and those with long memories noted that Germany, the historic enemy, was once again the most powerful force in the north. They had more pressing problems: with the economy, the mafia and the Moslem republics. But concern for the eastern Baltic went far back in Russian history, deep into the Russian subconscious. There was a chance, if only an outside chance, of old-fashioned trouble in the north. I asked myself whether the Baltic was perhaps not so much a sea of hope as a flash-point.

It was clear that I would have to think again about this book. I had imagined myself travelling through stable societies, describing old towns and lonely islands and fishing ports, but the newspapers trumpeted elections, demonstrations, storms in parliament, and the expulsion of Russian troops from training grounds they had ravaged for four decades. I had to add today's politics and economics to my excursions into history and society in order to give some account of peoples caught up in the fear of change and the excitement of new beginnings.

I set off on a series of Baltic journeys: through Poland and Germany in 1992; around the Nordic coastline in 1993; to the eastern

Baltic and back to Denmark in 1994. Poland was vibrant with uncovenanted opportunity; eastern Germany was stupefied by change,
waiting for knights on white chargers to ride to the rescue. A year
later Swedes and Finns could talk of nothing else but their changing circumstances and their ambitions to join the European Community. In 1994 the Baltic states were still euphoric, celebrating a
sublime Monday morning, but growing warier. And Denmark, which
I thought I knew well and had believed unchanging, had altered too,
bolder by far than I remembered her, and embracing new commitments in the Baltic.

Back home, I reflected on what I had seen. I remembered Gdansk
crouching like an old lion by the water. The ships would still be filing
past Bo's telescope in the blue light of the Sound. My photographs of
Estonian folk dancers showed them in their thousands, expressing
their sense of nationhood in movement and music. I recalled the
magical seascapes of the Åland islands in a light as clear as gin, and a
Gotland sunset over the towers and roofs of Visby. At home I faced
another kind of reality: four years of press cuttings and tottering piles
of books from the London Library. Events still crowded in upon my
story. There were referenda in Finland, Sweden and Norway, news of
fresh horrors and fresh hopes from St Petersburg. It was clear that the
cities, the islands and the people of the Baltic would not be contained
in amber. The societies which face onto it were committed to change.
So the time had come to commit my enterprise to paper. These pages
record my impressions of a changing Baltic and of its recovered importance in a changing world.

2

The Baltic

One Midsummer's eve I stood at midnight at the very tip of the Skaw, the northernmost point of Denmark. A mile-long ribbon of sand ran away behind me to the mainland, sombre in the twilight. There glimmered the lights of Skagen, supplemented on Midsummer's eve by bonfires on the beach. Beyond Skagen, Jutland stretched away to the south, Germany and the Continent. On the other three sides, below the horizon, lay the cape of Norway and the long flank of southern Sweden. Beyond them Scandinavia extends all the way to the North Cape, 800 miles distant, as far away to the north as Corsica to the south.

The unseen embrace of the Norwegian mountains and the Swedish coast gives Skagen a microclimate of its own. The combination of brilliant light, sea, sand and fishing port attracts holidaymakers to picnic among the dunes and watch the fishing fleet come home. A century ago it summoned a group of Nordic painters such as P. S. Krøyer and Michael Ancher whose work distils a particular northern spirit. So Skagen represents at least the Scandinavian part of Baltic life.

The sea at the Skaw that night was flat calm and almost luminous. A ripple of water from the west, from the Skagerrak, the North Sea and the ocean, fluttered softly across the point of sand. Another ripple came from the east, the Kattegat and the Baltic. The ripples met, crossed, and for a moment printed a herring-bone pattern on the sand. The movement, the sibilant whisper of sea over sand, reminded me that I stood at the meeting of the waters, the very entrance to the Baltic.

For most of recorded history, ships have felt their way into the Baltic round the Skaw. Approaching it from the west they are on a dangerous lee shore, with no land this side of Scotland to protect them from westerly gales. Beyond it they enter 150 miles of narrow and crowded waters. Technically these constitute the Baltic approaches and not the sea itself; but they are an essential preliminary

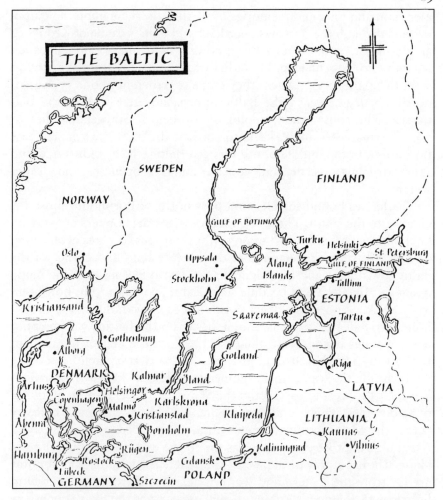

to the Mediterranean of northern Europe. The Kattegat comes first: 120 miles by 80, punctuated by no more than scattered islands. But across the southern end of the Kattegat you run up against Sjaelland, the chief of the Danish islands, which all but stops the narrow neck which forms the entrance to the Baltic.

You can pass to the west of Sjaelland, feeling your way through the Great Belt and a tangle of Danish islands before you turn east into the Baltic proper. In the summer you are among yachts all the way, in some of the sweetest sailing grounds in the world. Alternatively, you can bear away to the east when you reach Sjaelland. This is the classic, direct route into the heart of northern Europe, fraught with merchant shipping and memories of warlike descents upon the Baltic. It leads through the narrows guarded by Hamlet's castle of Kronborg at Helsingør, and on into the gradually widening Sound between Malmö and Copenhagen. On either of these routes you have land in sight throughout. But where they come together, at about 55 degrees north, 13 degrees east, the Baltic approaches give way to the Baltic sea. The southernmost point of Sweden at Smygehamn lies to port, Germany's Cape Arkona to starboard. And once you are past Bornholm, in the middle of the western Baltic, the Scandinavian and southern coasts recede, and you are entering open sea and deeper waters.

The ferries bound for Helsinki pass north of Bornholm, those for Gdansk to the south. These are not cross-channel hoppers but stately, liner-sized ships embarked upon serious voyages. It takes a very long day to sail from Travemünde at the bottom left hand corner of the Baltic to Gdansk, and two nights and a day to Helsinki. As the Baltic opens out the distances become significant: 200 miles from Bornholm to Gdansk, almost 400 from Bornholm to Stockholm. Even Stockholm, at 18 degrees east, is only halfway up the Baltic. St Petersburg lies 400 miles beyond it to the east; the northern end of the Gulf of Bothnia even further distant, just short of the Arctic Circle.

So the Baltic is not an insignificant little sea. It pierces northern Europe from west to east. From the Skaw to St Petersburg is a voyage of 1,000 miles. This is a distance which would only take you halfway across the Mediterranean: from Gibraltar to Sicily, or from Sicily to Istanbul. Yet St Petersburg lies as far to the east as Istanbul, and the Skaw is indisputably of the west. And whereas Istanbul and Gibraltar are far from the eastern and western hearts of Europe, St Petersburg lies close to the north Russian heartland, just as the Skaw opens the way to industrial western Europe around the North Sea. So for much of every year the Baltic has over the centuries carried ships and ideas, raw materials and manufactured goods from west to east and east to west as effectively and with quite as much significance for European history as the Mediterranean, and in half the sailing time.

Fourteen thousand years ago the ice cap covered northern Europe as far south as the German and Polish coastlines. Over the next 5,000 years it receded northwards, leaving a vast freshwater lake roughly where the Baltic lies today. A breach opened between the North Sea and the Baltic 6,500 years ago. Land rise and fall, changes in sea level, waves, wind and sediment have completed the geographical picture we see today: a relatively shallow sea, more or less tideless, almost salt-free.

The Baltic is unquestionably a northern sea. Stockholm lies just short of 60 degrees north. Oslo, St Petersburg and Helsinki are the only other major cities to be found at such high latitudes anywhere on the globe: 600 miles further north than London and 1,800 miles further than New York. The last climatic consequences of the Gulf Stream bring some relief even to the eastern Baltic, but summers are short; winters dark and cold. Snow and ice come in November or December and linger until March, and before the age of steam and ice-breakers, ice closed much of the eastern Baltic to shipping for four months in the year.

The Baltic has its gentle coasts and its harsher ones. Denmark is a low-lying country that has grown over the centuries from the sand bars that almost close the mouth of the Baltic. The German coast is flat, all the way from Schleswig to the point where the long offshore island of Usedom reaches the Polish frontier. The Polish coast, the shore of Kaliningrad, and the beaches of the Lithuanian and Latvian coasts as they march northward to the Estonian border are likewise flat. Their monotony is broken not by cliffs or distant mountains, but by long offshore spits of fine sand and delicate vegetation, and by the lagoons that form behind them. These are gentle, sandy coasts, along which medieval navigators depended on church spires for landmarks. Inland the soil is relatively fertile, with a predominance of wheat giving way to woods and pasture as one moves eastwards.

The true north begins in Estonia: the fields stonier, the coast more rugged. St Petersburg famously stands on marshland, but beyond it the coast of Finland is iron-bound and the land behind it unforgiving. Nature relents a little in the Gulf of Bothnia, where you again find sandy beaches and patches of poor pasture. But most of the Swedish coast is rocky, replete with narrow inlets, skerries and navigational hazards, and so is most of the coast of southern Norway where it curls around the mouth of the Baltic at Skagen.

Most of the great rivers of central Europe north of the Harz mountains and the Carpathians drain into this inland sea. The Elbe is the one exception, passing within forty miles of Lübeck on its way to Hamburg and the North Sea. The Oder and its two Neisses flow northwards from Bohemia to Szczecin. The Vistula washes the walls of Krakow and Warsaw on its way to the Bay of Gdansk. Further east

are the Neman and the Dvina and the Neva, between them draining
much of European Russia. Together, these rivers and the Baltic have
shaped the geography, history and trade of northern Europe. Today
they bring to its enclosed, tideless waters the industrial pollution that
is the biggest threat to the long-term future of the Baltic.

A major part of the history of the Baltic countries is the story of how
their peoples came to terms with the problems of land and climate.
The Scandinavians needed salt from Lüneburg to cure the fish that
sustained them through the winter. Åland seamen brought firewood
to Stockholm in all weathers in open boats. Polish farm labourers still
travel down the Baltic every summer for the money they can earn
in the short Danish harvest. The Swedish inheritance of religion,
discipline and self-improvement owes much to climatic influences,
just as the heathen faiths which persisted for so long in Estonia and
Latvia found their symbolism and their gods in the dark northern
forests.

   Baltic navies have always fought their campaigns in the summer
months, and when Nelson attacked the Danes at Copenhagen in
April 1801 he was taking advantage of the season to engage one
hostile fleet at a time: with their ships still locked in the ice of the Gulf
of Finland the Russians could do nothing to help their Danish allies.
Traditionally, northern armies have preferred to do their fighting in
winter, when marshes and woodland freeze underfoot and even
heavily-armed soldiers can take to the ice. In the seventeenth century
Swedish armies crossed it on foot to attack Copenhagen. During the
Finnish-Russian war of 1939–40 – the Winter War – Finnish troops
slipped silently through the birch woods on their skis to attack the
Russian columns. At the end, when things turned against the Finns, it
was the Russians who profited from the cold, sending tanks and
artillery across the sea ice to outflank the defences of Viipuri. And for
the defenders of Leningrad a year later cold was as much a part of the
horror of the siege as starvation, disease or German bombardment.

   Throughout Baltic history, ice-free ports or ports that freeze late
have had a special value. Peter the Great's window on the Baltic at St
Petersburg was opaque with frost for nearly half the year. For him
and for his successors a major part of the importance of the Baltic
provinces was the possession of ports like Liepaja and Ventspils
which froze late, or in kinder years not at all. Today the Finns deploy
powerful, 8,000-tonne ice-breakers, orange-painted, slab-sided, as

tall as two houses. They can cut through ice five metres thick, and in the worst of winters they keep channels open for the ferries between Helsinki, Turku, the Åland islands and Stockholm. But ice remains a factor in Baltic calculations – maritime, commercial and political.

At the beginning of this chapter we stood at the point at the Skaw where the Baltic meets the open sea. But there are other approaches, for it is not just the Danes and traders from the west who have poured their energies into the Baltic. Every northern nation has a different view of the sea which binds them together. As Oliver Warner put it in his book *The Sea and the Sword* (1965):

> The enchanting Danes, who once ruled Norway, the serious Swedes, the resilient Finns, the all-enduring Russians, the unpredictable Poles, the obedient Germans, look out upon the Baltic from their various windows and points of vantage.

The Germans, for example, think that the history of the Baltic starts at Lübeck, where German merchants and the Holy Roman Empire first broke into what is still to them the *Ostsee,* the eastern sea. They can claim that their traders and warriors have done more than most to shape the story of the Baltic: for centuries Germans for all practical purposes ruled its southern and eastern shores. But the Poles have another view: the Vistula is their river, whose very Polishness demands that it flow untroubled by foreigners to the sea, and the struggle to control its estuary is the essence of their endlessly troubled relationship with the Germans. The Swedes, at the heart of the Baltic, see it as their sea: Gustavus Adolfus fought all over Germany to keep the Habsburg monarchy out. For Peter the Great, the sea was his way to the west, and he sacrificed more lives to build St Petersburg than were lost in the siege of Leningrad. And for the Finns and the peoples of the three smaller Baltic states, the sea has an altogether more fundamental significance: this is where they live and where, despite diasporas in North America and Australia, they mean to die.

A few breathless paragraphs of history will help to explain how all these Baltic nations arrived at 'a local habitation and a name'. By global standards their stories start relatively recently. You can find traces of the Stone Age in northern Poland and Germany, but evidence of settlement further north does not go back much further than 10,000 years. The origins of agriculture go back 6,000 years; of

manufacture and of artistic creation 4,000; and the traces of all these
things remain fragmentary. But towards the end of the pre-Christian
era, the Mediterranean world began to discover the Baltic. In 330 BC
the Greek geographer, Pytheas of Marseilles, reached Norway. He
wrote of the short summer nights and of Ultima Thule, a land at
whose shores the seawater itself thickened 'like a jellyfish' and which
marked the northern limit of the world. And by the first century of
the Christian era Pliny the Elder was using names we recognise, writing of islands in the north called Nerigon and Scatinavia.

A few years later Tacitus described the tribes of Germany in a tortured mixture of contempt and admiration. His descriptions naturally
become sketchier as he moves north and east, but he identifies the
main Baltic tribes: the Goths on the lower Vistula, the Rugii and the
Lemovii of northern Germany, and the Cimbri, whom the Romans
had driven into Jutland from the lower Rhine. He tells us that the
Suiones of southern Sweden used boats with a prow at each end, which
sound very like the forerunners of Viking ships. He refers to the Aestii,
who must have been Balts, who share many customs with the Suiones
but whose language he describes as 'more like the British'. He men-
tions also Baltic amber, which the natives neglected, 'unheeded like any
other refuse of the sea, until Roman luxury made its reputation'. On
the Fenni, living in today's Estonia, he waxes eloquent. Their appearance is repulsive, their savagery astonishing, their poverty disgusting;
they live not by husbandry but by hunting, in which the women join on
equal terms; but they have peace of mind:

> Unafraid of anything that man or god can do to them, they have
> reached a state that few human beings can attain: for these men
> are so well content that they do not even need to pray for any-
> thing.

For the classical world these northern barbarians would have
remained mere purveyors of amber and exotic curiosities had they
stayed where they belonged. Instead, some embarked on the fighting
migrations which eventually devastated the waning civilisations of the
Mediterranean. Gibbon describes the Goths' migration from the Baltic
to the shores of the Black Sea. From there they launched a series of
marauding expeditions in which they sacked most of the Greek and
Roman cities of the Black Sea and the eastern Mediterranean. They
were driven back eventually, but they remained a dynamic force,
lurking on the edge of the Empire. Repeatedly they penetrated the

frontier defences, invading the provinces and eventually Italy. The Goths were to remain a force with which the legions had to contend, unsuccessfully more often than not, and when the legions had departed the Goths haunted the uneasy dreams even of the great city of Constantinople.

The Vandals were neighbours of the Goths. In the fifth century they marched against the western Empire. They stormed the Rhine and invaded Gaul, Spain and Africa. They besieged Hippo, where St Augustine lay dying; and nine years later they conquered Carthage. Like the Goths in the east, they took to the sea, becoming the terror of the declining cities of the western Mediterranean. In AD 455 they sacked Rome itself, and in another quarter of a century the western Empire was all over, with the banishment of its last ruler, Augustulus, to a villa in Campania. Hard men from the Baltic had destroyed the soft living of the south.

Others came to fill the northern spaces that the Goths and Vandals had abandoned and many of them went raiding in their turn. About the time of the fall of Rome, Angles, Saxons and Jutes invaded Britain. Like the Goths and Vandals, they adopted something of the culture and civilisation that they laid waste and, in time, Christianity. So it was Anglo-Saxon monks who raised the alarm when the next wave of northern raiders, the Vikings, fell upon Lindisfarne in AD 793. Little sea-borne armies followed: 'ruthless, wrathful, foreign, purely pagan people', as an Irish monk called them, descending on the coasts of Ireland, England and northern France.

The Viking era lasted for 300 years. In the course of it, strong and eventually Christian kingdoms emerged around the Baltic, linked with Norse kingdoms in the British Isles, Normandy and Sicily. The Baltic and its eastern rivers provided Swedish adventurers with a way to the east and into the heart of Russia. There they founded the first Russian kingdom and pushed southwards to reach the awe-inspiring grandeurs of Constantinople. As it expanded, the Baltic's trade became a significant factor in the calculations of soldiers and missionaries, merchants and statesmen.

In the tenth century, the Poles came to challenge Scandinavian power. In AD 966 King Mieszko I was baptised and set up a recognisable Polish state at the mouth of the Oder. But soon German expansion eastwards began. It started with groups of migrants cultivating virgin land across northern Germany and into Pomerania, but over the next

200 years other, more sophisticated forces became involved: Hansa merchants, episcopal soul-savers and knightly crusaders.

Lübeck had its beginnings in shipping Lüneburg salt to the Baltic herring fisheries. Cloth, weapons and beer from the cities of the Rhineland and the Low Countries followed. In return Lübeck's ships brought timber and tallow, tar, furs and amber from the east. In 1160 Lübeck merchants trading with Gotland formed an association which reflected the importance of the eastern trade and their desire to monopolise it. This association developed into the Hanseatic League, with outposts as far afield as Novgorod in Russia, Bergen in western Norway and the Steelyard in London. Regularly challenged, the Hansa nevertheless remained the strongest commercial force in the Baltic and a major political factor there until the end of the middle ages. It embraced non-German cities, but its predominant weight and voice was German.

German churchmen and knights followed. In 1201 a little fleet led by Bishop Albrecht of Bremen arrived at Riga. Albrecht established a bishopric and the knights who accompanied him went crusading against the pagan Livs and Latvians. German merchants followed and set up in business. The country around Riga became a province of the Holy Roman Empire; the knights became the Livonian Order. A little later, other German crusaders arrived in the eastern Baltic. In 1225 the Teutonic Knights established themselves in northern Poland and drove northward into pagan Prussia. The Livonian Order rode south, and the two orders joined hands. In time they established an essentially German spiritual and temporal presence, encroaching on the Kingdom of Poland, campaigning against the Grand Duchy of Lithuania, buying Tallinn from the Danes, and subjugating or exterminating the pagan Baltic peoples. In 1308 they captured Danzig and themselves became members of the Hanseatic League. The mutually supportive structure of German trade, church and power in the eastern Baltic was complete.

As always, a counter-force emerged. The Lithuanians had never been decisively defeated by the Teutonic Knights. They were the last major heathen people in Europe, but in 1386 they concluded an alliance with the Poles. They converted to Christianity and their ruler married the infant queen of Poland. In 1410 Poles and Lithuanians set out together to do battle with the German knights at Tannenberg.

Fought five years before Agincourt, Tannenberg was one of the decisive battles of the Middle Ages, and it crippled for good the aggressive power of the Teutonic Order. The knights clung to their possessions, however, and when a century later the Reformation came to northern Europe the Order was still in place all the way from Danzig to Tallinn. Its officers and knights embraced Protestantism, and built a purely temporal authority on the threefold base of their military prowess, German settlement and Baltic trade. Over the years their authority developed into the rule of the Baltic barons in what are today Latvia and Estonia; and into a temporal principality which was to become Prussia, and which in turn was to play a critical part in the growth of the German Empire.

Throughout the Middle Ages the Danish and Swedish kings competed for supremacy in the western Baltic. Denmark ruled Norway; Sweden ruled Finland; and they repeatedly went to war with one another. Then, in 1397, they tried co-operation instead, creating by the Treaty of Kalmar a Union which should, if it had been respected and supported, have given mastery of the Baltic to a united Scandinavia. But the Union never achieved its founders' intentions, and limped its ineffectual way through the history of the next 100 years, while Sweden and Denmark returned to their old struggle for preeminence. By the time of the Reformation, which they embraced with Scandinavian calm, each had created strong Renaissance monarchies which remained locked in rivalry.

Christian IV, king of Denmark in the first decades of the seventeenth century, was the *beau idéal* of Renaissance monarchy. He built and beautified cities all over Denmark, throughout Denmark's provinces in southern Sweden, and in Norway. He fought bravely, in land battles and at sea. He gave his sister in marriage to James VI of Scotland. He tried to lead the German Protestant princes against the Counter-Reformation. But he bankrupted his country, and the Swedes seized pre-eminence in Scandinavia.

The Swedes had Spartan virtues, and Swedish power was the wonder of the seventeenth century. From 1630, when Gustavus Adolfus landed in Germany to lead the Protestant fight against the Habsburgs, to 1718, when Charles XII was killed in a pointless siege of a Norwegian fortress, Sweden raged around the countries of the north. She was rarely at peace, in turn fighting the Habsburgs, German princes, the Danes, Poland and Russia. But she lacked the resources of greater powers, and after Charles XII's death she was forced onto the defensive, anxiously watching the growth of Russia and Prussia.

The Polish-Lithuanian Commonwealth was also caught between these emerging powers. In their time the Poles and Lithuanians had barred the way to the west against Mongols, Tartars and Russians in turn, but the Swedish wars fatally weakened them, and now Peter the Great, determined to fight his way into the Baltic world, threatened their very existence. In 1703 he founded St Petersburg. In the following year he took Narva on the Gulf of Finland from the Swedes, and in 1721 he occupied the Baltic provinces, today's Estonia and Latvia. The Poles and Lithuanians would once have met force with force. Now, like the Swedes, they could only watch.

As Russia grew stronger, so also did Prussia. During the course of the eighteenth century, the Hohenzollerns built the kingdom of Prussia on foundations laid by the principality of Brandenburg and the Knights beyond the Vistula. They turned what had been the poorest of the German states into a new centre of power. It gradually became clear that only Prussia had the strength to challenge Russia in the Baltic, and that in time she would have to. At first Poland separated the two, but three partitions in twenty years led to her extinction. Russia and Prussia seemed doomed to fight one another for domination of the Baltic.

But with the nineteenth century came Napoleon, and his moral and military force imposed itself upon the Baltic powers. They formed the Confederacy of the North, whose essential purpose was to conciliate France by keeping the British out of their ports. But in April 1801 Nelson descended on Copenhagen and sank the Danish fleet. Five years later, Prussia turned unsuccessfully against France. Napoleon marched east, fought the Russians and Prussians at Eylau and Friedland and imposed terms of peace on them at Tilsit. He took Sweden's last remaining possessions in Germany and brought hope to Poland. For a short historical moment Napoleon came as close to uniting the Baltic as any man ever did.

The French empire was overstretched. British ships and agents and their subsidies were at work. In Berlin, Stein began to introduce the reforms which were to turn Prussia into a modern secular state, capable of inspiring resistance to Napoleon. Yet the Emperor embarked on his last great northern adventure. He assembled his troops on the Vistula, and in May 1812 crossed the Neman. By the autumn he reached Moscow, but in October the retreat began. The Grande Armée came back as a starving rabble, abandoned by its leader. What was left of French military might was harried away from the Baltic down the long road that was to lead to Waterloo.

In the treaties which tidied up the consequences of Napoleon's defeat, Sweden lost her last possessions in Germany, and Denmark ceded Norway to Sweden. Russia's suzerainty over Poland was confirmed and Prussia strengthened her position still further. Order had been restored in the Baltic, and most of the excitements of history departed from it. For many of the countries of the north the nineteenth century tells a quiet story of economic and social progress out of the glare of the world's political limelight.

But the Baltic saw its own political dramas. In 1831 the Russians put down a gallant and hopeless Polish uprising. Eighteen years later came the year of revolutions, with scattered troubles all over the north. The Crimean War brought convulsions 1,000 miles away from its main battlefields, when a combined British and French fleet in the Gulf of Finland bombarded Russian coastal fortifications, threatening, had the war dragged on, to attack St Petersburg itself. Seven years later the Poles again tried to throw off Russian rule, again unsuccessfully. In 1864 Denmark, the first victim of Bismarck's drive to create a powerful Germany, lost Schleswig-Holstein to Prussia. In 1871 the King of Prussia became Emperor of Germany and in 1895 the Kiel Canal was opened, simultaneously creating a new entrance to the Baltic and increasing Germany's power in it.

The twentieth century brought to bloody fulfilment the struggle between Germany and Russia for Baltic domination, for which the scene had been set 100 years earlier. In 1914 the Russians marched into East Prussia on their way to Berlin. Hindenburg and Ludendorff destroyed their invading armies on the historic battlefield at Tannenberg. Thereafter Russians fought Germans in eastern Poland and the Baltic countries until at last the collapse of Habsburgs, Romanovs and Hohenzollerns gave the smaller nations of eastern and northern Europe their opportunity. The end of the First World War saw Finland, Estonia, Latvia and Lithuania emerge as independent Baltic nations, and Poland was reborn.

For the next twenty years Poland struggled to reinforce her new-won access to the sea while the Baltic states nurtured their tense and nervous identity. But Adolf Hitler's many grievances included a Baltic grievance. For him, the status of Danzig and the Polish corridor were unendurable offences. In 1939 he went to war to resolve both, and Poland was divided between Germany and the Soviet Union, her fourth partition.

Stalin made his own dispositions for the coming conflict.

Molotov's butcher's agreement with Ribbentrop had given him eastern Poland. Now he attacked Finland and occupied the Baltic republics. When world war came to the Baltic in 1941, the Nazi war machine rolled across eastern Poland and up through the Baltic states to the gates of Leningrad. Finally the tide turned. The Red Army marched into East Prussia, victorious Poles advanced along the coast of Pomerania, and Montgomery's armies from the south reached Lübeck only hours before the Russians. The Baltic was divided where the fighting ended: in the forests of Karelia on the Finnish frontier and at the gates of Lübeck between Mecklenburg and Schleswig-Holstein.

The division thus imposed on the Baltic world was to last for nearly half a century. In the east, Moscow absorbed Estonia, Latvia and Lithuania and its half of East Prussia. Germany was formally divided. The Poles tried to assert their will for freedom and real sovereignty, but their country remained a subordinate nation. The Swedes and Finns in their different ways found their own accommodation with the Soviet Union. Denmark and Norway, both cautious members of NATO, completed the Nordic balance, and Denmark hesitantly committed herself to the European Community. Economies prospered in the north and west, seemed to prosper in East Germany, and dragged their weary way forward in Poland, in Russia and in the Baltic republics of the Soviet Union.

Attitudes and relationships around the Baltic reflected this division. Königsberg, now Kaliningrad and a Soviet province, bristled with Soviet tanks and warships, a threat looming over the whole Baltic which NATO armed itself to meet. Trade continued, but it was commerce between different systems, embarked upon cautiously, trammelled by politics, a pale shadow of the robust business of the past.

Eventually, however, the 1980s brought change to Europe, and the Baltic saw early signs of it. Sweden and Finland grew steadily closer to their natural western political and trading partners, if always with an eye to Soviet reactions. Solidarity, born in Gdansk, was gathering strength throughout Poland. The Federal Republic had come to terms with the East in the 1970s, and her influence along the Baltic continued to grow. The Soviet Union's Baltic republics found a voice on issues like the environment, folk traditions and religious observance. As Communism's failure became ever more apparent there were signs of change even in the Soviet Union, and Leningrad seemed more eager than Moscow to embrace it. Then came 1989, the year of miracles, and the will to dominate seeped away from the Soviet Communist leadership.

For years, Poland had led the resistance in central and eastern Europe, and it was the Polish elections of June 1989 which brought the first glimpse of a miracle to the Baltic. Solidarity won 99 of the 100 seats in the Senate; and in the following year Walesa himself, the electrician from Gdansk, was elected president. Poland was reborn as a fully sovereign and independent north European power, the first of the many changes which in the next five years would re-shape the political geography of the Baltic.

Change in Germany came close behind. Reunification presented the Federal Republic with many challenges. In the north she found the length of her coastline tripled. Bonn now faced responsibility for the backwardness of Mecklenburg and western Pomerania, the poorest of the eastern *Länder*, and for the industrial and social wreckage of Rostock, Wismar and Stralsund. But at the same time the Germans saw tempting new prospects in the north.

As Communism entered its death throes south and east of the Baltic, Social Democracy in Scandinavia was also threatened. The enviable social and personal standards it had brought were too heavy a load for the economy to carry. First Denmark, then Sweden and Finland braced themselves to face the need for change. Sweden looked outward, as membership of the European Community beckoned. But it was the change in the Finns' position which was most remarkable. Neutral they remained; but now they were free to think in terms of western links stronger than the European Free Trade Area could offer, all the way to membership of the European Community .

Yet even Finland's changes were tame by comparison with those taking place on the Baltic's eastern coast, where 1990 and 1991 saw the re-creation of three sovereign, independent nations. Each looked back on twenty years of nationhood, extinguished in 1940. Now they struggled to reassert it. In August 1991 came the failure of the Moscow coup, the collapse of Communism and an exodus of republics from the Soviet Union. By their courage and their exertions, Lithuania, Latvia and Estonia made themselves indisputably sovereign states.

Russia, the giant among the republics, was left to cope with the aftermath of the Soviet Union's collapse. Russian troops came home from Germany and central Europe, and then slowly from the Baltic republics themselves. The troops in Kaliningrad were powerful yet impotent, separated by Lithuania from the motherland. In their demoralisation they turned to trading in arms and drugs and to extortion.

Leningrad, now St Petersburg again, remained to play a central part in Russia's turbulent development. It was the country's second city, and by Russian standards it was relatively prosperous, relatively progressive, relatively open to the world. But St Petersburg was caught up like the rest of the country in the social, economic and political chaos that followed the break-up of the Soviet Union.

By the beginning of 1993, therefore, all nine of the nations round the Baltic enjoyed in their different ways a freedom they had not experienced for half a century. Each nation set itself goals which clearly would have been beyond its reach before the year of miracles. Since then, these nations have advanced by different roads and at different speeds. But they share the belief that they face new opportunities, and that the experience of their history – by turns co-operative and confrontational – now provides a basis for them to work together. It is this belief which today brings a specifically Baltic sparkle to their politics and business and society, to match the individual sparkle of countries which are at last free to be themselves.

3
Lübeck, Mecklenburg and Vorpommern

I started my exploration of the Baltic in the ancient city of Lübeck, home of the best marzipan in the world. It was a wet evening in the summer of 1992, and in the rain I could not find the dirty old Lysia hotel which I remembered standing four-square and perdurable outside the Holsten gate. But I tracked it down in the sunlight of the following morning, transmogrified into an apparently brand-new member of the Mövenpick chain, its pastel hues calculated to attract Swedish travellers on their way home from sultry Mediterranean beaches via the Baltic ferries at Travemünde.

The evening rain also veiled the classical view of the old city across the Trave: no St James' spire, no twin spires of the Marienkirche were to be seen, and away to the right no trace of St Peter's and of the cathedral. But as I crossed the footbridge the steep gable ends of the warehouses beside the river loomed out of the rain. In Mengstrasse the street lights and their flickering reflections in the puddles revealed the old houses on either side. At the top stood St Mary's church and the Rathaus. And on the other side of Mengstrasse lay the merchant's house in which Thomas Mann spent his boyhood and which he described with such perfect recall in *Buddenbrooks*. Lübeck began to seem itself again.

The old city stands on a low hill between the River Trave and the Elbe-Baltic Canal. It rises clearly above the new city and the suburbs, perhaps a mile long from north to south, less than a mile east to west. There is just room for a main street running the length of the hill from the city gate to the cathedral, and for a dozen steep sidestreets at right angles to it. Crowded within this little oval city heart are many of the jewels of the Baltic, medieval in origin, smashed in war, mostly well-restored, their importance certified by the city's three Michelin stars and by its inclusion in UNESCO's catalogue of the great achievements of civilisation.

The greatest of Lübeck's wonders is St Mary's, the Marienkirche, a great brick cathedral with a soaring white-washed interior. It was built in the late Middle Ages, laid waste in the British air-raids of 1942, and lovingly restored thereafter. The second greatest is perhaps the Rathaus, an elaborate celebration in Baltic brick of the glory of the city, completed – as is the way with such monuments – just as Lübeck was beginning its descent into long decline.

Lübeck offers other splendours also, but the bishop's cathedral is a sad one. Even in its heyday the burghers of Lübeck kept their bishop at arm's length, and now, dutifully restored but with what feels like less love than was lavished upon the Marienkirche, the cathedral has been made over into an unconvincing centre for the arts and crafts. The other Gothic brick churches, St James's near the north end of the city and St Peter's near the Holsten gate, pack a more powerful punch. So, in their different ways, do the great brick gates themselves, the old warehouses along the Trave, the seventeenth-century merchants' houses that Thomas Mann brought to life, and the medieval Hospice of the Holy Ghost. Restored and fraudulent they may be, marred by twentieth-century uglinesses scattered between them, these jewels reflect back to you something of the splendour of a great city, perhaps the greatest of the Hansa cities around the Baltic.

You can find that splendour distilled in the Schiffergesellschaft across the street from St James's church. Here, in a half-cellar, a restaurant has been carved out of the old hall of the Seamen's Guild. It is essentially a single cavernous room, long and dark, at once intimidating and welcoming, with its oak pews and tables stained by four centuries of sweat and polish and candle grease. The place throbs with life. On my wet summer's evening a party of noisy pensioners monopolised the high table, calling for North Sea sole and Baltic herring, for Rhine wine and Holsten beer. Waiters bustled between the customers with their measured blend of courtesy and busyness. The low lights glimmered on the vast ship models hanging from the ceiling. With my knees under a table in the Schiffergesellschaft I felt I was properly back beside the Baltic.

Lübeck is the right place for travellers from the west to start their exploration of the Baltic. The Vikings, Wends and Slavs made their mark on the northern sea long before twelfth-century Lübeck started its long voyage towards Baltic pre-eminence. But when the Lübeckers opened their market, set out their stalls and welcomed others to do

business with them, they founded a trading-post which came to represent the northernmost presence of the might of the Holy Roman Empire and of the commercial weight of Germany.

Lübeck became Germany's trading window on the east. Emperors recognised its significance, making it one of the members of the Council of the Empire. Its merchants helped to establish German trading cities further east: Wismar, Rostock, Stralsund, Greifswald.

Traders from Lübeck travelled to Visby in Gotland and Bergen in Norway, to Stockholm and Novgorod and Bruges, and out of their determination to defend their profitable monopolies the Hanseatic League was born. They sold cloth and beer and wine and weapons from the Rhineland and Saxony, from the Low Countries, France and England; and in return they brought hemp, wheat, amber, pitch and wax from the east. For two centuries east-west trade depended on the Hansa. Within the League, Lübeck was always weighty; usually pre-eminent. And even when the League had been forced, painfully and reluctantly, to surrender its monopoly of the Baltic trade and admit the Dutch, the English and the French, Lübeck in its long decline nevertheless remained a bridgehead for Germany's eastern trade.

But on 2 May 1945, Lübeck found itself central to modern history. This is where the division of the Baltic between East and West, Communist and free began. On that day the 11th Armoured Division of the British VIIIth Corps advanced into Lübeck. On 29 April the British had forced a crossing of the Elbe at Lauenberg, forty miles to the south. They did so against stubborn resistance and under heavy artillery fire. Even the Luftwaffe joined in – in what must have been its last operation on the western front. The next day Hitler committed suicide and the British troops moved forward into Schleswig-Holstein. Montgomery had fought his last battle, and the object of the advance was to keep the Russians out of Denmark and to deny them control of the entrance to the Baltic.

As Churchill put it, VIIIth Corps 'headed for the Baltic, so as to place themselves across the land-gate of Denmark'. A fortnight earlier, signals had been flashing between Churchill in London and Anthony Eden in Washington. They were clear that the Russians must not be allowed to control the Baltic approaches. In Montgomery's words: 'We reached the Baltic at Lübeck and Wismar on 2 May and thus sealed off the Danish peninsula with about six hours to spare, before the Russians arrived.'

The events of that day shaped the Baltic for the next half century. The victorious allies moved into their agreed zones of occupation, as a great convoy of American and British tanks and trucks advanced up the autobahn to take over their sectors of Berlin and western troops across Germany withdrew to their agreed positions. On the Baltic, Montgomery's troops pulled back from Wismar to the line of demarcation between the British and Russian zones, which ran along the border between the old duchies of Mecklenburg and Schleswig-Holstein.

Very soon this border became a part of the dividing line between East and West. In time, frontier guards of both German persuasions took the place of the British and Russian soldiers who faced each other along it in 1945. Watchtowers went up and belts of mines and barbed wire were laid all the way from Travemünde on the Baltic to Lauenburg on the Elbe – and for another 600 miles to the Adriatic. From the Elbe the border ran northwards close to the Elbe-Baltic Canal. Then it swung away a little to the east, to enclose the little towns of Ratzeburg and Mölln of the old duchy of Lauenburg within Schleswig-Holstein and the western world. It ran through the woods just beyond Lübeck's eastern suburbs. And from there to the sea the border followed the eastern bank of the Trave, so that for forty years holidaymakers on the beach at Travemünde looked up from their ice creams to contemplate the guards in the watchtowers across the water. Nowhere else except in Berlin did the Iron Curtain run through the back yards of a major city. On 2 May 1945 Lübeck, heart and centre of the Baltic for centuries, found itself on the very edge of a great divide.

The city itself was in ruins, devastated by British bombing. A quarter of the old city was totally destroyed. Into this battered shell flooded 100,000 refugees. The first wave came from East Prussia and Pomerania, the eastern Baltic provinces lost by Germany to the Russians and the Poles. A second wave followed, as refugees poured into Lübeck and Schleswig-Holstein from neighbouring Mecklenburg.

Photographs give some impression of Lübeck in the late 1940s, before reconstruction began. So until very recently did unreconstructed places like Wismar and Stralsund, Hansa cities in the old East Germany. But Lübeck now shows nothing of the damage of those days. Throughout the city the glories have been restored with loving precision, except where, along Breitestrasse, intercourse between retailer and shopper has bred bleak shopping boxes in the place of the old merchant houses. In the Hospice of the Holy Ghost you can see how Lübeck's successful merchants provided for the needy; how in the Schiffergesellschaft they found captains and seamen for the voyages on which their wealth was based. In restaurants and museums carved out of their old mansions you can capture a sense of their domestic and business lives, and the towers of the Holsten gate, where they posted the city's sentinels, remind you of their vigilance in protecting the wealth which their argosies brought home.

The centre of Lübeck, the old oval city on its little hill between the Trave and the canal, offers us a sense of one Baltic world, the late medieval world of city states, of traders and the Hanseatic League. Greater Lübeck, a sprawling city of 250,000 people, reflects the Baltic of today. With Travemünde a few miles away at the mouth of the river, the city was for nearly fifty post-war years West Germany's main trading window on the Baltic. Its gritty industrial and commercial prosperity is as much bound up with the Baltic as was the old city's 600 years ago. Lübeck handles the bulk of Germany's sea-borne exports to Scandinavia, Poland and the Baltic states. Ferries sail out of Travemünde all over the Baltic, to Gedser, Trelleborg, Rønne, Helsinki and Gdansk: if you want to go ferry-hopping around the Baltic, Travemünde is the place to embark.

The division of the Baltic in 1945 seemed likely to be fatal to Lübeck, cutting it off from much of its distant eastern trade and from its neighbour, the province of Mecklenburg. But that division concentrated in Lübeck and, to a lesser extent, in Kiel all the Federal Republic's seaborne business with the Baltic world, which before the war had been shared with Rostock, Wismar and Stettin. Now a united Germany can look to a wider range of options. So Lübeck, with the Iron Curtain at its back gate lifted and with its citizens free once again to spend their Sunday afternoons on the beaches and lakes of Mecklenburg, may yet suffer from the changes which have made the Baltic whole.

Of this there is little sign as yet. And even if Lübeck loses business to Germany's eastern ports it will remain a lively and dynamic place. Rostock and Wismar will win back some of the importance Lübeck enjoyed when Communism cut them off from the rest of the world, but in tomorrow's Baltic there will be business enough for all. Perhaps Lübeck will benefit from losing to a restored Wismar some of the tourists who comb its medieval buildings. Its southern suburbs, up in arms against plans for a new autobahn, may be relieved to see traffic and business going elsewhere. Whatever its destiny in the new Europe, the city can face the future with more confidence because Montgomery got there to close the land-gate of Denmark just before the Russians drove in.

In the 1970s and early 1980s I lived for six years in Bonn. I came to know the Federal Republic well. But western diplomats in the western half of Germany lived strangely cut off from the German Democratic Republic. The obstacles to contact grew out of our own rules, not the East Germans', but were real enough for all that. Security was part of the problem, the fear that a car accident might give the *Stasi* the opportunity to prise secrets from our shaken diplomatic skulls. But there was also the problem of status, the particular position of the wartime allies who still in theory, whatever the realities, exercised by right of conquest ultimate authority in both parts of Germany. You could – and we did – spin ever more tangled webs of theory about all this. Such theories seemed important in principle and there were moments of crisis when they were important in practice too. But they had the effect of restricting us to our own patch, and only British diplomats accredited to the German Democratic Republic were licensed to explore the eastern provinces of Germany.

So I crossed the old border behind Lübeck on that summer morning in 1992 with a double sense of discovery. I was exploring territory long closed to me and discovering what freedom and change were doing to it. In the past I had walked with German friends right up to the dividing line, awed by the wire, watch towers and threat of sudden death that lay beyond. Now every trace of that threat has been eliminated. Today's archaeologist must go all the way to Lauenburg to find relics of the old system: the deserted frontier-control building and the road-bays for cars awaiting their turn to cross from one Germany into the other. And if he wants to see its extravagant complexity he has to go still further, to Helmstedt, where the abandoned infrastructure of control spreads out like a vast deserted marshalling-yard beside the Hanover-Berlin autobahn.

But in 1992 German thoroughness had been less successful in eliminating the differences on either side of the vanished border. As I left Lübeck I was carried back half a century. The roads were as they were in the years before Weimar fell, when Berliners set out in their two-seaters with a dickey behind to explore the Baltic coast. The villages were just beginning to sprout shop-fronts, bill-boards, modern filling-stations. An Opel dealer had set up camp in a field, his advertising flags speaking of the brash Germany down the road. Bulldozers tore into the earth behind an announcement of a business centre to come. But these were rare 1990s impositions on 1930s

Germany, on which the intervening decades of war and Communism had made no visible impact. Hens scratched in a dusty back yard, a horse and cart lumbered almost imperceptibly towards its unimportant destination, and when I found petrol it came courtesy of a dignified old man from a hand-pump. This was not eastern Poland – I was to find much greater dynamism when I got there – this was Mecklenburg, only a hundred miles from Berlin. Mecklenburg-Vorpommern is not unrelieved Rip Van Winkle country, but first impressions as I entered its north-west corner were of slumber scarcely stirred by change.

I turned briefly inland to visit Schwerin, capital of the old duchy of Mecklenburg, in which an old tooth-fairy castle rises above a handsome, nineteenth-century town. Here I came upon the first of the sub-plots that enrich the Baltic story. Schwerin stands among lakes, part of a necklace of inland waters which stretches right across north Germany between Berlin and the Baltic. These lakes are part of a longer chain which runs pretty well right round the Baltic. If you weary of the Baltic's beaches and fishing ports and strike inland, you will find yourself before long among lakes. Finland's are so numerous as to be indecipherable on any map. Mazuria in north-eastern Poland has a thousand more, many of them lost in the forest wilderness. Kashubia, just west of Gdansk, is punctuated with sunny, welcoming stretches of water, big ponds rather than lakes. Sweden's lakes are grander by far, with at least one – Vänern – big and stormy enough to have reduced a delegation of visiting American naval dignitaries to seasick misery. And Lake Ladoga behind St Petersburg is the mother of all the lakes of the Baltic basin. If pollution eventually drives the holidaymakers off the Baltic's beaches, they can still turn to its lakes.

In Schwerin I discovered the first traces of another sub-plot, which has developed vigorously all over the southern and eastern shores of the Baltic: post-Communist business enterprise. On a bridge in front of the castle, Russian dolls and lacquer boxes were laid out for sale. The bulky young man behind the stall was clearly Russian. Even today, when the Russian military have gone home, you can find more spectacular Russian enterprise elsewhere around the Baltic, with caps and belts and badges for sale along with more traditional handicrafts and, they say, with Kalashnikov assault rifles in Kaliningrad for those who ask. But this was my first Russian huckster, and he was clearly a soldier. Modestly, he confirmed this. Today was his day off. What was his unit? He named a Guards Motor Rifle Division.

My mind went back to briefings at Danish Defence Headquarters, only five years earlier. They started, as military briefings do, with the threat: East German warships, Polish sea-landing brigades, Soviet divisions, poised for a massive attack on Schleswig-Holstein or the Danish islands across Mecklenburg Bay. The most potent threat of all was my huckster's Motor Rifle Division, a match, some analysts said, for the German Sixth Panzer Grenadier Division which faced it on the other side of the Iron Curtain. God knows if this was true, or routine military exaggeration, but at the time I for one believed it. Now, a few years later, one of its officers was hawking Russian dolls. He had traditional dolls, dolls with Yeltsin's face in place of the babushka, and Gorbachev dolls – each with its strawberry mark – selling at a discount. If I had asked, he might have sold me a Kalashnikov. On my first day in eastern Germany he showed me dramatically how times were changing around the Baltic.

Times seemed to be changing more slowly in Wismar, on the coast north of Schwerin. It is no more than thirty miles from Lübeck, and for centuries their history has been intertwined: Hansa cities, trading partners and trading rivals, allies against the Danes. But the link was broken in 1945. Although in the last days of the war Montgomery's troops moved into Wismar as well as into Lübeck, within weeks the western allies pulled out, back to the agreed demarcation line on the Schleswig-Holstein border. Lübeck and Schleswig-Holstein prospered. For Wismar, things turned out differently.

As the west withdrew the Russians moved in. Hansa pride, which in the west is celebrated even on car numberplates, was crushed. Wismar's very closeness to the border became an extra handicap. It was too easy to escape in small boats or rubber rings across Mecklenburg Bay to Schleswig-Holstein, and special travel restrictions were imposed to limit access to Wismar from other East German cities.

If you come to Wismar today you feel that it has slept its way through the last half century. Its great brick churches are broken, like the Georgenkirche, which the Communists blew up, or the Nikolaikirche, exhausted by decades of wear and tear. There are gaps where ruins have been cleared away but nothing put in their place. The whole city, over-sized and over-ambitious as it has been since the Swedes ruled there in the seventeenth century, is covered with a patina of dirt and mould and exhales a gentle, sleepy exhaustion.

It feels different down by the docks. Here are the beginnings of bustle. There is a ships' chandlery in a fine eighteenth-century house, its broad bosom decorated with proudly-painted lists of the goods it offers. Further on you find an old pilot station at the end of the quay, looking out over the harbour towards Wismar's offshore islands but overshadowed by the bulk of grain elevators and storage tanks in the docks, and by cranes and growing hulls in the shipyards. This was the Wismar that you looked for if you came here from the east before the Berlin wall came down. The GDR's second port and second biggest shipbuilder, Wismar still bears stark industrial witness to what the world used to think was the East German economic miracle.

Admirers came not just from East Germany but from further east. Russians in particular came to buy German shipbuilding quality. When I was there the dockyard was completing a great river cruise liner, built to sail the Volga and Danube under the old Soviet flag. You could see ships like these in Budapest, tying up in the late evening to let the tourists ashore for a night club visit and two complimentary Hungarian brandies. They were to be seen as far upstream as Dürnstein, majestically rounding the bends in the Danube between the Wachau vineyards. Work on this latest sister ship, sleek and white against the industrial detritus of the dockyard, seemed to be advancing with infinite slowness, as if completion could only bring disillusion.

Reasons for that disillusion could be seen moored further out in Wismar Bay, two spanking new freezer ships for the Arctic fisheries, held in limbo because the Murmansk company that had placed the order could no longer find the cash to pay for them. They should have been at work beyond North Cape, catching Arctic cod to buy hard currency to fuel the Russian economy. Instead they were slumbering like so much else in Wismar, waiting for a prince to wake them with the kiss of money.

The princes are hard at work. We saw the Opel salesman camping out in a field until he could build his showroom. Since that brave beginning the showrooms and the banks and the supermarkets have gone up all over eastern Germany. The Treuhand, the organisation created at reunification to privatise eastern German industry, has found dynamic western businessmen to breathe new life into old factories. And the glories of the past are being rescued too, but like many other things that followed reunification, the process made an uncertain start. Four years ago, work was going on to restore the Georgenkirche, and in churches all across West Germany the

Friends of Wismar's Georgenkirche were collecting money for it. In the Marienkirche in Lübeck, St George's twin, they had planted a huge copper tank to receive offerings, but when I saw it, two days before I came to Wismar, it held two Deutschmarks and thirty pfennigs.

The less than whole-hearted commitment to the rebuilding of the Georgenkirche seems in a way typical of a hesitancy about the eastern *Länder* which long affected east and west Germans alike. The heady days of unification were gone. Disillusion and a sense of disappointed hopes had taken their place. Even more than the rest of eastern Germany, Mecklenburg-Vorpommern paid a high price for Helmut Kohl's pretence in 1990 that one Ostmark was worth one Deutschmark – easy politics and bad economics. In the catastrophe that followed, east Germans seemed to their western compatriots incompetent, slothful, scarcely German. To east Germans, the westerners who came to advise and patronise them destroyed the old east German economy and put nothing viable in its place.

For a time the east Germans' position seemed paradoxically worse than that of their neighbours further east. Poland and the Baltic states, infinitely poorer than the old East Germany and just as crippled by the Communist seizure of all initiative, celebrated their sudden freedom with innovation and self-help. People in Mecklenburg-Vorpommern seemed shell-shocked when I was there, consumed by an embittered sloth. But with time and the money that has poured into eastern Germany, things are changing. Traditional German characteristics – hard work, obsessive thoroughness, arrogance, attention to detail and to quality – are spreading to east Germans also. They are being absorbed into a western European world, and detached from the east Europeans who seemed for a time to be overtaking them.

The changes Mecklenburg-Vorpommern has gone through are most evident in Rostock. This is the old East Germany's biggest port, which was for forty years an industrial showpiece. Rostock goes back to the Middle Ages as a Hanseatic university city, but today it is a big and sprawling place, forgetful of its past and neglecting its little historical heart on a hill above the Warnow. Factories and dockyards and ten-storey block after block of modern workers' housing march across the urban landscape. This is the city whose long summer nights of rioting against foreigners in 1992 set people talking about the old Teutonic Adam and *Kristallnacht*.

That summer, Rostock seemed to me a desperate place, wholly charmless, bleak and characterless, a city where headlong expansion had overwhelmed what little had been spared by war. I had to look hard for something better to say about it, and a sleazy surplus equipment market apparently specialising in US army body-bags was not a promising start. Nor was an endless flight of stone steps up from the level of the Warnow to yet more workers' flats upon a bluff. But some anonymous city planner had implanted a delight into this urban wilderness. At the top of the steps I found a fountain, gently burbling water forth and sending it hopping and skipping beside the steps down to the river.

Rostock's efforts at city improvement did not stop with fountains. Outside the Kropliner Gate a line of strange metallic objects descends to a little park. In a different setting you might think them containers for hazardous waste, but here it seemed that someone had inexplicably taken sections of the city wall and sheathed them in rusty steel. Enlightenment dawned an hour later. In the museum in the Convent of the Holy Cross a German woman volunteered to be my guide. She loved her work, willing me to share her delight in the convent's medieval beauty. I asked her, this professional woman so full of splendid German seriousness, about the objects outside the Kropliner Gate. 'They are art,' she explains, 'an experiment.' People do not like them, demand that the city fathers take them away. But we must be humble, says this middle-aged woman so head-over-heels in love with her convent's marvels, and we must seek the artist's meaning. Her heroic tolerance of damnable, ugly pretension was the best thing that happened to me in Rostock.

For the rest, Rostock seemed full of dangerous extremes. It is by far the biggest city in Germany's poorest *Land*. All East Germany's investment in making Rostock a showpiece had turned to ashes. The shipyards were precariously dependent on European Community subventions, and local cunning held that Hamburg and Bremen were determined to bury Rostock's competition. The Federal Government and German industry have decided that things shall change, and now, in Rostock as in other east German cities, change is afoot. Investment, order, logic, a fresh start, all these are marching across the eastern *Länder*. But it will be a long march.

In Rostock there are still a few traces of a more glorious past on which to build. The old city above the Warnow boasts a great Marienkirche and a fine complacent Rathaus, as well as the Convent of the Holy Cross. It has its intellectual glories, with a natural history society founded forty years before London brought forth the Royal Society. Today, the city fathers are seeking out a long-rejected past, and striving to give the place a new sense of its old identity. They have restored its proud title of Hansestadt, and when I was there the main hotel was being refurbished room by room to make it fit for the white knights from the West. Backed by money and German earnestness, Rostock may in time defuse the resentment and anger that smouldered in the apartment blocks in 1992. At the moment it seems, like all of the old East Germany, poised between hope and cynicism, sloth and vision, bitterness and creativity.

So the people of Mecklenburg-Vorpommern feel sorry for themselves: bewildered, impoverished, at a loss. But, though they may not acknowledge it, they have much to be thankful for. They have education, skills and resources. The chances are that, given time, they will succeed in making themselves rich and become good *Bundesbürger*. The process is well under way. But in 1992 respectable East Germans seemed to be content to wait and see what was to be done for them; in the journalist Marc Fisher's haunting words, they bore their wounds like solemn, dutiful children.

Meanwhile, there are good things to encourage them in the wilderness that East German Communist rule left behind. The road from Wismar to Rostock takes you through Bad Doberan, the summer residence of the dukes of Mecklenburg that in the nineteenth century was turned into a newfangled, now very old-fashioned, health resort. Bad Doberan is laid out around what remains of a twelfth-century Cistercian monastery. There is a lush stretch of grass that would grace an English cathedral close, and beyond it the minster. It is tall, as big as a cathedral, powerful and dignified in its glowing red brick. From the outside it deserves to be considered among the great churches of Europe.

Sadly, restorers have been at work in the interior, and with a heavy hand. Someone has painted the brickwork a deep unnatural red, with the sort of thick, clogging paint which Lancashire housewives used on their doorsteps in the years before Coronation Street. He has picked out the groins of the arches in an unearthly blue. He or an earlier vandal has decorated a great medieval crucifix with what look like tin-foil scallops.

Despite such barbarism, the minster at Bad Doberan is a worthy member of that splendid family of northern European Gothic brick churches which march from northern France, through Bruges and Hamburg to Lübeck, along the southern Baltic coast through Wismar and Stralsund to Gdansk and Frombork; and northwards through Riga to Tartu in Estonia. There are outposts of Gothic brick on the other side of the Baltic: the great cathedral of Uppsala, for example; and in Denmark in Roskilde, the burial place of her kings. As the sacred, so the secular: the Rathaus, the merchant's mansion, the blank-walled warehouse – all bear brick witness to the world of medieval mammon. Red brick persists into the seventeenth century, in buildings such as Christian IV's Stock Exchange in Copenhagen or his Holy Trinity church at Kristianstad in southern Sweden. Gothic brick – *Backstein Gothik* – is in its way as great an architectural achievement as the stone Gothic cathedrals of France and England. Like them, it defines a civilisation.

The minster at Bad Doberan needs a miracle to restore its interior to grace, yet the town has had its miracles before. On one medieval occasion, divine intervention saved it from a great wall of storm-driven water that swept in from the Baltic across the flat pastureland. The monks and nuns went down on their knees to storm heaven. Heaven answered, and laid across the fields a miraculous dam that turned the waves aside. Heiligendamm, holy dam, they christened it. By the time Beau Brummel was regulating Bath, a Duke of Mecklenburg had turned Heiligendamm into a seaside resort. For a century and a half it attracted summer wealth. For a further half century, East German trade unionists monopolised its splendours. It fell into decline, was put up for sale; and in 1992 the Treuhand advertised in the British press for a buyer for a complete Baltic seaside resort.

Bad Doberan is almost a suburb of Rostock. So is Warnemünde, at the mouth of the river on which Rostock stands. Warnemünde started as a fishing village. In the nineteenth century it became a fashionable resort like Heiligendamm, and kept its reputation well into the twentieth. In 1907 it attracted Edvard Munch, bruised by rejection at home in Norway but elated by his success in German artistic circles. He painted his self-portrait on Warnemünde beach, brush and palette in hand, a look of almost sexual exaltation on his face. Behind him is the canvas on which he painted his huge study of male nudes advancing up the beach and striding out of the frame. It proved too advanced even for German critics at the time, but nearly a century later, glowing with power in a Helsinki gallery, it tells a story of the Baltic, not merely of Munch and the stalwart Warnemünde lifeguards he took for his naked models.

The Communist years took their toll of Warnemünde's beach, just as the capitalist years have taken their toll of beaches further west, but there is an area around the fishing harbour which preserves the charm of the old Baltic. Brightly-coloured cottages facing the water remind you of Thomas Mann's description of Travemünde a hundred years ago, when Toni Buddenbrooks met, loved and lost the estuary pilot's son who alone among her lovers might have brought her happiness. But varied uglinesses press in upon this unspoiled heart of Warnemünde: the 1930s hotels along the front, long since converted to trade union holiday homes and now converting back again; further on, a great slab of a hotel built in the 1970s to part Scandinavian tourists from their hard currency before they took their ferry home; and up-river the truck parks and the warehouses and the ferry docks themselves.

There is much more of the German Baltic east of Rostock before you come to the Polish border. A long off-shore finger of land, which in German is called a *Nehrung*, marches most of the way to Stralsund, trapping a long shallow lagoon behind it. This feature is a characteristic of the south Baltic coast, which is fringed by spits and lagoons all the way to Lithuania. But at Stralsund, where Mecklenburg gives way to Vorpommern, the mainland faces not a lagoon but the island of Rügen. We shall visit Rügen later, look at it with other Baltic islands such as Fehmarn and Gotland, Bornholm and Öland and the Åland Islands in the mouth of the Gulf of Bothnia; and we shall come back at the end of this chapter to Stralsund, which may yet become another jewel of the Baltic. For the moment, western Pomerania, stretching all the way to the Polish frontier, beckons.

Beyond Stralsund the coast turns south-eastwards. It leads to Greifswald, a Hansa city saved from destruction by the rare wisdom of a commander who had the sense to surrender in 1945; it has been threatened since by a looming nuclear power station; and it is now restoring and reviving itself with the lugubrious earnestness of so many east German cities. From the coast nearby you look out on a great Baltic bight, shut in by Rügen in the north and the point of Peenemünde to the east.

Peenemünde stands at the tip of Usedom Island. In the golden days of the 1920s, it was a fishing village and seaside resort, a place to enjoy in the short Baltic summer and avoid for the rest of the year. Now it is a broken-down, wretched sort of place, to be avoided all the year round. But it has twice played a part in history, if only in the long, miserable story of European war.

Gustavus Adolfus of Sweden disembarked his army here in June 1630; and if that sounds today like a remote, irrelevant event, fit only for a continental version of *1066 and All That*, it felt very different to the men of the time. To the Protestants of Germany, his intervention in the Thirty Years War was nothing less than God's doing. For five years the Habsburgs' Catholic general, Wallenstein, had dominated the war, carrying imperial rule and Catholicism right into the Protestant north. In 1628 the emperor made him Admiral of the Baltic. In 1629 he drove Christian IV of Denmark out of the war. For his co-religionists in northern Germany, Gustavus Adolfus was a last hope, the Lion of the North coming out of Scandinavia to defend their faith and put the emperor's general to flight.

Summer thunder and lightning accompanied his landing at Peenemünde, and Gustavus stumbled as he stepped ashore. Propagandists on both sides made much of these signs of divine favour or disapproval. Gustavus, a practical man, was undeterred and his army drove Wallenstein all the way back to Bavaria. Finally, he himself was killed at Lützen in the very act of defeating Wallenstein again. Two years later Wallenstein himself was murdered. Yet Sweden and the Habsburgs continued to fight for pre-eminence in Germany for a further fourteen years

In trying to save Germany for their respective faiths the protagonists all but destroyed it until, at the Treaty of Westphalia, the idea of weary accommodation overtook the passion for supremacy. The struggle should have been too much for Sweden, at bottom an impoverished northern kingdom for all her military glory. But from the Treaty of Westphalia she carried away control of much of the north German coast. For another half century she remained a factor to be reckoned with in continental calculation, and the people of this part of the Baltic coast still talk of it as Swedish Pomerania.

Peenemünde made its second appearance on the stage of history in the twentieth century. Wernher von Braun needed a quiet stretch of coast for rocket research and the choice fell on Peenemünde. Here he developed Hitler's Victory weapons, the flying bomb and the rocket. Left undisturbed, his work might perhaps have tipped the balance Hitler's way. But his foreign labourers smuggled word to the West and 600 British bombers descended upon Peenemünde. Even so, the Germans put their rockets to effective use against London and Antwerp for six months through the last winter of the war. With nuclear warheads they would have snatched victory out of defeat – but that is another story for which, thank God, there is no script.

By the time the Russians reached Peenemünde, von Braun had taken care to fall into American hands. He helped build America's missile programme, then its space programme. Other Peenemünde men did as much for the Russians. Long after the war, after the bleak laboratories and factories on the peninsula had been abandoned or turned over to low-tech East German military uses, the knowledge gained there still sharpened the weapons which East and West levelled at one another.

There are prettier places on Usedom Island than Peenemünde, but it is time to turn back westwards. Stralsund is a big place, a major fishing port. Like Wismar it is run-down, decayed. Like Rostock it has had its share of soulless Communist-era development. But the old city stands proudly, between the sea and an encircling series of lagoons. And it is packed with historic buildings whose importance UNESCO will surely certify as it has those in Lübeck: great medieval churches like the Nikolaikirche and the Marienkirche, a wonderful Rathaus with a tall, perforated facade rising above its state rooms, a marketplace of merchants' houses not yet laid waste to make way for department stores.

When I was in Stralsund a post-Communist clean-up was under way, and by now it must be emerging as a place once more to be reckoned with. But there was a particular wildness about the streets of Stralsund that summer of 1992, going well beyond the raffish swagger you find in fishing ports anywhere. I saw anger flare up sporadically, the sort of anger that comes with uncertainty and frustration. I felt that round the next corner anything might happen. Someone who believed in the old order or feared the new had daubed upon a doorpost LAST CHANCE FOR THE GDR.

But Stralsund does not suffer from Rostock's legacy of decaying industrial investment. It does not have to find jobs for a bloated industrial work-force. Its scale is moderate, and ordinary life in Stralsund has a market-day feel to it. It has all the essentials of a decent living city: beauty, evidence of history, everyday bustle, and reasons for hope about tomorrow. In time it could surpass Lübeck. It could replace Schleswig as the most beautiful German city on the Baltic. In Stralsund I felt that if Teutonic panic in the face of Germany's new problems can be kept in check, five years of constructive Teutonic seriousness will change the place fundamentally for the better. In Mecklenburg-Vorpommern, Wismar may stand for sloth and Rostock for the anger of despair; but Stralsund seems to offer reasons for quiet confidence.

4
Poland

For almost half a century, the western frontier of Poland has followed the line of the Oder and the Western Neisse rivers. The line was fixed in 1945 by the victorious allies, when they shifted Poland westward and transformed her from an eastern to a central European state. Thus Poland acquired territories historically German: rough but not inappropriate recompense for what Germans had done to Poles for five long years. Five million Germans moved out, and Poles from regions lost to the Soviet Union moved in. Poles of every political complexion, whether in Paris, London or Warsaw, have insisted ever since on the validity of the Oder-Neisse line. Associations of ageing Germans displaced from the old provinces of Pomerania and Silesia dispute the frontier in vain. For forty years Federal Germany's reluctance to accept the line *de jure* in the absence of a peace settlement kept diplomats happily occupied, and academics and jurists made a cottage industry of the issue. In my first year in the Foreign Office, when there was talk of resignations over Suez, the only thing I could see myself resigning over would be British connivance in undoing the Oder-Neisse frontier. Fourteen years later, when Willy Brandt made his pilgrimage to the Warsaw ghetto, he still could not deliver absolute clarity on the issue. Now at last it is fixed beyond a peradventure, or at least for as long as Federal Germany respects her treaty obligations.

So it comes as a surprise on the autobahn from Berlin to Szczecin to find you have reached the Polish frontier a good ten miles before you reach the Oder. You are plunged at once into a different world, a different tempo. The strange blend of Teutonic discipline and uncertainty which we tasted throughout eastern Germany gives way to frantic hustle. The passport controllers and customs men are overwhelmed by traffic, while German and Polish police struggle, angrily or fatalistically, to impose some sort of order. There are Germans setting out for Poland in their Mercedes, Poles returning home with their Ladas, motor bikes and sidecars; little vans and crashed German

BMWs on trailers. Beyond the frontier stretches a long line of
shacks like an oriental bazaar: money-changers, freight-forwarders,
Marlborough cigarette-sellers and dubious-looking investment ad-
visers. A rich Polish spiv in a Mercedes 600 arrives to visit one of his
runners. From the moment you enter Poland you get a taste of her
post-Communist vigour. After the catatonic calm of eastern Germany, everything here is businesslike hysteria.

The frontier lies firmly west of the Oder because fifty years ago the
allies decided that it should. Looking back, there is something almost
studiously indirect about the language in which they said so, as if
they wanted to make policy by sleight of hand. In August 1945 a
Potsdam Conference communiqué recorded: 'The three heads of
Government agree that, pending the final determination of Poland's
western frontier, the former German territories east of a line running
from the Baltic Sea immediately west of Swinemünde, and thence
along the Oder River . . . shall be under the administration of the
Polish State.' Drawing the line from the Baltic to the Oder had the
effect of including the city of Stettin within the new frontiers of
Poland. Yet Szczecin – as it has become – stands indisputably on the
west bank of the river. And although the Poles deny it, for most of its
1,000 years of history Stettin has been indisputably a German city.

The 1945 settlement and the expulsion of the Germans changed all
that. Poles from the eastern territories poured into Szczecin. Today
its life, language and population are purely Polish, quite as completely as Warsaw's or Krakow's or Poznan's. All the same, if the
neutron bomb, which destroys all life and leaves all property un-
harmed, were to fall on Szczecin tomorrow, you would be left with a
dignified if run-down German provincial city.

There was a time when that last sentence would have had Poles
shouting about revanchism. No longer. After fifty years in occupation, Poland today feels secure in possession of Szczecin, as of all her
Baltic coast. All the same, the story of Szczecin, like the stories of
Wolin or Gdynia, Gdansk, Torun, Malbork and Elblag, tells much
about Poland's relationship with the Baltic over 1,000 years. It is not
as self-evident a story as Poles would have us believe.

If you look at the map of Poland today you see a manifestly Baltic
nation. Poland is a solid block of a country, standing squarely behind
her Baltic coastline, a 200-mile frontage to the sea. Two great Polish
rivers empty into the Baltic. Poland has three major Baltic ports. She

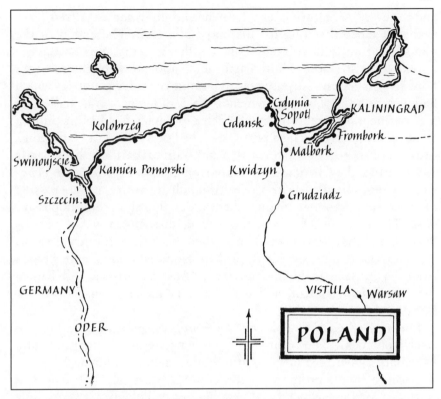

has, it is true, bigger rivals on the Baltic, but Russia, Germany and Denmark have other openings to the sea. Finland and the three Baltic states are smaller fry. Only Sweden compares with Poland as an exclusively Baltic power.

Earlier maps show a different picture. Throughout history, Poland has been a nation on the move. Today she reaches within fifty miles of Berlin. In the seventeenth century the Commonwealth of Poland and Lithuania stretched almost to the Black Sea. From after the First World War to the beginning of the Second, the Poles held what is today the capital of Lithuania. Yet between 1795 and 1918, Poland was wiped off the political map of Europe. The great powers made of Poland in turn a laughing-stock, a whipping-boy, and a sacrificial victim. Just as the forces released by the French Revolution spread out to change Europe for good, Poland's neighbours decided on her liquidation. The Third Partition divided what was left of her between Russia, Prussia and Austria and decreed that 'The name or designation of the Kingdom of Poland . . . shall remain suppressed as of now and for ever.' A century later a French schoolboy named Alfred Jarry needed a fanciful setting for his play, *Ubu Roi.* 'The action of the play', he wrote, 'takes place in Poland – that is to say, Nowhere.'

Not long after the Third Partition, Napoleon brought renewed hope to Poland. His purpose was to humble the three countries which had partitioned Poland and which, in their different ways, challenged his continental hegemony; but French diplomacy is adept at putting an altruistic gloss on selfish purposes. The Poles rallied to Napoleon's cause. Polish regiments formed a substantial part of the Grande Armée, and they believed in Napoleon's star. In *War and Peace* Tolstoy describes the death ride of the Polish cavalry at the crossing of the Neman, content if they died under the Emperor's impassive gaze. The Poles believed that the war against Russia was a war for Poland, and that victory would give them back their country. Instead the Grande Armée retreated broken from Moscow, and French troops were seen in Poland no more. Austria, Prussia and Russia reasserted their control, and for a century gallant Polish uprisings failed to shake them off.

But in 1918 each of Poland's three oppressors came comprehensively unstuck. The eclipse of Hohenzollerns, Romanovs and Habsburgs gave Poland her nationhood again. Woodrow Wilson's Thirteenth Point, promising her free and secure access to the sea, started a process which, at Versailles, gave Poland a twenty-mile frontage on Danzig Bay and access to it through eastern Pomerania. On 20 January 1920, when the Treaty of Versailles came into effect, enthusiastic Poles celebrated their nation's fulfilment. As Norman Davies records in his marvellous history of Poland, *God's Playground*, they 'waded into the icy waters of the Baltic, and with upraised hands saluted the renewal of Poland's ancient "Betrothal to the Sea"'.

However, most of Pomerania remained German, a great salient reaching beyond the Oder to within twenty miles of Danzig. So did East Prussia. Only the Polish corridor to the sea and the Free City of Danzig under a League of Nations commissioner interrupted German control of the southern coast of the Baltic. But for Hitler the corridor and the Free City were unpardonable offences. His war destroyed Poland as a nation and as a Baltic power. Only his defeat restored her nationhood and her access to the sea.

You can explore the history of Poland's struggles for a share of

the Baltic's riches 1,000 years beyond the eighteenth-century partitions, without ever reaching a conclusion satisfactory to both Polish
patriots and German irredentists. Polish historiography points to an
early king of Poland, the Piast Mieszko I, who captured Szczecin in
the tenth century. It celebrates the Polish and Lithuanian defeat of the
Teutonic Knights at Tannenberg in 1410, and it reminds us that the
Jagiellonian union of Poland and Lithuania ruled the Baltic coast as
far north as Riga. And Polish geography calls Poland the land of the
Vistula and argues the need for Polish control of its estuary.

But this scholarship has to be set against the trading monopoly of
the German Hansa; against the power of the Teutonic Order before
Tannenberg and the persistence of a German presence afterwards;
and against the grip of German estate owners and settlers along the
Baltic coast almost all the way to the gates of St Petersburg. The fact
is that for most of her history Poland was a major land power in
central and eastern Europe, her frontiers endlessly shifting, her reach
expanding and contracting, but she rarely secured a firm grip on the
Baltic coast.

Of course, the Poles see their history differently; and in any case,
for them all this is dead and done. They have made their coastline
Polish, and the facts speak for themselves. To travel from Swinoujscie
to Braniewo is to see how completely Poland today has imposed
herself on German yesterdays. German visitors may nurse a sense of
injustice. To other travellers, pondering German crimes in Poland,
there is a rough-and-ready justice in how things have turned out
along the Baltic coast.

So we drive on from the border-crossing at Kolbaskowa over indisputably Polish roads. Mercedes carefully pick their way around
the potholes but ancient Polish cars charge across them like Polish
cavalry. The trucks are matt mud-beige like all eastern European
trucks. As we turn into Szczecin the trams grind and the buses thump
painfully in front of us, as they do all over eastern Europe. Blocks of
flats rear up, the same woebegone workers' homes that flank our
route all the way from Wismar to St Petersburg. Beyond them we
are in nineteenth-century streets: scruffy shops and curtained cafés
and, rearing above them, the handsome, down-at-heel mansion flats
created for the old bourgeoisie of a German city.

But Polish life overflows these relics of an old Germany.
Guidebooks point you to the Gate of Prussian Homage and the
Harbour Gate. They will tell you that Catherine the Great was born

here, a German princess of Anhalt-Zerbst. The two great Gothic churches of St James and SS Peter and Paul are places for tourists, and they admit their German origins. But, these apart, Szczecin is Polish, with no concessions to the past or to the West. The street names are impenetrably Polish; the restaurants, if you can find them, list Polish food on Polish menus. The American lyrics at the pop concert in the castle courtyard are pumped out in Polish accents. Polish pride and self-sufficiency start in Szczecin. They escort you without a break all the way to Russia. Poland is a big country, that feels no need to explain herself to visitors.

A visit to a museum, high on a bluff above the river, illustrates this self-sufficiency. Its collection specialises in the maritime history of this part of the Baltic coast, everything from early seafarers to nineteenth-century ships' bells. All is Polish and Polish captions. At the kiosk they are selling a little print of the Town Hall and Stock Exchange of Stettin in the 1860s. It is a steal at five pence, but takes half an hour's negotiation to acquire it. Weary, you emerge into the calm, tree-shaded avenue in front of the museum. On the other side of the road is a coffee bar. It has little to offer except coffee, fly-blown fruit, chocolate, and a view across the river into the infinity of the Polish plain. You are ravenous. Coffee is as universal as Esperanto. You ask for a Mars bar to go with it. Incomprehension, a proffered postcard. 'Mars,' you say. They offer you a street map. 'Mars,' you say. They offer you a newspaper. 'Mars,' you say. A torrent of Polish is your reward. 'Mars,' you say. 'Mars,' they reply, handing you a Mars bar. Even on the doorstep of a museum, Poles see no pressing need to communicate with foreigners, most of whom are likely to be Germans anyway.

Mars bar in hand, you raise your eyes to the port stretched out before you. Szczecin should be a major outlet to the Baltic. Berlin is only eighty miles away down the autobahn, and the Oder flows here from the industrial heartland of the old East Germany and Bohemia. But the Oder, like the Vistula later, seems to carry little traffic, and the port of Szczecin seems a quiet backwater. With all the splendour of her autobahns, western Germany still sends great processions of barges endlessly up and down the Rhine and the Mosel. She has linked the Main and the Danube, and German barges swing round the Danube's bends on their way to the Black Sea. The idle tourist, playing at economic geography, can only wonder why Poland does not make more use of the Oder and the Vistula.

There is another kind of economic mystery to be seen beside the road towards the Baltic coast. This road runs straight, between dark pine woods. A sign-board in English promises a ranch with twenty horses. Another points the way to the airport. A hut beside the road calls itself a Drink-Bar. On the grass beside the road men take their ease, offering bottles filled with berries to passing motorists. No-one stops. This is the sort of economic madness sensible Germans were accustomed to despise as peculiarly Polish, until they discovered similar slothful madness in their own eastern *Länder*.

You come to Kamien Pomorski, a sleepy little town looking out over a lagoon. Shops offering amber and second-hand clothes face the overgrown churchyard in which Kamien's cathedral stands. A cathedral it has been for 800 years, but in size it is no more than a modest parish church. Kamien Cathedral offers beauty in a small space: brick, stone, wall paintings, organ, triptych altarpiece. You imagine yourself in a quintessentially Polish setting, removed from the bustle of the frontier-crossing beyond Szczecin, until you remember that until 1945 this was Pomeranian, not Polish.

The same tranquillity is to be found across the lagoon in Wolin, one of a line of off-shore islands that almost close the mouth of the Oder. Wolin's story stretches back to the very fringe of recorded history, with memories of pagan gods and a trading post in the eighth century. Today its back roads through the pine woods seem to be empty of everything except the sense of peace. Then you notice trickles, then torrents, of holidaymakers emerging from the woods on their way home to tea. Through the trees you see glimpses of camp sites, trade union rest-houses and holiday cottages, and beyond, the cool glimmer of the sea. Travemünde and Warnemünde offer two kinds of Baltic holiday-making, Wolin an older and gentler third.

Swinoujscie, across the water from Wolin, is the Swinemünde which the Potsdam allies decided to include in Poland even though it lies on the otherwise German island of Usedom. It was on Swinemünde that the German novelist, Theodor Fontane, modelled his little port of Kessin, to which Instetten took his new bride, Effi Briest. In *Effi Briest* Fontane created a Baltic Madame Bovary, as bewitching and finally as tragic a figure as Toni in *Buddenbrooks*. And in Kessin he gives us a nineteenth-century Baltic port even more sharply delineated than Mann's Travemünde.

By that time, the Baltic's glory days of trading were over, but Fontane has left an imperishable impression of one of its little ports.

Kessin still had its links with the big world: a ship from Sunderland is wrecked off the coast and a mysterious Chinese seaman once died in Effi's house. There is still a row of consuls' houses, where local tradesmen fly the flags of the countries whose interests they represent. Now visitors from Berlin take houses in Kessin for the summer, and it is a natural place of retirement for the major who so lightly encompasses Effi's undoing. Kessin is a place of deep provincial peace. But Instetten has his official responsibilities, his visits to Bismarck himself, which fatally distract him from his bride. There is a zest of tension between Germans on the coast and Poles inland. The ancient introverted snobbery of the Pomeranian landowners humbles little Effi, and then the major's wiles and her husband's inhuman sense of order destroy her. Fontane's *Effi Briest* captures a lot of Baltic history.

Eastern Pomerania, like Szczecin, is now entirely Polish. In 1945 the Soviet armies poured in, with Polish administrators close behind. The great changes were clearly, even brutally foreseen. At Tehran, Churchill wrote: 'I demonstrated with the help of three matches my idea of Poland moving westwards. This pleased Stalin. . . .' At Potsdam discussion went beyond matchsticks to human beings, and it was agreed that the 5 million Germans living within the new frontiers of Poland must be expelled; in the north they were shifted at the rate of 2,500 a day through Szczecin to Schleswig-Holstein.

The Germans lost their homes and everything but their baggage. They suffered the grief and indignity of the conquered and the exiled. Many have recorded their experiences, often in memoirs of distinction. Some treat their sufferings at the hands of the Red Army and of the Poles as uniquely appalling. Their readers need to be reminded that by the standards of eastern Europe in the Second World War most of them got off relatively lightly. In Norman Davies's cool words: 'For the first time in their lives, a great mass of ordinary and decent Germans were reduced to the sort of predicament which most ordinary and decent citizens of Central and Eastern Europe had come to regard as normal.'

You can still find in Germany old people who remember the Pomerania from which they were driven in 1945. They have golden memories of what they have lost, as golden in their way as memories of England before 1914. Pomerania was a land of estates and comfortable country houses, of orderly villages with cherished churches, of woods and cornfields, of an unchanging rural society. Two young Englishmen who were to become eminent men of letters discovered Pomerania in the early years of this century. An Englishwoman of uncertain temperament and literary aspiration, who later made a name and an income for herself as Elizabeth von Arnim, married a Pomeranian landowner. She found him uninspiring, and satisfied her own taste for literary conversation and her daughters' need for education by employing two young Englishmen to coach them: E. M. Forster in 1905 and Hugh Walpole a season later.

Forster remembered warmly the three daughters and the rural beauty of Pomerania. He obviously found Elizabeth von Arnim herself, with her moods and exaggerations, more difficult to come to terms with in her Pomeranian exile, and he used his pen to take a cool revenge. He wrote to a friend in England that he 'couldn't find the precious garden', which as *Elizabeth and Her German Garden* formed the basis of the Arnim literary reputation. And with his employer clearly in his sights he wrote, in a tone of exasperation that even today many a male might echo if he dare: 'Women are not, I think, sillier than men, but more shameless; as each mood . . . arrives, they base a view of life on it, and pour out opinions which they must inevitably contradict.'

The Pomeranian idyll ended abruptly in 1945. Poles came from the east, displaced by the great shift westward of Poland's frontier with the Soviet Union, to replace the Germans. The Arnims' estate at Nassenheide became a Polish farm. Throughout Pomerania the Poles found a country which, even at the end of a long war and after Russian depredation, seemed to them unimaginably rich: fertile, varied land, which had been cosseted by careful husbandry for centuries. The towns and villages still show traces of that old prosperity, interleaved with the bleak evidence of the drive to build here as elsewhere a Peoples' Poland.

If he speaks Polish the visitor can identify not just the children and grandchildren of the immigrants of 1945, but side-by-side with them the native country people whose families lived for centuries as marginally second-class citizens in German Pomerania. If he does not, he has to take it on trust that this man's family came from Grodno in the great migration, that this old woman was born in the corner cottage in which she will surely die, and that this couple are not Poles at all, but Kashubians from the gentle hill-country just west of Gdansk, whose predicament Günter Grass anatomised in *The Tin*

Drum and summarised as 'not German enough for the Germans nor Polish enough for the Poles'.

The towns of Polish Pomerania make less impact than the countryside. They are sleepy and scruffy in a Polish-Irish kind of way. Inland from the little coastal resorts there is a sense of time-lessness and gentleness. A woman and a five-year-old wobble on their bicycles through a country town. She wheels suddenly to the other side of the street, in search of conversation and sausages. The child wobbles on, until he too turns across the street to pat a dog. No one is surprised.

I ask three children the way to Szczecinek. They listen carefully, eyes solemn, and unlike the Mars bar dealer they understand. Further on a hairdresser's is fenced in by a row of diversions for children: coin-in-the-slot-controlled helicopter, go-kart, motor bike and jet fighter rides at 600 zlotys a go. Out in the country a fisherman stalks preoccupied across the road, on his way from one little lake to another. In the next village an ancient man is perched high up on the roof of an ancient church, creosoting it back to health. In a field a man is sieving grain, a woman raking it into heaps. A gigan-tic, road-blocking piece of farm machinery trundling to a new field speaks of more serious farming, action, economic activity; but Pomerania mostly sleeps as deeply as did Mecklenburg a week ago.

One of the coastal towns of what is now Pomorze has a particular story to tell. Kolobrzeg sits on a bleak bit of Baltic coast seventy miles from Szczecin. Its history goes back 1,200 years, but now it is nothing more than a middling seaside resort, patronised by Poles who cannot afford to go further afield. Like everywhere else on this Pomeranian coast, it used to be a German town, and in 1807, as Kolberg, it wrote itself into Prussian history.

In that year the otherwise unknown General Nettelbeck stood a long siege here against the armies of Napoleon, in an act of deter-mination that symbolised Prussia's recovery and reassertion of herself as a nation. The siege of Kolberg became the stuff of German history books, and in 1944 Goebbels, casting around for ways to motivate the German people, decided to make a film of it. Somehow he extri-cated 100,000 troops from the fighting on the eastern front. With them he made a glorious historical extravaganza, in which German troops doggedly resisted the might of Napoleon to make a powerful propaganda point. By the time the film was ready at the beginning of 1945, Germany was on her last legs. But Goebbels's film was distributed nevertheless, flown intrepidly even to German garrisons cut off, hundreds of miles behind the lines, on the French Atlantic coast. It showed them and other German audiences how Germans could fight against all odds, when all seemed lost.

But another story came to cap Goebbels's propaganda extravaganza. In March 1945 Polish troops advanced to the sea at Kolberg. They came determined to celebrate the recovery of Pomerania. Soldiers and civilians advanced breast-deep into the icy waters to celebrate Poland's reunion with the Baltic, just as they had in 1920, in as solemn a celebration as the Doges' annual reconsecration of Venice's marriage with the Adriatic. Ever since, Kolobrzeg has belonged to them, not to the German defenders whom Goebbels conjured out of celluloid, nor to the Germans living out their retirements, remembering their farms and the society that their forebears created in what used to be German Pomerania.

We drive on from Kolobrzeg into the Kashubian hill and lake country, and from there down into Gdansk. Gradually, activity accumulates: thumping buses, groaning trams, crowds at bus stops, a sprawling hospital. It is a big city, its suburbs spreading inland from the Bay of Danzig and reaching out to the west and south. There is muck and murk in the sky, dirty weatherstains on the concrete flanks of the blocks of flats. The foreigners are lost until a railway station punctuates the streets; beyond the tracks lies the main town, which looks like the heart of a medieval city, and the old town, bits of which look even older. Beyond the main town you reach the canal and the harbour; beyond the old town lie the shipyards which put Gdansk's mark on the modern world. Gdansk is populous – 750,000 people if you throw in Gdynia and Sopot up the coast. Seedy and down-at-heel as it is, it throbs with life. Leave aside its history and it is no mean city. Weave in the history and you have one of the great cities of the Baltic.

Gdansk stands close to the point where the Vistula empties itself into the Baltic. To the Poles, the Vistula has always been the quintessence of Poland, linking as it does Krakow, Warsaw and Gdansk. Poles will tell you that there were Poles around Gdansk and the mouth of the Vistula at the beginning of recorded history, rubbing shoulders with Kashubians and pre-German Prussians and Pomeranians, with the people of Warmia and Chelmno and Mazovia. And the German merchants who set up shop in Danzig did so by permission of the Poles, just as the Teutonic Order came to the Vistula by Polish invitation.

But by the end of the thirteenth century the German presence had grown to dominate the area. Danzig became unarguably a German trading city, linked along the Baltic to the other cities of the Hanseatic League. It monopolised Poland's sea-borne trade. Polish wheat, amber and timber flowed westwards through the hands of German merchants, and they imported in return the cloth and weapons and luxuries of the west. Meanwhile the power of the Teutonic Knights grew in Danzig's hinterland. In 1308 they seized the city, and from then on the Order lived in incongruous association with the trading cities of the Hansa. The relationship between Poland and the Order, between the Teutonic Knights and Danzig, fluctuated. But for centuries Danzig's mercantile prosperity endured, and it grew to be one of the greatest of Hansa cities. The Hansa shared a common interest in controlling the trade of northern Europe by serving the interdependent needs of east and west. For its part Danzig served both Poland and the west; and in so doing it served itself.

Danzig survived the Teutonic Order's defeat at Tannenberg. It survived the Swedish wars. The steady expansion of Russian power challenged Danzig's prosperity but did not cripple it. The successive partitions of Poland did little to discommode it. Napoleon's Continental System failed to choke off its trade with England. In Seton Merriman's romantic and sentimental *Barlasch of the Guard* you can read how the Danzigers watched the French set off to march on Moscow and lived through a bitter siege on their return.

In the centre of Gdansk today you can see satisfactory replicas of the relics of all this history. Replicas, because there is next to nothing here that dates back very far except ideas: the city was almost entirely destroyed in the war. What you see today is a reconstruction, as perfect as and, in its grime, perhaps even more convincing than the reconstruction of Warsaw. The main street and the main square run from the city gates to the canal which opens onto the harbour. In 1945 they were flanked by rubble. Now they are bounded by Gothic and Renaissance houses and the great mass of the Town Hall, with the Upland Gate closing one end of the promenade and the Green Gate the other.

Behind the Town Hall is St Mary's Church, as pre-eminent in the world of Baltic brick churches as the Marienkirchen and Georgenkirchen we have seen in Germany. City gates, fine warehouses and an ancient timber crane line the canal. A street of merchants' houses running down from St Mary's to the canal would not be out of place in Amsterdam or, strangely enough, on New York's Upper West Side. Yet almost all these buildings in their infinite variety date from the 1950s.

The shipyards are not as remote as you might imagine: you can walk to the monument to the workers killed in the 1970 riots in no more than twice the time it takes to walk down to the canal. Its date reminds you that the great Polish political stand-off lasted for over thirty years: successful resistance in 1956, riots in 1970, martial law in 1980, the avalanche of change in 1989. It demonstrates that Gdansk has made itself central in Polish affairs, a chief protagonist of Solidarity's long struggle, a major architect of post-Communist Poland. Behind the monument are the shipyard gates and the great stretches, most of them empty now, of the shipyards themselves. This was the industry Communism built and this is the industry, inspired by an out-of-work electrician called Walesa, which destroyed Communism. Now, ex-President Walesa is back at work in a shipyard which, like those in Rostock and Wismar, is still looking for investment in an enterprise which seems unlikely ever to return a profit.

If its shipyards represent old men's ideas of business, the visitors' Gdansk displays their grandchildren's enterprise. In the town square and St Mary's Street, eager young saleswomen offer you amber and antiques, videos of the city, designer clothes and old tat. A teenage businessman runs rides in golf runabouts from the Upland Gate to the Green Gate and back again. You can get coffee and ice cream in a restaurant built into the flank of the Town Hall. Before too long, tourism will be Gdansk's leading industry.

For the moment, however, the tourist trade makes little of Danzig's curious twentieth-century history. But in a second-hand bookshop you can buy mementoes of the Free City of Danzig, that strange creation of the League of Nations which survived for nearly twenty years until it was swept away by war in 1939, an absurd little kingdom under its League of Nations commissioner, in which the world tried to make sense of conflicting national passions and self-assertion. The Free City pleased no one in particular: not the Poles, who believed that they should control Poland's port and the mouth of Poland's river; not the Germans, who believed that they should control the Baltic; not the Danzigers, who for the most part thought of themselves as Germans. But the League of

Nations formula seemed something with which reasonable men might reasonably be asked to live. The Poles could comfort themselves with the corridor and Gdynia; the Germans and the Danzigers with the city's special status. But from the beginning Hitler in his unreasonable way was determined to sweep away the corridor and the Free City. Throughout the 1930s Nazi agitation challenged the compromise, and war in 1939 destroyed it.

At 4.40 in the morning of 1 September 1939, the German warship *Schleswig-Holstein*, moored in the port of Danzig, opened fire pointblank on Westerplatte, a Polish military base on a spit of land between the harbour and the city. It was garrisoned by a major's command of 182 men. Like Polish troops everywhere in that autumn of 1939, the major and his men astonished the Germans, holding an indefensible position against naval gunfire and infantry assault for seven days. Broken fortifications and inscriptions on the spot tell you their story, as Günter Grass's *The Tin Drum* tells the story of the defenders of the Polish post office in Danzig, executed for resisting the victorious Germans. Danzig returned to the Reich; the offending Polish corridor to the sea was obliterated; Poland was partitioned yet again. On 2 October, a month after the onslaught on Poland began, when resistance elsewhere had been overcome, Polish troops on the Hel peninsula, which curves in a long arc round the Bay of Danzig, finally laid down their arms.

Gdansk is a good place to reflect on the story of Poland's endless struggle with Germany for access to the sea. It is a good place, too, in which to turn one's mind to Poland itself, that mad, marvellous, indomitable country which, more than any other and with all her faults, brings a kind of glory to the Baltic.

Poland is a big country, bigger than western Europeans think any country in eastern Europe outside Russia has a right to be. She has as many people as Spain, nearly 40 million, and is not much smaller in area than united Germany. Her history as a state goes back beyond the Norman Conquest. Her borders have shifted endlessly, she has been repeatedly extinguished as a nation. But nothing has extinguished the elements which give the Poles their passionate sense of identity: a blend of patriotism, language, personal dignity, Catholicism, championship of Europe against Tartars and Turks, and heroic resistance to Russia and Germany.

You can trace the story of that resistance as far back in history as your antiquarian instincts lead you. There are Poles who talk about the victory at Tannenberg in 1410 as if it were yesterday. The eighteenth-century partitions, which extinguished Poland as a state, confirmed her identity as a nation and a people. The nineteenth-century risings against the Russians ingrained Poland with a hopeless kind of heroism. And in our own time Hitler's attack on Poland, Stalin's stab in the back, the Warsaw uprising and the Soviet betrayal, sharpened still further the image of Poland as heroine and victim. The Poles themselves see their country simultaneously as a mother in the likeness of God's mother and as a sacrificial victim in the likeness of Christ, for they are not a people given to half-measures, especially when they think about themselves.

The tragedy of Poland's subordination to Moscow and to Communism is perhaps even more poignant than that of other eastern European countries. Czechoslovakia did not fight for her freedom. Hungary fought on the Germans' side. Bulgaria welcomed the Russians. But Poland fought from the first day of the war to the last, in Poland itself, in Russia and Italy, in the Atlantic and the Battle of Britain. And at the end of it, Poland's freedom and integrity were swept into Moscow's grasp. Yet the Poles were the first of the eastern Europeans to emerge from that subordination. Successful diplomacy backed by national unity carried them successfully through the first great eastern European crisis of 1956, in which the Czechs were cowed and the Hungarians shattered. Ever afterwards, the Poles succeeded in keeping the Russians, at least by the standards of that world, at arm's length. Through riots, strikes and martial law they preserved a sense of Poland's interests as distinct from those of the socialist world, and of the Polish nation as distinct from its Communist rulers. The church was unmistakably Polish. So was the army. So was Solidarity. Poland may have achieved her freedom more as a consequence of Gorbachev's heroic realism in Moscow than of any action taken in Warsaw or Poznan or Gdansk. But thirty years of national assertion had prepared Poland for the freedom that came in 1989.

Certainly, everywhere you go in Poland you sense that the Poles are prepared for liberty in a way that the east Germans are not. The Poles have abused their freedom since 1990, but they have used it fruitfully too, enjoyed it, enlarged it, explored its possibilities. No one in Poland is going to hand it back, to Zyuganov or to anyone else. Poor, vulnerable, chaotic she may be, but Poland is back as a sovereign independent power upon the Baltic. Once again she demands to be accepted as an equal among European nations.

For the moment the Polish agenda is a conventional one. With the other members of the Visegrad group – the Czech Republic, Hungary and Slovakia – Poland seeks European Union membership. With most of the countries of central and eastern Europe she seeks membership of NATO, and meanwhile does her best to promote and develop the Partnership for Peace. She wants to keep pan-European mechanisms and forums in place, but is suspicious of those who see them as a substitute for more muscular co-operation.

Poland fears Russia, both in present weakness and in a possible revival of strength. Russia has threatened Poland for 500 years, fought her often and dominated her for the best part of two centuries. The Russian province of Kaliningrad is packed with troops and guns on Poland's northern border. Like the three Baltic states, the Poles feel vulnerable to any revival of Russian imperialism, old style or new.

But in a quite different way, Poland fears Germany. She welcomes Germany's friendship, her support for Polish membership of the European Union, her bilateral help and investment. But she will not forget her sufferings at Germany's hands. She sees a Germany economically pre-eminent in Europe, the weightiest force in the European Union, a country with interests extending deep into the eastern Baltic. Poland fears not the intentions of a decent and benevolent Germany, but her capabilities: political and economic today, conceivably taking more threatening forms the day after tomorrow. *Jamais en parler, toujours en penser* speaks even more for the Poles than for any other of Germany's neighbours.

Poland's traditional answer to her situation of vulnerability between Russia and Germany has been to reach out to the west. Napoleon brought her only short relief; Britain and France could do nothing for her in 1939; and the West sold her into Soviet captivity in 1945. But the sense of affinity still lingers, and with it the desire to lock the West into Poland's destinies. Membership of NATO and of the European Union would give Poland that western reassurance which she craves. But European Union membership is several years away at least, and full membership of NATO perhaps unattainable. In the meantime Poland looks for friends where she may, and sees encouragement in Finland and Scandinavia. Denmark, for example, has a defence agreement with Poland, and Sweden and

Finland in their different ways reach out to her, as to the Baltic republics. Beyond this, Poland would like to see herself building further bilateral relationships. For Britain, committed to European Union but so regularly at odds with her major partners, closer links with old friends around the periphery may not be the quixotic things little Englanders or users of small-scale maps might think them.

If you drive northward away from Gdansk up the coast, you come to other relics of the years between the wars. In the 1930s Sopot, just outside Danzig, was eastern Europe's most fashionable sea-bathing resort. Today it is a down-at-heel Blackpool, packed on a summer's evening with promenaders: fathers pushing prams, children surging to and fro, cherubic babies in the arms of respectable young mothers dressed like whores. When I was there it seemed intent on feeding its visitors ice cream and, as far as the foreigner could establish, little else. Its grand hotels were decrepit, echoing, crepuscular as the northern light faded outside. Now, to see the new rich and the beautiful people of Poland at play you must go to Hel, the scene of Poland's last stand in 1939, fifteen miles away across Gdansk bay.

Beyond Sopot is Gdynia, a handsome, rather anonymous city created out of a fishing village in the 1920s to give Poland her own port on the Baltic. The economics were shaky even then, and foreigners said that the Poles were being absurdly Polish, putting politics and dreams ahead of economics and common sense. But in Gdynia the Poles created their Baltic port and with it a fighting navy, most of which made a miraculous escape in 1939 and went on to fight the Germans beside the Royal Navy in the battles of Norway and the Atlantic. They cherish it today, with a polished and burnished old destroyer and a venerable three-masted training ship moored at the quayside to remind visitors of Poland's real if improbable maritime past.

The road eastward out of Gdansk crosses successive branches of the Vistula on their lazy way to the sea. This is low-lying country, marshland reclaimed for agriculture. There is a Dutch look about it, long flatnesses and huge skies. Indeed, Dutch settlers in the seventeenth century had a hand in the reclamation, but here the fanatical tidiness of Holland is overlaid by Polishness. You leave what was the Free City of Danzig and enter what was East Prussia.

Elblag comes next, with a canal and a fine brick church and much less industrial blight than the guide book threatens. This is the Elbing of history, where in 1579 the English merchants of the Eastland Company, chartered to trade with the Baltic, first established a depot. They did not prosper as the Hansa had done, even though Queen Elizabeth withdrew the Hansa's privileges in England to give the Eastlanders a competitive advantage. But British merchants persisted all along the southern and eastern Baltic, in Danzig, Elbing, Königsberg, Riga and Tallinn. The English House is a landmark in Gdansk today. Samuel Pepys recorded a conversation in a London coffee-house with Eastland merchants, who told him some tall stories about life near Königsberg. English merchants remained in the Baltic to challenge Napoleon's Continental System: their presence in Riga was so malignant that he called the city a suburb of London and threatened to burn it to the ground. But he never captured Riga, and it still had an English lord mayor in the last years of peace before the First World War.

Beyond Elblag the land rises, as you drive deeper into what was the old East Prussia and is now a remote and largely forgotten corner of Poland. Our goal here is Frombork, a fly-blown little town squeezed between a lagoon and a precipitous hill. The hill is crowned by a fine little cathedral, canons' houses and an observatory, embraced within a perimeter wall which dominates the town. Frombork today stands only ten miles from the Russian border. It was firmly closed for forty post-war years and though the border is more or less open now, even today Frombork feels very close to the end of the line. Yet there was a time when it could claim to be the centre of the universe.

For fifteen years in the sixteenth century, Nicholas Copernicus lived and worked on the hill above Frombork in the cathedral close. He was a canon of the cathedral, administrator of the diocese, a sound ecclesiastical bureaucrat. But he was no provincial; rather a true European who had studied widely and who kept up his studies when he came to the little cathedral city. It was he who built the observatory, and there he established that the earth went round the sun rather than the sun around the earth.

There is, when you come to think about it, an irony about that Frombork discovery. It has a central place in the flowering of modern thought, part of the process of putting the mind of man rather than faith in God at the centre of things. But Copernicus established paradoxically that man's only habitat was peripheral, not central to the universe. Having raised man up, Renaissance science cast him down. And, as Hans Küng suggests in his book *On Being a Christian,* science has continued the process ever since. Marx subjected man to economic circumstance; Darwin located his origins in the sub-human; and Freud subordinated his intellect to his instinctive subconscious.

It would be overdoing things to burden little Frombork with that intellectual luggage, but it really did have its moment as the centre of enquiry about the universe. And its place was taken after Copernicus's death by an even more improbable place we shall pass later in this expedition. We have seen the little island of Ven through Bo's telescope. There, safely isolated from importunate visitors, lived for twenty years the eccentric sixteenth-century Danish nobleman, Tycho Brahe, presiding over an observatory of his own and cataloguing the stars.

I drove on beyond Frombork to the Russian frontier, and in that wooded, northernmost part of Poland, I saw two remarkable things. At the edge of a field a house reared up, large, grey, built of breeze blocks, apparently doomed by the complications of Polish taxation to remain forever unfinished. A balustraded terrace at ground level and a balustraded balcony above stretched themselves across its long, unkempt face. On the left, a grand balustraded staircase ran up from terrace to balcony. On the right, a similar staircase ran down from balcony to terrace. Here, in the back of beyond, a proud Polish builder was putting the Fiddler on the Roof's practical philosophy to work.

A mile further on, my little back road passed over another, deep in a cutting twenty feet below. I went exploring down a steep slip road, half hidden by blackberry bushes. The main road at the bottom had all the characteristics of Hitler's early autobahns that you can still find in quiet corners of the Federal Republic. Signposts pointed to unknown villages. I had found what was left of the autobahn, built to lead arrogantly from Königsberg to Berlin but which now led humbly, even diffidently, from Slupsk to Plonsk.

The Baltic coast from Gdansk to Narva is marked by the presence of the Teutonic Knights, but their story belongs particularly to Königsberg and the old East Prussia, a subject to be explored in the next chapter. But they had their beginnings in what is now firmly

Polish territory. So one more excursion is needed before we can say we have explored the Polish Baltic: up the Vistula to the Teutonic Order's first strongholds, then east to the scene of their defeat at Tannenberg.

The Knights first established themselves in a place they called Marienwerder, which is today's Kwidzyn. They were invited there in the early thirteenth century by an injudicious Polish prince, who looked to them to keep at bay pagan Prussian incursions from the north. In Kwidzyn they built a little brick castle on a steep slope above the river, and from it they moved methodically down the Vistula against the Prussians, building fortresses as they went.

They moved up the Vistula also, to Grudziadz, Chelmno and Torun, edging steadily deeper into old Poland. Even after the Teutonic Order's decline, German influence persisted here almost until our own times, through Hanseatic trade, German settlement and Prussian rule after the partitions of Poland. The Germans have been swept from Kwidzyn and Chelmno, Grudziadz and Torun, but the Protestant flavour of the German Baltic persists half a century after their departure, mixed intriguingly with Polish Catholic flavours, and even with Orthodox ones. Torun and Chelmno in particular offer handsome squares, fine medieval and Renaissance houses, red brick Gothic churches, the remains of city walls, and long views over the Vistula. Torun also boasts the Zajazd Staropolski, a real hotel with real food which shone like a good deed in a country which four years ago offered the traveller little except Communist-era hotels and the tedium of food to match. The city also offered me a conversation with a Polish patriot and economic realist, a young man in charge of a car park. 'Is my car safe here?' Of course, he said, especially as no sensible thief wanted a car with the steering wheel on the wrong side. 'Do you want Deutschmarks or Marlboroughs or zlotys?' Zlotys, he said; zlotys were convertible, so why trouble oneself with cigarettes or funny money. The pride and release of business energy implicit in that reply goes a long way to offset the impoverishment and inequality which economic freedom has brought with it.

The Teutonic Knights established themselves in Kwidzyn, Chelmno and Torun in the first half of the thirteenth century. Towards its end they set about building a new headquarters, much further down the Vistula valley at what is now Malbork. They built their Castle of St Mary – Marienburg – on the very edge of Prussia.

The castle of Malbork with its red-brick walls and steep, red-tiled roofs glows in the sunlight; but even on a twentieth-century summer's day, with tourists clambering on the ramparts, Marienburg is a place of menace, claustrophobic like the Tower of London, packed with memories of armed men. The town beside it lacks the urbanity of the cities further up the Vistula. Malbork is marked by its history as a one-company town; and the business of the company, the Order of the Hospital of Our Lady of the German House in Jerusalem, was conquest, exploitation and control.

To visit the scene of the Teutonic Knights' discomfiture you must drive sixty miles south-east from their old headquarters to Tannenberg, on the fringe of the Mazurian lake country. Here in 1410 the Poles and the Lithuanians effected a combination that defeated the Teutonic Knights in open battle. It was one of the greatest battles of the Middle Ages, and Poles and Lithuanians to this day argue as to who played the greater role in the victory, like Germans and Englishmen disputing Waterloo. Tannenberg did not destroy the power of the Knights, but it checked their insolence, reasserted that more than mere words was expected of their fealty to the Polish kings. After Tannenberg they were never again all-powerful warriors of Christ. Eventually they moved their headquarters from Marienburg on Polish territory to Königsberg, deep in the Prussia they had conquered. The rivalry between Poland and the Order, between Poles and the German settlers who came in the Order's wake, continued – part of the frontier relationship which kept Germans and Poles at odds for centuries.

In the end, on the same battlefield of Tannenberg, the Germans also won a splendid victory. In August 1914, faithful to their agreement with the French, the Russians launched their military steamroller into East Prussia. The weight of the German army had been flung against Belgium and France; in the east the Germans stood on the defensive; and panic spread as it does in the first days of war, with the cry that nothing stood between the invaders and Berlin itself. Old General Hindenburg was recalled from retirement, wily General Ludendorff from the western front. Together they hurried east to meet their staff in Marienburg. Plans were confirmed, adjusted. The Russians, without motor transport, without air reconnaissance, their communications an open book to the Germans, lumbered forward. One of their armies had moved into East Prussia from the east, another from the south. The lakes and woods of East Prussia separated them. Solzhenitsyn's *August 1914* tells the story of their terrible destruction.

The Germans had avenged on the Russians the defeat which the Poles and Lithuanians had inflicted on them 500 years before. Overnight the great victory at Tannenberg became a legend. But the medieval defeat still rankled, and when Hitler's troops marched into Krakow in 1939 they razed to the ground the city's memorial to the Polish victory of Tannenberg. But so far at least, the Poles have had the last word. No German today holds land within 300 miles of Tannenberg. East Prussia is cut in two between Russia and Poland, its towns and farms peopled by Russians and Poles. Poland is free and independent. And to legions of visiting Polish children, Tannenberg is the site of a Polish victory just as Marienburg is a Polish castle, recaptured from defeated invaders long ago, when even their grandfathers were young.

5

Kaliningrad and Prussia

On a map, the frontier between Poland and Kaliningrad looks more North American than European. It runs due east in a straight line from the Baltic coast for 120 miles. North of it lies an area of 5,600 square miles, which until 1945 formed part of the German province of East Prussia. In that year the Potsdam powers divided East Prussia between Poland and the Soviet Union. Today its northern half forms the Kaliningrad region of the Russian Federation. To the north and east lies Lithuania, separating Kaliningrad from mother Russia. To the north-west lies the sea, fringed here by the two largest lagoons of the Baltic. Between the lagoons stands the city of Kaliningrad, which once was Königsberg.

On my journey along the southern side of the Baltic, Mecklenburg-Vorpommern, for all its woes, left me with the feeling that one day all will come right, and Poland brought the intoxication that accompanies all things Polish. Later we shall be sustained by the euphoria of the three Baltic states, now that they are nations once again. But Kaliningrad greets you with despondent surliness and sends you on your way with a sense of hopelessness and defeat. The scars of war and conquest half a century ago are etched upon its face, which bears too the scabs of fifty years of careless abuse and absolute neglect. Look for silver linings as you may, tell yourself that effort and the human spirit can turn the worst things round; all the same you will find it difficult to escape the conviction that this is the armpit of the Baltic.

Nature is not easily laid waste for long, and the Kaliningrad countryside, despite polluted water and poisoned air, asserts itself as it has always done. There are avenues of lime trees and chestnuts beside the roads; deep woodland beyond the ragged, deserted fields; marshland and quiet rivers. The long spits that enclose the lagoons along the coast offer deserted dunes. But the country towns, which once stole the hearts of inhabitants and visitors alike with their old churches and remains of castles and their careful Teutonic husbandry, are now abandoned to mud, dust and neglect. The fifteenth-century church at Drushba, which once was the neat little German town of Allenburg, has become a warehouse, and the church at Bagrationowsk, the site of Napoleon's defeat at Eylau, is now a factory. In the country towns the detritus of collective farms crowds in upon abandoned churches and sad, broken castle ruins. Round a corner you come across a bleak Soviet memorial to brave young men who died here in that last savage assault upon the Nazis. If in 1945 hope was mingled with fear, now there is only despairing lethargy.

The city of Kaliningrad itself is the bleakest place of all. There are supposed to be 400,000 inhabitants, but usually the streets echo emptily. Soldiers and sailors idle on windswept corners, a drunk dribbles in a gutter, and groups of aged German tourists shuffle past in search of lost memories. The old Königsberg is gone, laid waste by western bombers in the summer of 1944. They left the cathedral a burnt out shell; the Rathaus, the university and the castle shattered. Then, for three months at the beginning of 1945, the Russians and Germans bitterly contested the ruins. Most of the population of East Prussia had fled, but Königsberg still had more than 100,000 people at the beginning of the siege, only 25,000 when it was over. The end of the war brought the deportation of the few Germans who still cowered among the ruins. Gradually the ruins themselves were levelled, covered in concrete, and the memories they represented buried.

Kaliningrad today is a Russian city, a place of cracked and stained concrete buildings, of oversized empty squares and desolate streets. A House of Soviets, built in the 1960s, looms like a giant Dalek over a concrete wasteland. The rubble of the castle lies under concrete, and beneath the rubble, they say, is hidden the famous Amber Chamber, purloined by the Nazis from the Pushkin Palace when they finally abandoned the siege of Leningrad. A statue of Schiller survives amid this wilderness. There is a memorial to Kant, Königsberg's most famous son, a Kant museum in the university, and the great man's tomb in the partially and incompetently restored cathedral.

In the city's offices you can find optimists and opportunists, promoting Kaliningrad's attractions for western investors, making you offers no wise man can refuse, talking about wonders to come. But there is no optimism among the people in the streets. They are Russians or Ukrainians, settled here in the post-war years, most

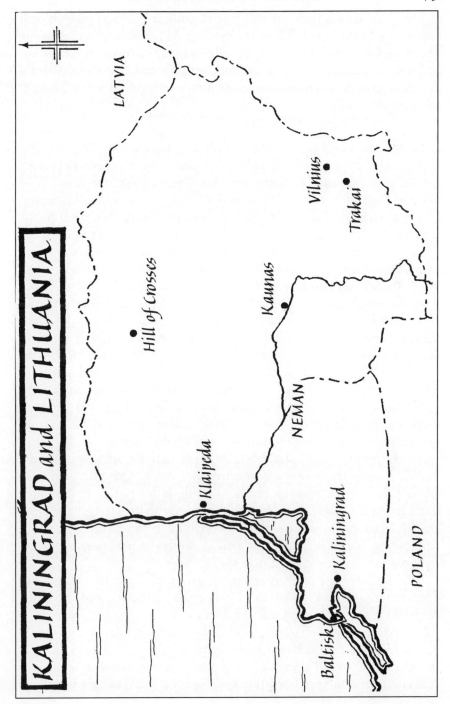

LATVIA

Vilnius

Trakai

KALININGRAD and LITHUANIA

Hill of Crosses

Kaunas

NEMAN

Klaipeda

Kaliningrad

Baltisk

POLAND

of them as dependants of the Soviet military society which still dominates Kaliningrad. They live in a city which was recreated in the Soviet image, which lost its essentially military purpose six years ago and whose leaders now cast around, optimistically or despondently depending on their temperament, for a new purpose to put in place of the old.

For 500 years before its destruction, Königsberg was a German city, perhaps the greatest of the Baltic. But there were people here long before the Teutonic Knights and the German settlers came. The original Prussians were a Baltic people, cousins of the Latvians and Livs and Lithuanians. Gradually Christianity established itself to the west and south, but not among the Balts. The Prussians, like the other Baltic tribes, formed self-sufficient heathen societies of their own. They farmed, traded, hunted and raided their enemies. When the Eastland merchants told Samuel Pepys in a London coffee house how the people around Königsberg caught fish, froze them living and revived them in the spring, how they smoked bees out of their tree-hives and how they hunted bears, they were describing a way of life that went back 1,000 years, that of the old Prussians, not of the German newcomers who ruled Prussia in the seventeenth century. These were the people who first built a fortress on a hill beside the river Pregel where it flows into the Kaliningrad lagoon. Here a market sprang up, a magnet to Viking traders and merchants from Lübeck, which attracted western interest in old Prussia.

The Lübeckers would have been content with a trading post on the Pregel, such as those they established all the way into northern Russia. But there were other Germans at work in the eastern Baltic, most notably the Teutonic Knights. We have seen their legacy in Poland, and will see more of what they left behind in the Baltic states. But Königsberg was the centre of their power, and Kaliningrad is the right place to explore their astonishing career.

At the end of the twelfth century a group of German knights and of merchants from Bremen and Lübeck who had followed Frederick Barbarossa to the Holy Land established a hospital for the care of wounded crusaders. Their organisation flourished and they determined to form themselves into an order of chivalry. The result was the Order of the Hospital of Our Lady of the German House in Jerusalem, and in 1199 Pope Innocent III took it under his protection.

But the Germans had come late to the crusades, and the great days of the crusaders in the Levant were over. There was no clear and glorious role for the German knights to play in the Holy Land.

Their lay patron, Emperor Frederick II, turned his mind from the Levant towards the Baltic, where he saw German expansion as a counterweight to papal authority. He sought a role for the German knights, and found it in Prussia. There was trouble on its ill-defined border with Poland. It was the old story of action and reaction, attack and counter-attack that can be found along any unsettled frontier from the Romans' time to our own. The Prussians had violently rejected the first Christian missionaries, who turned to the Poles for protection. But the Prussians proved too much for the invading Poles, and invaded Poland in their turn. In the previous chapter we saw the Teutonic Knights responding to an appeal for help from a Polish prince, Duke Conrad of Mazovia, and establishing themselves in northern Poland.

In 1226 they went over to the offensive against the Prussians. The Emperor appointed the Grand Master a Prince of the Holy Roman Empire, and authorised him to invade and conquer 'the lands of the Prussians'. The Teutonic Knights advanced down the Vistula and into Prussia, building fortifications as they went. Twenty years later they built a castle on the site of the old Prussians' fort on the Pregel. To honour the most distinguished of their number, King Ottokar of Bohemia, they called it Königsberg.

The Knights continued to extend their territories. They joined hands with another group of Christian adventurers, the Knights of the Sword of the Livonian Order, who had accompanied Albrecht of Bremen's expedition to Riga in 1201. By the year 1252 the Orders held a fortified base on the Lithuanian coast at Memel, today's Klaipeda, eighty miles north of Königsberg.

The native Prussians resisted the Knights for another fifty years, but they were pitted against a supremely effective military machine. Only once did the Knights find themselves seriously challenged. In 1260 a Prussian freedom fighter, Herkus Monte, led his people in a mass uprising against them. For fourteen years Monte sustained a guerrilla campaign against the invaders, but by 1274 he was finally defeated, and with that defeat the Prussians lost what remained of their lands and liberty, and eventually their name. Groups of old Prussians lingered, marginalised like American Indians, occasionally sustained by help from the Lithuanians across the Neman. But in the end even the Prussians' language was extinguished, and no trace remained of the conquered people. The story of Prussia became a German story, which lasted until 1945.

For another two centuries the Knights sought to win souls for Christ and land for their Order. Each year they rode out from Königsberg and Memel to do battle against the Lithuanians. Time after time the Lithuanians beat them off and eventually made common cause with the Poles. So it was an alliance of Poles and newly Christian Lithuanians which took the field at Tannenberg against the Knights on 15 July, 1410, and finally defeated them. Two hundred knights, their principal officers and the Grand Master himself fell in battle that day.

The Teutonic Knights never fully recovered their authority and reputation after Tannenberg. They abandoned their annual campaigns against the Lithuanians and, in a shadowy kind of way, acknowledged the suzerainty of the Polish kings. Much of the lower Vistula fell to Poland, but nothing could loosen the Knights' hold on Prussia. They made Königsberg as formidable a headquarters as Marienburg, and built castles throughout Prussia to reinforce their authority.

Any attempt to probe the motives of men who lived seven centuries ago is doomed to frustration. Piety, glory, a lust for souls or for property, escape from debt and wife at home, the craving for indulgences to shorten time in purgatory – among these motives and many more we shall never know for certain what drove any single knight to commit himself to the Teutonic Order in its crusades against the heathen. In any case, the medieval world did not make the tortured distinctions to which we subject ourselves when we question motives. To conquer the heathen, seize his land and enforce his labour, baptise him and bring his soul to God, all these desires coexisted in the medieval mind, interlarded with true piety and equally profound hypocrisy. The crusades had the pope's blessing and increased the harvest of souls. They promised land, power and fame to the victorious survivor.

Each individual knight was backed by the hierarchy of the Order, the princes and the bishops, the pope and the emperor, who calculated the political consequences of the crusaders' efforts: the shifted balance between heathen and Christian, between individual Christian princes, and within Christendom between pope and emperor. But for Christian gallants things were simpler. Chaucer based his knight on one of them, Henry of Derby. He tells us that his hero had fought in the Levant, in North Africa and in France. He joined the Teutonic Knights and campaigned with them in Russia and Lithuania. No-one, said Chaucer, had a higher seat at the Order's table when they gathered in Königsberg Castle. For Chaucer and his age, his knight was a model of Christian virtue and of manly bearing.

The adventures of the Teutonic Knights in the eastern Baltic had good effects and bad. They butchered heathens and brought other heathens to Christ. They enslaved their enemies and taught them the true faith. They stole land and settled German peasants on it, who brought to it a productivity unimagined elsewhere in the east. As members of the League they sold timber and tar, wax and hemp to the Hansa's customers down the Baltic, and returned bearing the west's weapons and luxuries and books. They destroyed pagan cultures and put Christian values in their place. Material progress accompanied them. Whether in the end they made things better or worse is anyone's guess, a value judgment none of whose terms can be defined. But the unbending rigour of the knights and the diligence of the settlers gradually created order, discipline and productivity in Prussia. The Knights transformed the eastern Baltic, profoundly and permanently.

The late Middle Ages saw the decline of the Teutonic Knights, and the Reformation brought an end to their order as a religious organisation. But the last Grand Master, Albrecht von Hohenzollern, transmogrified himself effortlessly into a prince of Protestant Europe. The Marshal of the Order, the Treasurer and many individual knights became lay magnates or squires, holding what had been the Order's estates and continuing to exercise the social and political authority which it had established. The diligence of German settlers provided the economic base on which the wealth and trade of the province depended. For more than 500 years after Tannenberg the lands around Königsberg remained a stable eastern bastion of the German world, even when that world was itself convulsed by change. These lands, with those of Brandenburg far away to the west, became the seed beds and nurseries of the German Empire.

East Prussia inherited the qualities which the Teutonic Knights

brought to the eastern Baltic: discipline and self-discipline were expressed in austerity of life, Lutheran religious observance, respect for
education and a willing subordination to authority. The East Prussian landowners zealously accepted their obligations. The province
was as much a land of churches as of crusader castles. Its farms were
ordered and productive, and its woods well-disciplined. It nurtured a
rigorous scholarship: we have seen that Copernicus, who would have
been welcome anywhere in Europe, spent his most productive years
as a scholar and churchman in East Prussia, and the university established at Königsberg in the 1540s produced over the centuries a long
line of scholars such as Herbart, Herder, Bazzenberg and Immanuel
Kant. Kant himself spent his whole life in and around Königsberg.
When he took his constitutional, neighbours set their clocks, so unchangeable was his routine. His qualities of intellectual rigour, self-
discipline and hard work were also Prussian qualities.

East Prussia also played a substantive and a symbolic role in a
wider eastern Europe. It formed a bold German salient on the Baltic.
It set standards for its Baltic, Polish and Russian neighbours. When in
the late sixteenth century the Counter-Reformation spread to northern Europe and the Jesuit university was established in Vilnius,
Königsberg University provided a Protestant counterweight. East
Prussian scholars studied the old Balt languages and when, in the
nineteenth century, the tsar forbade the Lithuanians the use of their
own language, East Prussia sustained them, printing books and
newspapers in Lithuanian and smuggling them across the Neman.
Neighbours enviously observed East Prussia's agricultural yields, the
fruits of German order, the benefits of progress under German
leadership.

Prussia's virtues were valued – and resented – throughout the rest
of Germany. The House of Hohenzollern came to provide a focus for
all Germany, and the Prussians became the foremost servants of the
emerging German state. The lower nobility and squirearchy – the
Junkers – produced officials and officers dedicated to the service of
Brandenburg, of Prussia and of the Confederation of German States;
and eventually of the German Empire and of the Third Reich. They
implemented the reforms that created the Prussia that stood up to
Napoleon. Their discipline, order, self-sacrifice and focused intel-
ligence gave nineteenth-century Germany a standard of public administration unique in continental Europe and an army and general
staff whose prowess frightened the world. Prussian generals and

officers held command on every front in the First World War and, in the Second, translated Hitler's evil genius into the reality of blood and iron.

The Junkers did not make themselves loved, in Germany or outside. To easy-going Rhinelanders or Bavarians they seemed inhuman in their dedication and self-discipline, inflexibly imposing north German standards on greater Germany. Germany's enemies and victims held them – in serving Emperor, Kaiser and Führer so effectively – responsible for Germany's aggressive wars. Attention turned to the East Prussians' defects, above all to their arrogance and ethnic consciousness. In the end it was army officers imbued with the Prussian tradition who led the attempt on Hitler's life in 1944; but it was East Prussia which, with Schleswig-Holstein, had voted most strongly for Hitler in the 1933 elections which brought him legitimately to power. When it was Germany's turn to be invaded, it was East Prussia which suffered first. In East Prussia's extinction at the hands of the Russians and Poles there was a kind of poetic justice, a final reckoning for the crimes that Germans committed in the east over the centuries, and most particularly between 1941 and 1945. But something of value died with it.

When the Soviet Union took possession of northern East Prussia she punished her enemies by expropriation and expulsion, and satisfied a psychological imperative by seizing a part of the hated Reich. There were military considerations too. Soviet defences on the Baltic were strengthened in 1945 by the reoccupation of the Baltic republics and the seizure of East Prussia. The Red Army secured a forward position on Russian rather than ex-enemy or satellite territory, and the Soviet Baltic Fleet acquired an ice-free base on East Prussia's Baltic coast. This new possession, named Kaliningrad after a seedy Bolshevik hero who became a figurehead Soviet President in the 1920s, served the Soviet Union as an armed camp much as it had the Teutonic Knights and the Prussian kings.

Armies rarely do much good to their training-grounds, as environmental activists and peace protesters have reminded the western world for thirty years. In Kaliningrad the reckless brutalities of the Red Army went unchecked by impertinent criticism, and civilian immigrants from the rest of the Soviet Union brought with them habits of Russian sloth compounded by Soviet inertia. Over the years the military on the one hand and the settlers on the other reduced Kaliningrad to Soviet squalor. The Pregel became an industrial sewer and military pollution poured into the Baltic. The Poles were as thorough in extirpating everything German from eastern Pomerania and southern East Prussia, but they put their own national pride in its place. Kaliningrad, remote from mother Russia, was consigned to isolated degradation.

The collapse of the Soviet Union in 1991, which brought uncovenanted relief to the rest of the Baltic, made matters worse. Despite its military might, Kaliningrad was totally dependent on Moscow. Equipment, spares, rations, pay, animation itself came from the metropolis. Now Moscow and mother Russia were preoccupied with problems at home. Next door, Lithuania achieved her joyful independence, and in her suspicious rejection of all things Russian challenged the military's overland access routes to Kaliningrad. The issue remains a bone of contention between Russia and Lithuania; and when, in 1996, the Russians sought an alternative route through Poland, alarm bells rang in Warsaw.

Whatever purpose the garrison and naval base might have served vanished with the détente that followed the eclipse of Communism. Morale and discipline collapsed. The black market took their place, blossoming into the sale of weapons and equipment, drug-dealing, corruption and extortion. The military were frustrated in Kaliningrad, fearful of a summons home. Civilians, dependent for almost everything on military initiative, dreaded their departure.

Kaliningrad has to find its own future. There is little to be hoped for from Russia, unless it be a desperate reassertion of great power status, a recovery of the 'near abroad' and honour for the armed forces once again. There are people in Kaliningrad who dream of such changes, and in the 1993 elections Zhirinovsky polled particularly well here. Officers in Kaliningrad will tell you that they could crush the Baltic states and recall the Poles to order in a week. But in today's world all this can be no more than a self-indulgent dream, fit only for nostalgic colonels. There is no fuel for the trucks, no spares for the tanks; and the ships of the Russian Baltic Fleet are sinking at their moorings.

Others look to the west, to ideas of liberalism and market economies, and the prospects of building in best capitalist style a free trade zone on the Pregel. A lugubrious academic in a run-down bar looks to the next generation: 'The best hope for Kaliningrad lies in the liberal conceptions of the daughters of colonels.' The Swedes, in their concern for Baltic security and environmental renewal, encourage anything that could lift Kaliningrad out of the mire, and Danish architects have offered to turn the House of Soviets into a business centre. But such ideas lack substance. Poland has her ambitions for Gdansk, Lithuania for Klaipeda, and each has a secure national hinterland. But Kaliningrad has no hinterland and nothing to bring to market but military contraband, smuggled drugs and Baltic amber.

Kaliningrad does have one asset. It has opened itself to tourism, and elderly Germans are beginning to respond, seeking out the old home or the farm or the site of the holiday cottage on the offshore spits. As the guests await their tourist buses, *meine Heimat* is a phrase that rings insistently round the lobbies of Kaliningrad's hotels. These people are seriously old, in their sixties at least. Their historical and cultural commitment to the eastern Baltic has roots that go back centuries, more than twice as long as the British commitment to Australia or Canada. Behind memories of East Prussia lies something both personal and substantial: the farm, the saw mill, the brewery which the Red Army laid waste in 1945. If such memories could be mobilised, rendered substantial by the émigrés' grandchildren, they could be the springs of economic hope for tomorrow's Kaliningrad.

But many Russians are hesitant, and so are many Germans. Some Germans want to rebuild not a Russian province in the back of beyond but the old East Prussia, epitome of a traditional German spirit. Yet for Russians Kaliningrad remains a spoil of war, agreed at Potsdam and guaranteed at Helsinki and by the German treaties. So the Russians and the Germans circle round one another, talking of German capital building a free trade zone; of old property rights restored; of a final settlement between old enemies.

All this reminds me of an allegory that Günter Grass set in another place on the Baltic coast where elderly Germans dream of their old homes. In *The Call of the Toad*, Grass teases out the story of a good German widower and a good Polish widow, both of them born and bred in Danzig, who meet by chance at a market stall in Gdansk. They fall in love – with one another, and with a scheme to advance human happiness by providing burial in the land of their birth for Germans driven out half a century ago. They see their scheme as a brain-child held in common and as a contribution to international goodwill. Others join them, and gradually turn the project into a vehicle for commercial profit and then for a polite German reconquest of historically Teutonic lands. It is a fanciful tale, driven by Grass's obsessive fear of his countrymen's recidivism. But it captures an aspect of political truth, and *The Call of the Toad* gives us a fictional version of something that could happen in Kaliningrad.

In January 1990 the *Financial Times* offered its answer to Kaliningrad's troubles. It reviewed the changes that had swept over Europe in the last twelve months, the year of miracles. It looked thirty years ahead and sketched an outline of the way Europe might come to be by the year 2020. It envisaged a United States of Western Europe; Balkan and Central European Unions; a Slavic Union; and a Scandinavian-Baltic Union. This last embraced the four Nordic countries (Denmark having defected from the United States of Western Europe to join it), the three Baltic states – and a Free City of Königsberg.

The twentieth century has seen two Free Cities on the Baltic. We have visited Danzig already and Memel is to be our first port of call in Lithuania. The League of Nations sponsored both in an attempt to resolve the age-old Baltic problem of reconciling a German presence along the coast with Polish and Lithuanian demands for access to the sea. Perhaps they show a way in which Kaliningrad, the orphan of the modern Baltic, might position itself between Russia and the west. Perhaps some day a Free City could house a free port and a tax-free zone – the improbable Baltic Hong Kong of which Kaliningrad's rare optimists talk so insistently today. Perhaps it could set itself environmental standards of which even the Scandinavians would approve. It might bind up old wounds, reconcile Germans and Slavs, and teach them mutual respect. It seems impossible to get there from here, but by 2020 Kaliningrad may be the Free City of Königsberg, patronised and protected by the United Nations or the European Union, and most of its burghers may be Germans.

6

Lithuania

As you enter Lithuania you are approaching the geographical heart of Europe. Paradoxical as that may sound, an atlas and dividers prove the point. Vilnius, the capital, lies midway between Iceland and the Caucasus, between Novaya Zemlya and Gibraltar, between North Cape and Cape Matapan and between the Urals and Tralee. The exact centre of Europe, Lithuanians will tell you, is to be found at Bernotai, sixteen miles outside Vilnius, on longitude 25 degrees 19 minutes east, latitude 50 degrees 54 minutes north.

You are also entering the world of the Balts, the peoples who lived along this eastern Baltic coast before the coming of the Germans, Swedes, Poles and Russians. We have seen that even the language of the original Prussians has been lost. But the Lithuanians, Latvians and Livs survive, proudly distinct from one another and from their bigger neighbours, filled with a new vigour since their recovery of their countries' independence.

Lithuania is home to the biggest of these tribes. Its language is Indo-European, somewhat akin to those of its neighbours, the Latvians and the vanished Prussians. Lithuanians, whose roots in the area go back at least 2,500 years, form eighty per cent of the population, predominating over Russians, Poles, Ukrainians and other minorities.

Lithuania is only one fifth the size of Poland, and a dwarf compared with Russia or the Ukraine. But it is the biggest of the three Baltic republics. It has more than 3.5 million people, 1 million more than Latvia and 2 million more than Estonia. More important, it is a historic nation as the other two can only pretend to be, with victories, cultural achievements and other props of national identity and pride going all the way back to the Middle Ages.

We have already encountered the Lithuanians persistently at war with the Teutonic Knights, challenging their expeditions beyond the Neman, besieged and besieging, often defeated but never conquered, and triumphantly victorious at Tannenberg. Before the Knights and after them, the Lithuanians fought raiders and invaders from the east, so successful in their wars with Russians and Mongols that at one time the medieval Grand Duchy of Lithuania extended all the way to the Black Sea. Like the Poles and Hungarians, the Lithuanians can claim to have stood in Europe's gate over the centuries with little thanks from more fortunate Europeans to the west.

Lithuanian pride was eventually humbled not by the Knights or the Russians but by the Poles. The Lithuanians may, as they still assert when they remember Tannenberg, have brought more than their share of military prowess to their fifteenth-century union with Poland, but the Poles brought a more advanced civilisation. The Poles did not let their new partners forget that Polish Christianity went back to the eleventh century, 300 years before the Lithuanians' conversion to the Cross, and Polish cultural sophistication and political assurance came to dominate the Polish-Lithuanian Commonwealth.

Poles and Lithuanians then entered a love-hate relationship of an Anglo-Irish kind which has marched through their troubled histories ever since. They suffered together at the hands of the Russians from the eighteenth century until the early twentieth, but independence – from Russia and from one another – after the First World War saw them at cross-purposes again, with a Polish occupation of Lithuania's principal city that lasted until Moscow and Berlin destroyed Poland and Lithuania yet again. Today the two countries get along better perhaps than ever before in their tangled histories, which is not to say that they get along very well.

I started my exploration of Lithuania in the west, at Klaipeda, where the conflict of history has been played out not against Poles but against Germans. Klaipeda, which nostalgic Germans still call Memel, stands at the mouth of the largest of the Baltic lagoons, the Kurisches Haff, which extends for eighty-five miles along the coast of Kaliningrad and Lithuania. Today it is Lithuania's third city, and its name is unmistakably Lithuanian. But for most of recorded history Klaipeda has been a German city, a stronghold of the Teutonic Knights, a Hansa port, and until 1920 an integral part of East Prussia, at times even its capital.

First impressions were alarming ones. The sticky summer's evening called for a beer, and I found one in the scruffy yard of a struggling café. But a ship of the French navy was paying Klaipeda a courtesy visit, and her sailors were on a run ashore. Suddenly my café was consumed by oaths and flying glass and urine and vomit, and I beat a retreat to bed. The morning after seemed safer and I took off aimlessly to explore a deserted back street. Out of an alley hurtled a car, reversing at fifteen miles an hour, the driver's eyes fixed not on his destination but on his point of departure. As I sprang aside, the rear of the car swung towards me, its driver still oblivious of the imminence of manslaughter behind him. He drove off innocently to some carefree destination, revving his engine and pooping his horn like Mr Toad, but I came close to dying under the back wheels of his car that sunny morning in Klaipeda.

Even on further, more reflective examination, Klaipeda turned out to be a dispiriting sort of place, with something of the squalor of Kaliningrad about it. The story of its desolation, like Königsberg's, goes back to the winter of 1944–45, when heavy air attacks followed by a protracted siege laid it waste. At the end of the war the few Germans who remained were expelled, and Lithuanians and Russians gradually took their place. Slowly the port was restored, the ruins cleared, factories and flats erected. Now a Lithuanian city, Klaipeda was detached from the East Prussia of which it had been a part; but Lithuania and Kaliningrad were linked together as integral parts of the Soviet Union.

With the collapse of the Soviet Union, Klaipeda serves Lithuania as her only port. Half of Lithuania's merchant fleet seems to lie permanently at anchor along the waterfront. Between the waterfront and the spit on the other side of the lagoon, the waters of the river Neman, called the Nemunas by the Lithuanians, roll past to the sea. Seventy cranes brood over the Nemunas, over idle ships and silent railway sidings, over warehouses and pilot stations. A terrible inanition presides over the port of Klaipeda.

The old town seems to be stricken by the same malady. The restorers have been at work, and here and there they have tried to recapture something of Memel's historic Hansa character. But there is something bleak and unloved about the houses and shops that line Memel's old streets and about its restored Hanseatic warehouses. On one corner a life-sized chessboard tries unsuccessfully to charm, but it is hard to imagine human pieces at play upon it. Nearby there is an ambitious, unsuccessful copper monument to Klaipeda's Hanseatic past. And round the corner you are back with the crumbling concrete of the Soviet 1970s, in a hangar of a department store displaying dispiriting pieces of grimy underwear pressed up against its equally grimy windows.

The heart of the old town, Theatre Square, is at first blush almost as desolate as the streets around it. But on one side stands Klaipeda's theatre, by comparison with everything else an almost absurdly successful modern building, the only one that I could find in the whole city that combines beauty with conviction. Here there is no attempt to reproduce medieval wood and stucco in today's concrete. Instead the form of the old theatre is re-expressed in a purely symbolic, modern idiom: blank walls focus the eye on the shadowed recess of the entrance, itself identified by a simple, free-standing arch. Confronted with this theatre, *Dramos Teatras*, my heart rose for the first time in Klaipeda.

And there is more pleasure of an older kind in Theatre Square. In its centre stands a statue of a young girl, Ännchen von Tharau, for whom Simon Dach, the seventeenth-century Prussian poet, conceived a hopeless passion on the very day she married another man. The love song she inspired became the best-loved piece of writing in Prussia and Ännchen became a literary heroine. The statue to her memory was the second lyrical thing I found in Klaipeda.

The city stretches well beyond the old town. What looks like a nineteenth-century barracks purports to be the beginnings of a university. A power station beside the river spews smoke over the heart of the city. Further along stands one of Intourist's building-block hotels. Away from the centre, trees soften the urban harshness, and you find the occasional dignified house from the old days of Memel. And out on the road towards the coast a row of new houses is taking shape – homes that, when the gardens have grown, would not be out of place in Virginia Water. They are houses for Klaipeda's prosperous few – the newly, mysteriously and seriously rich.

In the old German days Memel had a reputation for its Baltic charm, its Hansa intimacy, the vitality of its fishing port, the beauty of its surroundings. The long spit that divides the lagoon from the sea attracted summer visitors. At one time it grew great oaks for the Royal Navy's warships. Once they were gone, the winter wind off the Baltic whipped up great sandstorms and threatened to sweep the spit away. Replanting gave it a hope of survival, and it became a refuge for those who wanted to escape to an empty seaside. Thomas Mann spent a summer writing *Joseph and His Brothers* at Nidden, and in the years before the First World War, Max Pechstein went there to paint a series of Matisse-like pictures of stylised, idealised nudes gambolling among the dunes. Now the spit bristles with regulations to protect a fragile nature, but on the rare brilliant days of a Baltic summer it still offers sand, trees, and simple villages with long views over the water.

Like everywhere else along the south-eastern Baltic, Memel was caught up in the fighting at the end of the First World War, when Balts, Bolsheviks and Baltic Germans waged their separate campaigns for pre-eminence. It was a vicious war that ravaged much of the Baltic provinces, but when it was over it seems to have left behind surprisingly little ill-feeling between the city's German and Lithuanian inhabitants. But Germany and Lithuania both laid claim to Memel, just as Germany and Poland both claimed Danzig. Germany argued that everything about Memel made it German: its history and trade, its place in the very first stanza of 'Deutschland über Alles', and the wishes of the majority of its inhabitants. Lithuania pointed to remoter history, her need for a port of her own, and the wishes of the city's Lithuanian-speaking citizens.

It was the sort of problem thrown up all over eastern Europe by the collapse of empire. In 1920 the allies established a French trusteeship to hold the ring: a French general moved in, with French officials and a few French troops, in a Gallic occupation more urbane than the violence and vomit of my first evening in town; and in what pass for antique shops in Klaipeda today you can still find faded snapshots, taken seventy years ago in the dappled gardens of Memel's well-to-do, in which French képis incline gallantly over the gloved hands of ladies serving afternoon tea. The French established then that there were 71,156 German-speaking citizens in Memel, as against 67,259 Lithuanians; and of the total, fewer than three per cent wanted education in the city to be conducted in Lithuanian.

But Lithuania in the 1920s was full of the new-found joys and griefs of independence, patriotism and nationalism. Her sons wanted to be heroes. In 1920 they saw Polish freebooters steal away their capital, Vilnius, in a lawless *coup de main*. Three years later they took equally forceful action to recover Memel from the Germans. On 10 January, 1923, 5,000 Lithuanian volunteers invaded Memel. French policy was preoccupied elsewhere, and French troops were assembling that day to occupy the Ruhr. The French garrison in

Memel was only 200 strong, and after a perfunctory exchange of fire it withdrew into its barracks. Eventually the League of Nations acquiesced in the *fait accompli*, recognising Lithuanian sovereignty over Memel, on condition that the city keep something of its autonomy.

This was a proud but Pyrrhic victory for the Lithuanians. They had won their access to the sea, but the parties representing German interests in Klaipeda continued to win local elections. Its German inhabitants became increasingly nationalistic. Memel, like Danzig, offered Hitler a ready-made grievance, and propaganda and pressure for its return *Heim ins Reich* increased. Eventually, in March 1939, Hitler reinforced his demand for the return of the city with a threat of air attack on the Lithuanian capital. The surrender of Memel was unavoidable, and it came shortly after Hitler's occupation of the remains of Czechoslovakia, two days before Britain guaranteed Poland's integrity.

Memel was therefore the last of Hitler's gains to be won by threats alone, just as Danzig was the first he was to win by force six months later. At the time the recovery of Memel was a famous victory, the righting of another terrible wrong done to Germans at Versailles, and Hitler planned to make the most of it, by sailing up the Baltic in a German warship and presiding over the great celebration in Theatre Square to mark the city's return to German sovereignty. But seasickness laid him low, and the Germans of Memel were left to celebrate without him.

The Baltic has its own charms and fascinations, but it has to be said that few of its products can stand comparison with those of the Mediterranean. As David Kirby put it in his book, *The Baltic World*: 'The smell of tar and salted herring cannot really compare with the sweet scent of the lemon blossom.' The same is true of Baltic beer compared with the wines of the Midi, or Baltic pitch as against Italian olives. But amber is the exception, the Baltic mystery that captivated the classical world and whose mysterious potential Michael Crichton, aided and abetted by Steven Spielberg, launched on the modern world in *Jurassic Park*.

Poland, Lithuania and Kaliningrad share most of the Baltic's amber. For Poland, it is a commodity, traded by jewellers and novelty stalls all along the Baltic coast. Kaliningrad claims to have more of it than Lithuania, and fledgling businessmen there talk as if amber alone could make their fortunes. But Lithuania has good cause to be seen as the true heart of the amber mystery, with her amber museum and a thriving trade of her own. And from Lithuania comes the legend of Jurate's love for Kastytis and of Perkunas' revenge.

For a country which has had so much of her historical being in forests far from the sea, Lithuania has a surprising number of maritime legends. The story of Jurate and Kastytis offers one explanation of sea-borne amber. Jurate is a sea-goddess who is engaged to be married to the god of water; but she falls in love with a simple fisherman. She bears him away to her amber castle at the bottom of the sea. But the god of thunder, Perkunas, is incensed by this miscegenation. In his rage he destroys Jurate's castle and scatters its pieces across the sea bed, which storms and fishing nets bring to light to this day. The beachcomber who finds a sliver of amber holds in the palm of his hand a tear shed by Jurate for her lost fisherman.

More prosaically, amber is fossilised resin, excreted by pine trees 40 million years ago. Its beauty lies in its range of colours from yellow to orange to a tawny red and translucent brown. But most of its fascination derives from the objects trapped in the resin when it was liquid: the 'inclusions' of insects, spiders and plants. Three thousand species have been found in fossilised amber: a valuable documentation of natural pre-history and the potential – if you are persuaded by *Jurassic Park* – of new life. Alexander Pope called inclusions

> Hairs, or straws, or dirt, or grubs or worms;
> The things, we know, are neither rich nor rare,
> But wonder how the devil they got there.

The Assyrians mentioned amber in their cuneiform inscriptions 3,000 years ago. It has been found in the tombs of the pharaohs. Homer called the Baltic the Amber Coast. Tacitus describes a Baltic tribe who ransack the sea for amber:

> Like true barbarians, they have never asked or discovered what it is or how it is produced. For a long time, indeed, it lay unheeded like any other refuse of the sea, until Roman luxury made its reputation.

He goes on to speculate about this mysterious substance:

> I imagine that in the islands and continents of the west, just as in

the secret chambers of the east, where the trees exude frankin-
cense and balm, there must be woods and groves of unusual
productivity. Their gums ... are finally washed up by violent
storms on the shores that lie opposite.

Amber was the one thing about the Baltic that fascinated the
Romans, until the Baltic tribes themselves descended on them and
destroyed them. Today it offers the Baltic a rare touch of the exotic to
rival the lemon trees and olive groves of the Mediterranean.

Before we turn away towards Kaunas, Vilnius and Trakai, there is
one magical sight to see in north-western Lithuania. Just north of
Siauliai – a prosperous but unremarkable town near the Latvian
border – stands the Hill of Crosses.

The Hill of Crosses is no more than forty feet high, an insignificant hillock in the flat meadowland of northern Lithuania. A
reference in the fourteenth-century Livonian Chronicle suggests that
there may once have been a castle here. Now there is nothing more
than a car park, market stalls – and a hill clothed in and blanketed
with crosses. The guidebook talks of 2,000 crosses, and of more being
constantly added. A guess would put the figure at fifty times that
number. Some are powerfully carved out of massive timbers. Many
display the Lithuanian sunrise behind the cross, mixing pagan faith
with Christian. Others are the miniature crucifixes that hang from
rosaries, and there are smaller crosses mounted on bigger ones.
Lithuania's Catholicism, her obsession with wood and her skill in
wood-carving are vividly represented here.

The notion of planting crosses on this hillock goes back to the
fifteenth century, but the first written reference to the practice occurs
in 1850. The crosses ask for health and happiness, mourn the dead,
mark jubilees and give thanks to God. Catholicism encouraged such
pieties, and Lithuanian Catholics took them to lengths you do not
find in the west this side of Spain. Then came Lithuania's decades of
suffering, under Russians and Germans and Russians in turn. The
deportations in the 1940s attracted crosses of remembrance. The
deportees returning twenty years later brought crosses of thanksgiv-
ing. The Hill of Crosses became, in the guidebook's words, 'a kind of
manuscript of the people's life'.

The Hill took on a political as well as a religious significance.
Religion and politics became interwoven. To the Communists the

Hill of Crosses was a celebration of ignorance and superstition. For the people it proclaimed religious faith and political resistance. In 1961 the authorities destroyed the Hill of Crosses and put a guard upon it. Crosses reappeared, little ones, planted at night, then bigger ones. Repeatedly the crosses were torn down, repeatedly replaced. The struggle became a war of crosses, and one in which victory went to the Lithuanian people.

For the historically-minded, there is an irony here. The Lithuanians were the last heathens of Europe; and as heathens they fought the Cross to the death, defeating the knights who wore it as a blazon upon their armour. Seven hundred years later they again conquered their enemies, this time under the sign of the cross. When the miracle of 1989 came to Lithuania, the Hill of Crosses became an easy, even banal way for visiting journalists to illustrate the struggle for freedom and independence, alongside the heroics at parliament and the television station. In 1993 the pope came to Lithuania and made his pilgrimage to the Hill of Crosses. Today there are more crosses than ever, constituting in their infinite variety an improbable modern masterpiece of folk art as well as a place of religious and political pilgrimage.

The Lithuanians see most of their last half-century as years of tragedy: occupation, deportation, extermination, oppression, stagnation. For them the late 1980s were years of hope, which courage and stubbornness brought to a near-miraculous fulfilment. Now they are buckling down to the mundane tasks of reconstruction, reform and restoration.

Lithuania is a land of fields and forests and her wealth, such as it is, comes from agriculture and forestry. Industry in Lithuania, designed as a piece in the jigsaw of vanished Soviet economic plans, is devastated, abandoned or painfully adapting. The country is dependent on the outside world for every source of energy except wood-burning stoves. Yet there are paradoxes built into this economy. In purchasing power the Lithuanians come behind all other eastern Europeans. But the shops seem to be stocked as well or as badly as Hungarian shops a decade ago, and ordinary people use them. No doubt the unemployed and the old suffer a crushing poverty that escapes the tourist's eye. But almost everyone has his market garden or a patch of land or a helpful country relative. Lithuania is not going to starve, even if she comes near to freezing next winter.

Reconstruction on the International Monetary Fund's best market principles is the buzz-word, and a government led by former Communists is devoting itself to the worship of free markets. What everyone else calls privatisation the Baltic states call nationalisation, for the process started in 1991, the year in which they so surprisingly got their nationhood back again. But they bring to the chase the same vigour as privateers anywhere, celebrating the same joys and experiencing the same pain along the way. Foreigners – white-knights-to-the-rescue or shameless asset-strippers depending on your point of view – are buying in. Gradually a simple form of modern capitalism will be superimposed on a land of farms and forests.

The economic game has largely eclipsed the game of patriotism and national self-assertion which dominated the early years of Lithuania's new-found independence. The change came when President Landsbergis, an academic figure for whom Lithuanian identity and nationhood had a mystic significance that first thrilled and then puzzled his compatriots, gave way to Algirdas Brazaukas, an ex-Communist who claimed he could talk business with Moscow and who brought practical experience to the job of running Lithuania. At first there were fears that an ex-Communist might bring something beyond experience in his briefcase, but Brazaukas presented himself as being as patriotic as Landsbergis but without his predecessor's mysticism; as dedicated to economic reform as any Vilnius entrepreneur; and as a man who looked like everybody's favourite uncle.

The economic game now engages popular concern, just as the nationhood game did, and would do again if Lithuania's independence were to be threatened. But popular needs are straightforward: modest prosperity; freedom from the oppression and stultification which came with Soviet rule; and recognition of Lithuanian identity. Roman Catholicism is a part of this identity. So are Lithuanian roots, expressed in folk song and dance and language. So also is a suspicion of outsiders, sometimes indistinguishable from chauvinism. Leaders have to recognise these concerns, and ensure that the complexities of policy respect them.

Lithuanians do not forget the courage of the late 1980s and early 1990s which brought them their freedom. Each Baltic state takes pride in the way that it first challenged and eventually defied Moscow in those tense and dangerous years, but outside assessment must award the palm to Lithuania. Each state can take credit for the Baltic

Way, the chain of 2 million people who in August 1989 joined hands all the way from Tallinn to Vilnius in the name of independence. But it was the Lithuanian Communist party which was the first to split from the Soviet party. The Lithuanian Supreme Council was the first to declare independence. It was against Lithuania that the Soviet army first struck in March 1990. Ten months later Soviet troops seized the television centre in Vilnius, killing fifteen people. A referendum in Lithuania was the first to call for independence, and it was Lithuanian border guards who were murdered at their posts by Soviet irregulars, just a month before the defeat of the August 1991 coup in Moscow.

Most Lithuanians believe that they achieved their freedom through their own efforts, and only the coolly realistic recognise how much events in Moscow – first the rise of Gorbachev, then the coup whose failure destroyed the Soviet Union – contributed to the process. Thoughtful Lithuanians would say that the West played an unheroic role, distant when things were most difficult, preoccupied with Moscow rather than the three little Soviet republics, and recognising Lithuania only when the game was won.

But today Lithuania's aspirations face west, as her fears face east. Like Latvia and Estonia she values anything which focuses western concern on the eastern Baltic. She clutches at the Partnership for Peace as she cannot have NATO membership. She is diligent in her commitment to the Baltic Battalion, to be brought by western and particularly Scandinavian assistance to a standard at which it could play a role in United Nations peacekeeping. And Lithuanians believe – quite unrealistically if you look at the economic facts, but very sensibly if you think about the politics – that membership of the European Union lies somewhere at the end of the road, not far into the twenty-first century.

There is push as well as pull about this impulse towards the west. One way and another, Moscow has ruled Lithuania for 200 years. Russia thinks of the Baltic republics as hers. Russian nationalists talk about recovering something of what has been lost around the Baltic in the catastrophes of the last decade. In weakness or strength, Russia and Ukraine are potential threats to Lithuania. The position of Estonia and Latvia, with their larger Russian minorities, may be more parlous than Lithuania's. But she shares their fears, and has some of her own – energy-dependency and the issue of Russian military transit rights to Kaliningrad foremost among them. There is fear mixed with hope in the continued optimism with which the Lithuanians celebrate their independence.

From 1920 to 1940, while Vilnius languished in Polish captivity, Kaunas was the provisional capital of Lithuania. There have been Lithuanians in Vilnius for hundreds of years, but to the Poles it was a quintessentially Polish city and, even more important, they had possession. And Vilnius was a Jewish city too. The Lithuanians never abandoned their claim to Vilnius, and they shut their frontier with Poland for years in protest at its seizure. But they set about making Kaunas a worthy, if temporary, capital; and they reminded themselves that Kaunas had never been anything other than Lithuanian.

Kaunas today is a handsome city, standing at the junction of Lithuania's two main rivers, the Nemunas and the Neris. The Nemunas (the Neman) has always been a dividing line between west and east, Teutons and Balts, Germans and Russians. It was at Kaunas that Napoleon crossed it, his fatal Rubicon, on his way to Moscow. For a century Kaunas was a frontier city between the Kaiser's empire and the tsar's. All the same, it feels central, not peripheral. The Town Hall Square and the old city around it exude security and confidence. So does the government quarter, hurriedly laid out in the 1920s around the monument to Lithuania's hero, Vytautas the Great, to provide government offices, parliament and legations. But above all, this is a city of churches and monasteries and seminaries, where religious confidence and temporal assurance flourish side by side.

Kaunas has its curiosities. There is an art gallery devoted to the work of the turn-of-the-century artist M. K. Ciurlionis, whose work is a strange combination of mysticism, modernism and a numinous sense of space and of place. The Lithuanians say that Ciurlionis uniquely captures the spirit of their country, even though in his lifetime the artist found recognition only in St Petersburg. Across the road lies a museum given over to depictions of the innumerable devils to be found in Lithuanian folk tales. In the centre of the huge Town Hall Square stands a town hall that looks like a cathedral, in piquant contrast to the cathedral of Kalmar, on the other side of the Baltic, which looks like a town hall. Around the square are grouped the actual cathedral, the Jesuit church and a seminary. This central square of old Kaunas has the same ordered permanence about it as the square of Chelmno in Poland, a similarity which you might attribute to a shared German influence had not Kaunas always been so defiantly Lithuanian.

The government that sat in Kaunas from 1920 to 1940 started out with democratic good intentions but lapsed quickly into a rough-and-ready authoritarianism. In 1926 the president, Antanas Smetona, mounted a coup with army backing, and ruled the country thereafter as a one-party state. Looking back, and looking from west to east, it is easy to call such right-wing eastern European governments fascist, and historians have far to go before they arrive at a definitive view of such leaders as Smetona himself, Hungary's Horthy and Poland's Pilsudski. At least they succeeded where Hindenburg failed: they avoided the catastrophe of outright Nazism, if at the price of adopting some of its less objectionable features; and this in countries with little or no experience of democratic politics.

But there were political prisoners in Smetona's Lithuania, and many of them were confined in the Ninth Fort at Kaunas. In the late nineteenth century the Russian government had built a line of fortifications to guard the frontier along the Neman. These were defended, fought over and eventually abandoned in the First World War. Independent Lithuania put the Ninth Fort to penal use and when the Soviet authorities arrived in Kaunas in 1940, they filled it with a new generation of political prisoners.

A year later the Nazis turned the Ninth Fort, already a place of suffering and fear, into a place of horror. They brought to it Jews from the Kaunas ghetto for execution, along with Jews from other Lithuanian cities and from all over Europe. Today's visitor can see the casemates and the cells into which the prisoners were crowded, and the usual last sad scribbles upon the walls. There is a Way of Death leading to the place where 30,000 Jews were shot – mass graves, jagged concrete memorials, all the paraphernalia of the extermination industry and the ensuing industry of commemoration. The Ninth Fort marks the terrible culmination of the long relationship between Christian and Jew in Lithuania.

Lithuanians will tell you that historically their country has been a place of refuge for the Jews. They came here to escape persecution in medieval Germany and pogroms in nineteenth-century Ukraine. They made themselves economically valuable, and integrated to a degree while in other ways remaining utterly distinct, a distinction as much willed by the Jews as imposed on them by the Christians. While Poles and Lithuanians argued about supremacy in Vilnius, Jews built its trade and its intellectual reputation. The Jews were an integral and indispensable part of Lithuanian life. They were resented, Lithuanians will tell you, as Poles were resented, or Ukrainians, or Germans; and their particular role in the Lithuanian economy sometimes added a sharper edge to that resentment. They suffered under the tsars, much as Lithuanians did. The position of the Jews in Lithuania was, in short, much the same as their position anywhere else in eastern Europe; and if anything, Lithuanians will argue, rather better than the average.

The twentieth century brought graver threats to eastern Europe's Jews. Most Christian Lithuanians facing the choice between Nazis and Communists preferred the Nazis. Jewish Lithuanians inevitably preferred the Communists. To them the Soviet occupation in 1940 seemed a brutal kind of salvation, whereas to Christian Lithuanians it spelt the end of their country's independence, the extinction of personal freedom, economic helotry and, for many, deportation and death. The German invasion of Lithuania a year later brought liberation from Soviet rule to the Christians, coupled with easy promises – soon broken – of German favour. For Communists and Jews, persecution rapidly escalated into extermination. Lithuanian fascists joined in the hunt; Lithuanian traditionalists exhumed their latent anti-Semitism; Lithuanian Christians who had suffered under the Communists made scapegoats of the Jews who in 1940 had returned from Moscow with the Soviet invader.

Old men in the west today are, it seems, only spared prosecution for their war crimes in the forests of Lithuania because of the impossibility of proving them fifty years afterwards. Lithuanians resent what they see as a western preoccupation with the Jews' sufferings under the Germans and a neglect of their own sufferings under the Russians. In an effort to balance the two a museum at the Ninth Fort recalls the horrors of deportation to Siberia as well as Nazi extermination. Lithuanians, like Poles, are everywhere labelled with an anti-Semitism which many of them perhaps still entertain, but in a form different in kind as well as degree from the horrors which Nazism unleashed in eastern Europe half a century ago. And Lithuania, like Poland, Hungary and Slovakia, still bears the scars that Hitler inflicted. The Final Solution has left great patches of dead tissue in these bodies politic, for no Jews remain to imbue them with the sparkle, diligence and stimulus their forebears brought to the countries in which they made their homes.

We move on to the geographical centre of Europe; to Lithuania's old capital at Trakai; and to Vilnius, the focus of Lithuanian nationhood today. We are going further from the Baltic than anywhere else on our journey, almost 200 miles inland. There is no smell of the Baltic here. All the same, Lithuania is a Baltic country and Vilnius, after all its travails through history, is her undisputed capital. Vilnius is necessary to an understanding of Lithuania, as is Trakai a few miles outside the city. Ours is an essential excursion.

Trakai today is a picture-book castle on an island in a lake set among woods, a sort of Leeds Castle in Baltic brick. Here you admire a reconstruction of a fourteenth-century castle built by Grand Duke Vytautas, father and national hero of Lithuania. The museum documents Lithuania's glory days when she reached out the length of eastern Europe to the Black Sea. Vytautas brought a Karaite bodyguard home with him from the Crimea. Their descendants still live in Trakai: the smallest ethnic group in Lithuania, technically Turkic, religiously dissident Jewish, the most extraordinary of many such historical oddities to be found in eastern Europe.

Hidden among forests, protected by its lakes, Trakai was a secure capital for a Lithuania on the defensive. But a more confident fourteenth-century grand duke moved his capital into the open; and since Gediminas's time Vilnius has been, for most of the ensuing centuries, the capital of Lithuania. Half the peoples of Europe contributed to its making. Today its population is fifty per cent Lithuanian, twenty per cent Polish and twenty per cent Russian. Before the war there were more Poles in Vilnius than there were Lithuanians, and as many Jews as Poles. Vilnius was not only a Roman Catholic city, but an Orthodox one too, and simultaneously one of the great Jewish cities of Europe. And in the city's early days the grand dukes advertised throughout Germany for skilful immigrants, and Germans also came to Vilnius to work and prosper.

The Soviet years brought Vilnius its quota of concrete gigantism, in buildings which seem in better shape than they do elsewhere from Wismar to St Petersburg; but the heart of the city remains overwhelmingly baroque. This is a city of the Habsburgs, miraculously transplanted here from the Danube, into what once was the Romanovs' back yard. Czeslaw Milosz, the Nobel Prize winner who saw himself as Lithuanian and Polish and as a European writer with global obligations, once said that in Vilnius even the clouds were baroque. From the hill above the city you can see what he meant.

Vilnius is a city of curves and domes and billows, to match the generous clouds overhead, and on a summer's day it is a creamy city: cream in the colours of its stucco, clotted cream in the texture of its architecture and whipped cream in its lavish ornamentation.

The cathedral, oddly enough, is an exception. It stands on a site replete with numinous significance. But repeated disasters and an eighteenth-century rebuilding have bequeathed us a neo-classical Greek temple, stalwart and composed on its great square, with its detached bell tower stark as a lighthouse beside it. The pediment adorning its west front is supported by Grecian columns, and the interior is as cool as skimmed milk. The cathedral of Vilnius is magnificent in its way, but it is not baroque, and it seems at eternal architectural odds with the old town that lies behind it.

As you walk up into the old town, however, it is creamy baroque all the way. The Jesuits built the university as an outpost of the Counter-Reformation in north-eastern Europe, and endowed it with the central European character they had made their own. Its court-yards and library and its old observatory have a Viennese opulence about them. The west front of St John's church is like an outsize Biedermeier cabinet in stucco. When the tsars expelled the Jesuits and tried to put an Orthodox stamp upon the city, the baroque and cream survived. You can find Orthodox churches and a monastery in the old town, with old Russian ladies praying and begging and selling in and around them, just as you can identify the old ghetto among the res-torations of the city. But today Russian Orthodoxy is a minority faith and its monuments mere islands in a Roman Catholic sea. And the 70,000 Jews who made Vilnius the Jerusalem of north-eastern Europe are gone, shot to death in the forests or at the Ninth Fort at Kaunas. Roman Catholicism and Lithuanian nationalism, the lat-ter tempered by the wistful dreams of the Polish-speaking minority, prevail in today's Vilnius.

We must look at two other jewels in Vilnius's crown before we turn back to politics. The first is the church of SS Peter and Paul on the outskirts of the city, unremarkable without, a paradise of ornamenta-tion within. Two thousand stucco figures rampage across its walls and pillars and ceilings, varying in the quality of their detail but over-whelming in their numbers and exuberance. And the colourists have been kept at bay: from west front to high altar this is an interior of white stucco, lavish in form, uninhibited in imagination and virtuoso in execution, but firmly disciplined by its monochrome. The second jewel is the church of St Anne at the back of the old town. If Vilnius largely springs from the Danube, St Anne's has something of the feel of a Hanseatic Baltic city. It is a small church, built of the old Baltic brick, its west front corded with twisted ropes of brick like the rigging of a Baltic schooner. When Napoleon saw St Anne's on his way to Moscow he said that he wanted to take it home to Paris. When the remains of the Grande Armée retreated through Vilnius, they left it a char-nel house of dead and dying, and St Anne's remained untouched. If Napoleon had shipped St Anne's to Paris and some other admirer had moved SS Peter and Paul to Rome, the world would recognise them for the miracles they are. But they remain where they belong, in Vil-nius, and are in themselves reason enough to visit this shamefully dis-regarded city.

When the Polish Pope John Paul II came to Vilnius in 1993 he pleased the Lithuanians by describing the Poles of the city as Polish-speaking Lithuanian citizens. When the Poles and Lithuanians concluded a treaty of friendship it specified that Vilnius was the capital of Lithuania. The days of Vilnius's Polish captivity are gone, and with them the need for Czeslaw Milosz and his mother to slip clandes-tinely across a closed frontier when they went to visit their relatives in Poland. Today Poland and Lithuania fear similar dangers, and walk the same road towards the same salvation. Relations are as good as they have ever been, but edginess remains, the sort of familiarity mixed with suspicion that you find between the English and the Irish, for similar historical reasons.

In the same way, Lithuania is not entirely at ease with her Baltic neighbours. There is no habit of co-operation in north-eastern Europe, no instinct towards consultation. While we in the west were healing post-war wounds and growing painfully together, the east Europeans were locked into fraternal relations with their Com-munist neighbours: relations that were good in theory but in practice prickly with cross-purposes. Freedom now means freedom to go one's own way, to rediscover the joys of national idiosyncrasy. The east Europeans must learn the skills of sublimation if they are ever to reach their goals in the European Union and the Atlantic Alliance.

At the same time the east Europeans, and the Baltic states above all, will have to learn to live with the Russians, still in their weakness as in their strength a powerful influence in eastern Europe. Today they show little sign of even wanting to try: but that is a story to unravel not in Lithuania, where the Slavs are relatively few, but in Latvia, where getting on for half the population are Ukrainians, Belarusians or Russians.

7
Latvia

From Vilnius to Riga is the best part of 200 miles: a reminder that each of the Baltic states which the west dismisses as minuscule is in fact bigger than the Netherlands, Switzerland or Denmark. The road forms part of the Via Baltica: a scheme to modernise and link the roads of the eastern Baltic to provide Helsinki, St Petersburg and the three republics themselves with a direct route to the markets of central Europe. The plan has something to offer each of the participants and a wider strategic significance. St Petersburg is the fourth biggest city in Europe, and it could in time resume its old importance in trade not just with the west down the Baltic but with central Europe overland. The Finns want every link with the continent that they can achieve, and there is even talk, fanciful now, perhaps conceivable 100 years hence, of a tunnel under the Gulf of Finland linking Helsinki to Tallinn. As for Estonia, Latvia and Lithuania, they need better north-south links with one another, to complement their old east-west links with Moscow and St Petersburg. More than that, they are eager to put themselves on the map of Europe, to attract the business and the tourists hitherto denied them by Soviet rule.

The main roads in the Baltic republics date from the 1930s, pleasurable and interesting to the occasional visitor; but they would crumble and choke under the loads which in time the Via Baltica will bring their way. Petrol, a coffee shop, somewhere to eat, these are hard to find; and so far the main evidence of the Via Baltica lies in the rare service stations which a Finnish oil company is establishing, dispensing lead-free fuel, bad coffee and worse cakes throughout the three republics. But private enterprise can do little to reduce delays at the frontiers. Strict controls are necessary, Latvians will tell you, to keep out the drug dealers, mafia merchants and cigarette smugglers who threaten Baltic stability. And on the Lithuanian frontier with Poland, where hold-ups can stretch beyond hours into days, private enterprise, demanding backhanders in dollars in return for passport checks and customs clearance, makes things worse. All the same, the

Via Baltica is a worthy idea, charged already with symbolic value and perhaps with practical usefulness to come.

For the moment, even the main roads give you some idea of the deep tranquillity of the Baltic countryside. Pastures yield to long miles of dark woods, punctuated by streams and ponds. Away from the woods, the landscape smiles as benevolently as it can at so northerly a latitude. Cattle ruminate in the pastures, old men scythe grass with Tolstoyan deliberation. No-one has industrialised agriculture here, and the collective farms that were supposed to do so were swept away by the avalanche of freedom. Stephen Tallents's elegiac memories of the Baltics in the 1920s still hold good today:

> The countryside derives, like other plains, an air of tranquil spaciousness from the unbroken width of its luminous skies, and there rests upon it in summer a mellow and tranquil light. The colouring is subdued. . . . I recall its dun stubbles, pale grasses and grey willows; its grey-green corn touched delicately by the passing wind as by the shadow of flying smoke; the airy lightness of its birch trees, standing among dark pines like children in an old house.

Away from the industrial wreckage, away from the concrete blocks of flats and shell-shocked shopping centres, Latvia, Estonia and Lithuania remain delectable places.

The rural population of the Baltic states diminished spectacularly in the Soviet decades, and the countryside is no longer the essence of Baltic life. But still there are farmers and foresters, and people from the town returning to their old homes at weekends and holidays. The villages straggle untidily over great distances with no obvious centre, each wooden farmhouse isolated from its neighbour. In the Baltic, dignity consists in a farmyard that no one outside the family overlooks. There is something odd about the boundary hedges, wispy growths of Leylandia that could have been transplanted from an English suburb. There is poverty, but an air of peace and contentment too. This is the sort of rural idyll the west knew 150 years ago, but which turns hard and vicious in the long Baltic winters. Nothing interrupts the ageless landscape except the abandoned sheds and barns of failed collective farms. Individual dairy farming and forestry now provide a living, hard but just about adequate in countries which have not quite yet woken up to the acquisitive needs which western sophistication will bring them.

From the Via Baltica your first sight of Riga is across the Daugava,
Latvia's great river which flows as majestically as the Elbe to the sea.
First the television tower and headquarters come into view, absurdly
grand for their purpose in a country of under 3 million people. But
next you see the spires of the old town and then, as you cross the
Daugava, you appreciate the sheer size of the place. For Riga is a big
city, with a population of getting on for 1 million people, a third of
the whole country. It was a major Hansa city; for a time the largest
city in the Swedish Baltic empire; and throughout the nineteenth

century the Russian empire's most important outlet to the world. You can see the homes and warehouses and churches of the Hanseatic merchants in the old town; the evidence of the tsarist years in the centre of the city; and the wreckage of Soviet industrialisation stretching away mile after mile towards the east. Riga would be the natural capital of an unlikely federation of the Baltic states.

The ethnic Latvians, a bare majority of the country's population today, are a Baltic people like the Lithuanians, with whom they have much pre-history and early history in common. Like the Lithuanians, and for that matter like the Estonians and the few remaining Livs, the Latvians are inspired by a powerful peasant culture. Its outward signs are folk-song, folk-dance and folk costume of the kind the rest of Europe is near to forgetting; a religious sense which blends pagan and Christian influences; and a consciousness of the forest, with its dark places and ghosts and goblins, which survives more powerfully in the Baltic states than anywhere else in Europe.

Like all the Baltic tribes, the Latvians during the Middle Ages were exposed to onslaught from the west, and most particularly from the Germans. Like the others they resisted; and unlike the Lithuanians they were overwhelmed. For 700 years, to be a Latvian or a Liv or an Estonian was to be a serf or a peasant under a German or Swedish or Russian master. Their languages were the mark of the beast, despised by outsiders. Unlike the Lithuanians, the Latvians lost all claim to be a historic nation, but they preserved their own distinct identity. They became Lutherans when the Lithuanians persisted in Catholicism, but they also clung tenaciously to the traditions and attitudes that dominated this part of the Baltic coast before the coming of Christianity.

The arrival of the Germans, who destroyed the old Baltic world, is a precisely-documented event. In 1201 Bishop Albrecht of Bremen led a little fleet into the Gulf of Riga and up the Daugava. He was accompanied by German missionaries, by German knights who called themselves the Brothers of the Militia of Christ and the Order of the Sword, and by German merchants. They established themselves at the river mouth on the site of an old Liv settlement. The missionaries set out to convert the Livs and Latvians. The merchants bought and sold and shipped their goods. The knights, now re-named the Livonian Order, rode out from Riga in campaigns against the heathen tribes. They conquered Latvia; they bought authority over Estonia from Denmark; and they reached out to the south to join hands with the knights of Marienburg and Königsberg. The knights ruled the Baltic countryside, the merchants the ports and cities, the missionaries the souls they won for Christ. Knights, merchants and missionaries often quarrelled, but their presence supported one another .

The German stamp on the old town of Riga remains indelible. St Peter's is another of the great German brick churches of the Baltic, but officious guides are eager to tell you a Latvian version of its story. St John's, which for 300 years was the chapel of a Dominican monastery, has the same brick beauty. St George's Church behind St Peter's was founded by Bishop Albrecht himself when he first sailed up the Daugava to save heathen souls. To Hansa seamen these church spires, like spires everywhere on the Baltic, were essential landmarks. Seen from the Daugava they still pierce the skyline with the ancient confidence of the church spires of Lübeck or St Mary's in Gdansk, or the churches on the hill at Tallinn we have yet to visit.

On the northern edge of the old town stands Riga Castle, important in history, unimpressive today. Nearby is the Powder Tower, and behind it the Swedish Gate, all that remains of the walls of the city. Nearer the river, the Danish Embassy is a riot of Gothic – or more probably pseudo-Gothic – decoration, and beyond it stands the Anglican Church, for which the nineteenth-century English merchants of Riga imported the very brick from England to be sure of excluding alien influences. And all over the medieval city you find merchants' houses, a few done up to the nines in restorers' paint and rendering, but most still dirt-stained in the squalor of Soviet neglect.

Until the nineteenth century, Latvians and Livs were debarred from owning property within the city walls, and until Latvian independence in 1920 the old town remained essentially German. But most of Riga is a Russian city, a city of the nineteenth century and of the twentieth. Its buildings are bourgeois-respectable, grey-rendered, ornate, imposing on the main boulevards, sunk in squalor on the back streets. You might be in Vienna outside the Ring, or anywhere in Pest, or in the still-German streets of Szczecin. Some are lined with Art Nouveau blocks of flats, awaiting the admiration of western architects and rescue from neglect. There are Orthodox churches to remind you of Russian rule, and crude buildings of the 1950s which housed Soviet party officials and state trading companies. Even three years after Latvia's independence the headquarters of the Soviet North-Western Group of Forces lingered on in a fine old building beside a park, responsible for Russian troops and ships and aircraft in the Baltic and Kaliningrad and, until the last of them went home, for the troops who remained in Latvia and Estonia.

There is an air of discovery about the streets of Riga, as if the city has suddenly become aware of freedom and of the good things and bad that go with it. In a café a father and his little daughter are taking tea together. She has stepped from the pages of Louisa May Alcott, he straight from Raymond Chandler. She is demurely ladylike; he, with a gold Rolex and an ominous bulge at his armpit, drips sweat and reeks of the mafia. But they love one another, and he is going to do his best for her: solemnly he sets himself to teach her the proper way to eat ice-cream.

Around a corner an old lady is scavenging in a dustbin. In a language that might once have been German she asks where I come from. 'England,' I say. 'England bad,' she gestures, 'Hamburg, boom, boom.' I give her a guilt-laden dollar. 'What was she on about?' my companions ask. 'The bombing of Hamburg, I think.' 'What about Coventry?' they say. 'What a cheek. You should have asked her about Auschwitz.' As we approach the twenty-first century we are still a long way from pan-European understanding.

Between the old town and the nineteenth-century city stands the Freedom Monument. Stylised, soaring, with the kind of monumental Baltic blankness we shall see again in Helsinki, this is a key symbol of Latvian identity. Erected in the 1930s where a statue of Peter the Great once stood, it surprisingly survived Soviet occupation. But throughout the Soviet years it was politically dangerous to linger in its vicinity. It started to resume its national significance in the 1980s, when crowds took to gathering round it to make a dangerous point against the Soviet authorities. It formed a mid-point in the chain of linked hands which created the Baltic Way. And in 1994 came apotheosis, when folk-dancers, hand-picked for their beauty, three Baltic presidents and innumerable Latvians gathered here to greet President Bill Clinton, when he descended on Riga with an entourage 700 strong in search of a photo-opportunity.

Two cultures met: the shallow certitudes of American advance men and security men and cameramen on the one hand; the courteous simplicity of Latvian folk-dancers on the other. The pity of it was that the lessons were being transmitted from the vulgar to the dignified, rather than from the dignified to the vulgar: 'Hold it, guys', 'More leg, honey', 'Let's do it this way'. But Clinton was a

welcome visitor, and the Latvians were determined to hear him
respectfully. They cheered when he praised their freedom. But they
were subdued, even quietly resentful, when he urged them to respect
the rights of foreigners – meaning Russians – in Latvia. For Latvians, the Freedom Monument is a focus of Latvian freedom, not a
place at which to discuss the problems of a people who deprived
them of it for so long.

In 1721 Peter the Great annexed the Baltic provinces, driving out the
Swedes who had held the eastern Baltic coast for the best part of a
century. He guaranteed the rights of German landowners, whose
sons were to become some of his best generals and officials. These
German landowners, officers and officials created a place of their
own in the Russian empire, alongside but never quite a part of the
Russian élite that clustered around the tsar. Russians and Germans
lived side by side for centuries, never entirely easy with one another.
To the Germans the Russians were, in the end, unserious, soft-cen-
tred people, whose sentiment and spirituality worshipped the Russian
soul as much as the Orthodox God. To the Russians, the Germans
were soulless, efficient and inhuman. The Russians even saw a contrast between their own and German attitudes towards the serfs,
be they Russian or Latvian or Estonian. They, the Russian landowners, had an empathy, a warm humanity towards their serfs. The
Germans, by contrast, wanted to use their subjects as machines. In
Dostoevsky's *Crime and Punishment* Raskolnikov, faced with a sister
contemplating marriage to a man she does not love, finds the thought
so horrifying that he declares that she would be better off as the serf
of a German landowner on a Latvian estate.

Mutual incomprehension between the Russian and German aristocracies is expressed in many places. Tolstoy's *War and Peace* is one
example. Bennigsen and Barclay de Tolly are cold military careerists;
Kutuzov is the embodiment of Russian instinct and humanity. But
the more you investigate it, the more complicated the story becomes.
Tolstoy was as scornful of St Petersburg as of the Germans, yet the
relationship between the aristocracy and gentry of St Petersburg and
the Baltic provinces was as contradictory as that between Tolstoy's
honest Russians and the Germans. On the one hand St Petersburg
was a proud capital of empire, while the Baltics were newly-won and
still suspect provinces. On the other hand, St Petersburg was a recent
and artificial creation, never at ease with itself and the Russia which

it ruled, whereas the Baltic ruling classes enjoyed all the self-confidence and westernness which St Petersburg craved.

Despite these contradictions the Russians valued the Baltic provinces. The German aristocracy brought rationality and self-discipline to the empire. German businessmen contributed the commercial and industrial abilities which nineteenth-century Russia lacked. So Riga flourished as an industrial city as much as a great port. But perhaps above all the land-locked Russians loved the Baltic provinces for their coastline, with its long, beguiling beaches, pine-clad sand-dunes and glimpses of islands in the mist.

From the Kaliningrad frontier at Nida to the Russian border at Narva, the coast of the three Baltic states stretches in a great double curve for 600 miles. Parts of it were closed for Soviet military purposes for the best part of half a century. Others are menaced by military or industrial pollution. Nevertheless, this is a wonderful coast, by far the most extensive stretch of beaches and dunes and spits in the whole Baltic. The long spit south of Klaipeda offers one kind of summer heaven, the dunes that stretch northwards into Latvia another. The northern coast of Estonia is rockier and wilder, with wonderful views of the Gulf of Finland between the trees. In between, the Gulf of Riga bites deep into the Baltic coast between western Latvia and the Estonian islands. On its beaches, at places like Jurmala near Riga or Parnu in Estonia, the Russian upper classes in the late nineteenth century discovered that they too liked to be beside the seaside. You can still see traces of what they discovered a century ago. Parnu has its old town and its spa, and Jurmala parades long shaded streets of Chekhovian wooden houses.

A few miles to the south of Riga lies the town of Jelgava, which was a trading centre and fortification long before Bishop Albrecht's time. The Germans named it Mitau and built a castle here. Eventually it became the power-base of the Kettler dynasty, from which the dukes of Courland and Semigallia governed their little duchy.

Changing and overlapping names of provinces and districts are the gremlins which confound exploration of the eastern Baltic: try to find Warmia, Kashubia, Mazovia and Livonia on a modern map. But essentially Courland is the Latvian peninsula which juts northwards towards the Estonian islands to form the Gulf of Riga, and Semigallia is that part of southern Latvia which lies inland from it. Today, as Kurzeme and Zemgale, they form two of Latvia's three provinces. In the seventeenth and the eighteenth centuries they achieved more particular fame.

In the cellar of the old palace at Jelgava you can see the lead coffins of several dukes of Courland. The most interesting of them is Duke Jacob, whose character you can judge from the fierce portrait engraved upon his coffin. Duke Jacob ruled Courland at the time of Cromwell and the later Stuarts. From Ventspils, on the Courland peninsula, he shipped pine masts to customers as far afield as England and Venice. Courland grew rich. Duke Jacob built a navy of his own and determined to conquer a tropical empire. He took Tobago in the Caribbean and an island in the mouth of the Gambia. His ships sailed the oceans, his colonies sent tropical produce back to Courland. For a short time the flag of Courland flew along the trade routes of the world.

After Duke Jacob the fortunes of the Kettlers declined. Courland continued to offer the world certain coastal curiosities: the terminal of a sub-Baltic telegraph cable, landings by the Royal Navy in the Napoleonic Wars and the Crimean War, and the same navy's rescue of a Latvian Prime Minister in 1919. But later ocean-going adventurers from the Baltic came not from Courland but equally improbably, as we shall see four chapters hence, from the Åland Islands in the mouth of the Gulf of Bothnia. It was a duke of Courland who was not a Kettler who would once again attract the world's attention to the duchy.

In 1710 a young Kettler princeling contracted marriage with a Russian princess, Anna Ivanovna, the daughter of the imbecile Tsar Ivan V and a niece of Peter the Great. On the way home from their wedding in St Petersburg the duke died, leaving his seventeen year-old widow to live out an empty life among strangers in the Kettler palace at Jelgava. She found herself alone, far from St Petersburg. An obscure courtier, Johannes Ernst Biron, had the wit to catch her on the rebound. He gave her the comfort and the sexual release she craved, and became a Courland favourite. When on her father's death she became Empress Anne of Russia, she took Biron with her to St Petersburg, ennobled him, heaped wealth upon him, made him a count and then duke of Courland, and on her death in 1740 left Russia in his charge and care as regent for her infant great-nephew, Ivan.

In 1736 Biron set about building himself a palace at Rundale, south of Jelgava, putting Bartholomeo Rastrelli, the architect of the

Hermitage in St Petersburg, in charge of the works. A year after Anne's death, his regency was overthrown by rivals and he was exiled to Siberia, where he languished for over twenty years. But when at last he came home, work on Rundale was resumed and, more than thirty years after its beginning, was carried to a splendid conclusion. If it fell short of the standards of St Petersburg, Rundale nevertheless became one of the great rural palaces of eastern Europe, even grander than Esterháza.

Rundale was almost destroyed in the fighting that ravaged southern Latvia in the First and Second World Wars. But in the 1970s the restorers came to the rescue, and you can see it now in all its fresh magnificence. You approach it through fields beside a canal and enter a great courtyard between stable blocks. Columns crowned by coroneted lions point the way to an inner courtyard formed by the wings of the palace itself. Window follows window, pillar follows pillar with all the stately regularity of Versailles. Within, chamber succeeds stately chamber: the Golden Hall, the White Hall, room after room of ducal splendour. Rundale is an improbable palace to find in the middle of nowhere, and a superb memorial to the duchy of Courland and Semigallia.

There is a bright Monday-morning air about Latvia today, as there is about all three Baltic states. They have their improbably-recovered independence; Russian troops are gone; and though difficulties lie ahead there is a confidence that they can be mastered. People look forward; and they look back with almost as much passion to what received wisdom tells them were golden years between 1920 and 1940, their short period of free nationhood.

The recent history of the Baltic states starts with the collapse of the Hohenzollern and Romanov empires. Stirrings of nationhood stretch back into the nineteenth century, encouraged by academic exploration of Baltic language and folk legend, but a flourishing Russian empire could have contained them. By 1917, however, the German army had advanced deep into the Baltic provinces and in that year the Russian empire collapsed in chaos. At first it seemed as if Germany might take control of the eastern Baltic coast, but within a year the empire of the Hohenzollerns fell also. All over Europe small peoples, encouraged by Woodrow Wilson's support for self-determination, seized their opportunities.

In the Baltic states, nationalists found themselves challenging both

Russian Whites and Bolsheviks, regular German forces and levies raised by German Baltic barons. Finnish volunteers came to the help of the Estonians, and so did a German division that had been helping the Finns secure their own independence. Confused, vicious little wars ensued. The Russian Whites believed the Baltic provinces were theirs by right, and in any case needed them as a base for their attacks upon the Bolsheviks. Bolshevik policy and war aims swung wildly between conquest, peace between socialist brothers and world revolution. The allies sought the Bolsheviks' destruction in Russia, and saw Baltic independence as a subsidiary factor in the mad equation. For them the German levies at first seemed an effective force to send against the Bolsheviks, but they drew the line at dreams of a new German empire in the east, dreams which preoccupied the German commander, Rüdiger von der Goltz. The nationalists' goal was simple: nationhood, untrammelled independence, the expropriation of the Baltic barons and the establishment of bourgeois and peasant republics.

The stories of those who got involved in the fighting give an idea of the passions and cross-purposes of the time. Harold Alexander, later Lord Alexander of Tunis, was sent to the Baltic on detached duty and found himself commanding a German militia column against the Bolsheviks. He called his months in the Baltic some of the happiest of his life, and briefly entertained the wild idea of resigning his commission and buying an estate in Latvia where he would farm and paint. And he thought the Germans under his command were the finest human beings and fighting men he had ever known. Others thought as favourably of the Latvian Rifles, who served the tsar faithfully in the early years of the First World War and then went their different ways, some to serve the Soviet Bolsheviks, others to fight for Latvia's independence. To others the German Freikorps and the Latvian Rifles were at best ruffians and more frequently killers as bloodthirsty as the Black and Tans.

On all sides there was a tendency to shoot first and ask questions afterwards, and the Royal Navy's commander in the Baltic, a fiery little warrior named Admiral Sir Walter Cowan, whose men loved him until provoked to short-lived mutiny, was quick to turn his guns against Bolsheviks and Germans alike. In her short novel *Coup de Grâce*, Marguerite Yourcenar tells a convincing story which captures something of the convoluted horror of those days. She describes a love affair in a German country-house somewhere in the Baltic provinces. The girl is a daughter of the house, the man a member of its small German garrison. The Bolsheviks attack, the girl joins them and then is captured by the Germans to whom, days earlier, she had been serving afternoon tea in their front-line house party. Death by shooting is the drum-head court martial sentence, and in a tortured last act of love she forces her lover to pull the trigger.

Arthur Ransome, later to write *Swallows and Amazons*, experienced more whimsical hazards in these muddled wars. He was a correspondent in Russia during the First World War, and in the chaos at its ending drifted into the roles of propagandist and confidential agent. He fell in love with Trotsky's secretary, and embarked on a dangerous journey with her between Bolshevik and White lines. Three separate groups of irregulars took them prisoner, and each considers shooting Ransome, just to be on the safe side. On one occasion a chance acquaintanceship saves him. On a second he satisfies his interrogators. But it takes his mistress's offer of a favourite tea-pot in return for his life to save him from a third set of captors. It was that kind of war, viciously lethal at one moment, ludicrous the next.

In 1920 the Bolsheviks withdrew, the German irregulars were disbanded and the Royal Navy sailed for home. The three Baltic states had their independence. They inherited the ruins of war, deep animosities, economies that had been shaped by two centuries of Russian rule, and social traditions which had held Latvians, Estonians and Lithuanians in absolute submission to German, Russian and Polish landowners. Their leaders set about creating small bourgeois and peasant republics where previously only the tsar's and the landowners' authority had prevailed.

The Latvians and the Estonians, like the Lithuanians, set out with democratic intentions. Once the Baltic barons had been expropriated, the new countries enjoyed relatively cohesive societies: a few intellectuals, businessmen and administrators in the towns, a few landowners and a great mass of peasants and labourers in the countryside. Strong ethnic identities bound most of the people of these societies together and excluded minorities from the national circle almost as rigorously as the Baltic Germans had excluded the natives. Peasant traditions, extending back before Christianity and blending heathen and Christian pieties in a sometimes intolerant mix, reinforced political loyalties. They were, in short, closed societies, strong on intimacy, short on tolerance and political experience. And placed where they were in the shadow of the Soviet Union at the wrong end of the Baltic they had little room for manoeuvre.

The three little countries soon became caricatures of democracies, whose plethora of parties were innocent of concepts such as conciliation, accommodation and co-operation. Even in the Europe of the 1920s, their political preoccupations had a dated air, above all in their concern with ethnic identity. Like Lithuania, both Latvia and Estonia succumbed in time to authoritarian leaders. Karlis Ulmanis in Latvia and Konstantin Pats in Estonia avoided – like Smetona – the worst extremes of authoritarianism. They were not fascists, nor were they driven by fantasies of political engineering. Indeed, they argued that they had assumed power in order to defend democracy against its abuse; and in the Baltic states in the 1930s there was some justification for that familiar claim. These were not bad societies, but they were societies under pressure.

Lithuania, Latvia and Estonia found themselves in increasing political isolation. Each built a limited and very vulnerable prosperity. They had a fair degree of internal stability. Each was recognised as a sovereign European state. But they were as close to Russia as they had always been. Weimar Germany cherished resentments of losses in the eastern Baltic, and Hitler nurtured clear ambitions in the area. Britain and France had shepherded the Baltic states to independence, but they lacked the will to come to their rescue again. There was talk of regional groupings, but they were blocked by national antipathies. As the 1930s wore on the Baltic states were rabbits paralysed in the glare of totalitarian headlights.

Riga remained the cosmopolitan city it had been under the tsars. Its port suffered when the Soviet Union closed its borders, but Baltic Germans lingered there, as did foreign businessmen and Jews. And White Russians took refuge in Riga, swelling its already considerable Russian population and waiting for the day when they could repossess their palaces and businesses in St Petersburg. Throughout the 1920s, fading in the 1930s, there was an expectation of the great undoing of the Russian Revolution which came at last in the 1990s, long after the last refugee was dead.

Western Legations in Riga had two tasks: to follow at a distance developments in the Soviet Union and, less important, to conduct diplomatic relations with Latvia. George Kennan, the first of a legion of American experts on the Soviet Union, spent three years in Riga in the early 1930s, preoccupied with the rumours brought to him by refugees from the enigmatic mystery over the border. For him it was like living in a time warp. 'Riga was in many respects a minor edition of St Petersburg,' he wrote in his memoirs. 'The old Petersburg was of course now dead, or largely dead . . . But Riga was still alive. It was one of those cases where the copy had survived the original . . . it was, in fact, almost the only place where one could still live in Tsarist Russia.'

On 23 August 1939 the Molotov-Ribbentrop Pact was signed. On 1 September Hitler invaded Poland and sixteen days later Stalin did the same. Lithuania, Latvia and Estonia passed unambiguously into the Soviet sphere of influence. Washing his hands of the three countries, Hitler ordered the Baltic Germans back to the Reich, settling most of them in the territories he had just seized from Poland. On 17 June, 1940, Stalin invaded the three republics, and in August he annexed them to the Soviet Union.

There is no question of the horrors the Soviet Union inflicted on the Baltic states. They were absorbed into the Soviet Union and reduced to abject subordination to its Communist leadership. In rapid succession their peoples suffered loss of nationhood, expropriation, loss of personal and religious liberty, and deportation in their thousands to Siberia. During the mere twelve months that separated Stalin's annexation of the three republics from Hitler's attack upon the Soviet Union, Soviet actions made a reality of every fear that the Balts had nursed for twenty years.

So when Germans tanks came rumbling through the Baltic states, many welcomed them as liberators. The Wehrmacht expected to capture St Petersburg before the winter, and its interest in the three republics was confined to keeping lines of communication open. But here as in the Ukraine, the crass brutality of German policy brought disillusion, and behind the armies came the Gestapo and the *Einsatzgruppen*. The Jewish tragedy was acted out in Latvia and Estonia as in Lithuania. Leftists met the same fate.

The German occupation lasted for over three years. Then came the Soviet counter-attack, which by the spring of 1945 had swept right through the Baltic states and into East Prussia. Behind the Soviet troops came the security police. Many Balts had fought on the German side; many fled with the Germans or across the Baltic to Sweden. Now those who had remained were hunted down as Nazis or war criminals. Many partisans took to the woods, fighting a campaign against the Russians which lasted into the 1950s and cost the occupiers thousands of lives. Their resistance provoked more deportations and executions. In 1947 Soviet collectivisation of agriculture destroyed the rural heart of the Baltic world. And in March 1949 came mass deportations of more than 100,000 Balts, carried away in cattle wagons to Siberia and Central Asia. This was the Baltic Golgotha.

Soviet policy set out to destroy all political and social influence other than that of the party. National and religious sentiments were to be eradicated. A socialist economy was to replace private ownership. More extreme measures were needed in the Baltic republics than in the rest of eastern Europe, for they had to become mere constituent parts of the Soviet Union. Even after the deportations were over, oppression in the Baltics was harsher than in Poland, Hungary, Czechoslovakia and even Romania.

Russian immigration came in the wake of the militarisation of the Baltic states: to fill places emptied by the deportations; and to help build science-based industries to serve the Soviet Union's military needs. The immigrants added insult to deep injury. Latvians say that they brought the standards of the slum or the farmyard to what had been a fastidious, bourgeois republic. Their demands for housing, privilege and special treatment enraged the Balts. Their rate of reproduction threatened to outnumber them. As Soviet terror eased and a limited tolerance spread, permitting in the 1970s some measure of guarded expression of national sentiment, the Russian minorities came to be seen as the greatest threat to such hopes of nationhood as survived.

But in the 1980s the Baltics began to assert themselves. As elsewhere in eastern Europe, environmental concerns provided a first occasion for quasi-political organisation. So did a cautious search for roots, for truth about the past. The local Communist parties began to emphasise their concerns for Baltic identity and to play down their links with Moscow. Gradually the embers of hope were rekindled, ready to burst into flame when change in Moscow allowed. When millions joined hands along the Baltic Way they astonished the world. In the struggle for fulfilment of national dreams that followed, Latvia and Estonia marched with Lithuania. By 1991 they had recovered their independence.

We will look at the strengths and weaknesses of these three new societies and newly re-established nations when, at the end of the next chapter, we have had a chance to see them all. But the particular story of the minorities belongs in Latvia. It has clouded the years since independence; it harms the good name of the Baltic states as truly representative democracies; and it could provide Russian nationalists with an excuse if not a reason for a disastrous intervention in Latvia and Estonia.

Russians, Belarusians and Ukrainians amount to forty-two per cent of the population of Latvia. Latvians form a bare majority in their own country, and a mere third of the population of the capital. Estonians form sixty per cent of their country's population and under fifty per cent of their capital's. So there is fear of the immigrants as well as resentment and contempt, for only the Lithuanians, at eighty per cent, can feel themselves demographically secure. And Russian policy, reluctant to accept that its influence in the old Baltic provinces must yield at last to Baltic nationhood, has played the settlers' card with stolid determination.

If you are an Estonian or a Latvian, you argue that your forebears have lived here and nowhere else for thousands of years. The Russians are interlopers, and most of them came lately, as a consequence of the Soviet rape of the Baltic states. Now the world has changed. If the Russians can adapt to that change of circumstances, learn the language, show themselves loyal to the republics, the way to citizenship is open. But they were arrogant when they arrived, and their arrogance has been little moderated since their world was turned upside down.

The Russians sing a different song. They argue that some Russians have roots here going back two centuries and that even the newcomers have been here for twenty or thirty years. They paid their dues in the old Soviet Union and now have rights in the new republics. They are quick to complain of discrimination: A third of the people have no votes, an embittered guide from the Intourist era mutters. 'Is that what the West calls democracy?'

A western diplomat orders the arguments differently. The Baltics' emotions are understandable, but they live in the shadow of the Bear. They cannot afford to provoke him. Yet their policy towards the settlers encourages just the sort of sentiment that gives Russian nationalists a colourable reason to threaten the Baltic states. And the shortcomings of that policy diminish their reputation in the West, recalling Baltic involvement in wartime crimes, undermining western backing for their nationhood. In short, be reasonable, and bend policy to favour the Russians.

The answer is that such advice ignores the intensity of Baltic feelings. There is no family untouched by the deportations of the 1940s. The executioners of the Baltic Golgotha were Russians. Russians have impoverished the Baltics, reduced them to an environmental slum, resisted the reassertion of Estonian and Latvian nationhood, and done their best to frustrate the recovery of independence.

No one gets off such an argumentative merry-go-round satisfied, but for the moment a kind of balance prevails. Russian troops have withdrawn from the Baltics. Agreement has been reached on the Russian early-warning radar station in Latvia. The Baltics pay pensions to those retired Soviet officers who cannot tear themselves away from the countries in which they served. Settlers can achieve voting rights after several years' residence if they can pass a language test which the Balts claim to be reasonable and which the Russians protest to be impossible. And more and more Russians, particularly younger people, are throwing in their lot with the Baltic states.

But some of the Russians remain a time-bomb in the eastern Baltic. The poorly-educated live aimless, alienated lives, cut off from the Latvians and Estonians, more often than not unemployed, their young people at hazardous loose ends. They are numerous, often a majority, in the urban wildernesses which surround the major cities; and an overwhelming majority in places such as Narva, on Estonia's Russian border. The Russian presence in the Baltics is a time bomb which Russia's nastier nationalists may yet seek to explode.

8

Estonia

We now enter one of the smallest national societies in Europe. Estonia has a population of 1.5 million people. A third of them are Slavs, and less than 1 million of them speak Estonian as their first language. Estonian belongs to the Finno-Ugrian family of languages, spoken only by Magyars, Finns and Estonians; and by a group of north-east European tribes whose quiddities enthral anthropologists and philologists. All these groups came originally from the east. The Magyars reached the Danube only 1,100 years ago, and say wryly that their wiser cousins turned north towards the Baltic when they themselves went south to the cockpit of central Europe. But in fact there were Finno-Ugrian tribes on the Baltic 1,000 years before the Magyars first arrived in Hungary.

Like the Latvians, the Estonians learned their Christianity from western missionaries and conquerors, but their religion is shot through with older instincts, a turning to nature and particularly the woods, rather than to a personal god. So in Estonian churches a window onto the outside world sometimes attracts as much devotion as a cross. The best-loved burial places are not churchyards but forest glades, the grave marked not by a cross but a boulder. And it is folk-song, sung by great choirs in glorious costumes, with subtle differences between every district and every village, that best expresses the Estonian soul. In the summer of 1994, at the first nationwide folk festival since Estonia recovered her independence, they sang in their tens of thousands. You can find similar expressions of identity in the other Baltic countries; and even the sheer force of Lithuanian Catholicism has not blotted them out. But in this – as in so many respects – Estonia seems to express the purest essence of the Baltic states: it is more self-contained and less affected by outside influences than either Lithuania or Latvia.

Its capital is a smaller, simpler city than the other Baltic capitals. Whereas Riga is cosmopolitan and Vilnius a city of the east European plain, Tallinn keeps its provinciality. It has, as Arthur Ransome said,

'least of the vices of a town and most of the virtues of a village'.
Even though more than half its population today is Russian-speaking, it is essentially an Estonian city. Tallinn looks north to the sea,
not east to St Petersburg; and the heart of the city admits few
outside influences.

Yet Tallinn was largely created by non-Estonians. For the Estonians, like the Latvians, have been serfs or subjects for almost
all their history since the arrival of Christianity. Those with a
nationalist historical bent look back to a golden age of freedom, but
by the eleventh century their Scandinavian and Russian neighbours
were beginning to crowd in upon them. In 1219 a Danish fleet,
commanded by King Valdemar himself, appeared off the ancient
Estonian settlement that was to become Tallinn.

Valdemar had imperial and commercial ambitions in the eastern
Baltic. He was concerned that the Germans might pre-empt him. He
came as a crusader, with the pope's blessing, and he brought with
him the Archbishop of Denmark. The Estonians attacked, throwing
the Danes into confusion, and even stoutly agnostic Danes will
tell you of the miracle that followed. The invading archbishop fell
on his knees to pray, with two canons holding his hands aloft in
protracted supplication; eventually a red and white flag – the *Dan-
nebrog* – fluttered down from heaven as a sign of God's favour;
the Estonians were routed, Valdemar became the Victorious, and a
Danish fortress was established. The Estonians called it Tallinn, the
Danish town.

For over 100 years the Danes held the Estonians in uneasy sub-
jugation. Tallinn grew in size and importance and became a trading
outpost of the Hanseatic League on the Gulf of Finland. In 1343 the
Estonians attempted a last uprising against the Danes, but failed to
drive them out. But the uprising weakened the Danish hold on their
eastern province and three years later another Valdemar – this time
Valdemar the Evil – sold it to the German Knights. They impressed
upon it an indelible German stamp, which survived one century of
Swedish and two centuries of Russian occupation.

This medieval German stamp is most manifest in the old city of
Tallinn, known to Germans and foreigners for most of its history as
Reval. It divides into two parts, distinct from one another and from
the modern city which surrounds it.

The upper town was in turn the Danes' redoubt, the Knights'

fortress, and the nobles' town. At its foot is the merchants' city. Old fortifications surround the upper town, and their names are still redolent of Danish whimsicality. There is Long Hermann's Tower, Arrow Sharpener Tower, and a tower called Kiek in de Kok, because its garrison had an uninterrupted view into the merchants' kitchens below. Within these defences lies an enchanted little city, essentially medieval but embellished with the seventeenth- and eighteenth-century houses of the Swedish and German aristocracies. The dark cathedral was built in the time of the Knights, but it is filled with the graves and coats of arms of Swedish governors and later German noblemen. There are quiet streets and squares, and shabby alleys which open out to reveal large views over the lower town and the harbour and the Gulf of Finland. UNESCO, busy labelling beauty, should recognise the upper town of Tallinn for the jewel that it is: exquisite in its own right, and with its own particular, unspoiled Baltic quality.

The Danes built the castle which occupies one corner of the upper town, and the Germans and the Swedes made it their headquarters. But first Russian rule and now Estonian nationhood have obliterated its warlike purposes. Long Hermann's Tower still stands – in 1989 it marked the Estonian end of the chain of linked hands that ran the length of the Baltic states – but the buildings in its shadow house the parliament and government offices, as they used to house Russian governors. Across the street the strident ochre of the Alexander Nevski Cathedral shouts twice as loud as parliament's muted pinks and greys, proclaiming the icons, incense and chimes of Orthodoxy in this austere corner of the Baltic. The visitor may appreciate the touch of spice and verve that it brings to the old town; but Estonians are people of understatement and reserve. They dislike the cathedral, in large part because of their dislike for the Russia that it represents.

Estonia is obsessed with Russia and with her Russian minority. The frontier lies only 120 miles from Tallinn, and Russia's second city, St Petersburg, is just beyond it. For millions of Russians, and not just extreme nationalists, the Baltic provinces are historically and instinctively theirs. And 450,000 of Estonia's people, thirty per cent of her total population, are Russian speakers. The proportion is even higher in the capital, where fifty per cent of the population speak Russian, and where Estonians point out an urban wilderness of workers' flats, entirely occupied, they say, by unemployed and alienated Slavs. The countryside is predominantly Estonian and so is Estonia's second city, Tartu. But Narva, an industrial town on the Russian frontier, is overwhelmingly Russian. As in Latvia, the grievances of the Russian minority are met not with understanding but with the self-assertion of recovered nationhood. In short, Estonia is highly vulnerable to Russian nationalist pressure on behalf of Estonian Russians.

There are particular problems on the frontier. Lake Peipus plays a useful role in keeping Russians and Estonians apart, but south of the lake there is an area which the Estonians claim is historically and legally theirs, but which the Russians continue to hold. Their president wisely tells the Estonians to drop the matter or let it lie until times are calmer, but nationalism often speaks louder than wisdom or presidents. The frontier issue, like complaints about the legacy of pollution left by Russian sailors and soldiers, has joined the long list of Estonian grievances against the Russians.

The Finns, by contrast, are Estonia's most favoured neighbours. The linguistic links are treasured by a nation which has so few; there is a handsome monument beside the sea to the Finnish volunteers who came to the Estonians' aid in their war against the Bolsheviks; Finnish television gave Estonians a window on the West in the Soviet years; and Finnish ministers and businessmen have been swift to offer help since independence – and, some Estonians say, to take advantage of Estonian inexperience in putting a cheap but skilled labour force to profitable work in a capitalist world. The westerner who imagines that the three Baltic republics would be wise to federate with one another ignores the differences which separate them. If it were to come to regional groupings in the eastern Baltic, Estonia would look northward across the Gulf of Finland, not south towards Latvia and Lithuania.

The Finns have been good friends to the Estonians since they recovered their independence, as the Nordics have been to all three Baltic states. Recognition, technical assistance, political advice and investment came quickly. So did the diplomacy of meaningful gesture, with Danish and Swedish royals paying state visits of which you find memories all over the Baltics. When Russian nationalism talked about Russian interests in the Baltic republics, Carl Bildt, then Sweden's prime minister, spoke with unusual boldness about their significance for Sweden's security. Now companies of troops from the Baltic countries' little armies are twinned with Nordic battalions as they train for UN peacekeeping. The Nordics had different starting points: Denmark within NATO, Sweden coolly neutral, Finland traditionally checked by its concern for Russian sensitivities. But they had a common interest in helping the new democracies, building Baltic institutions and focusing outside attention on the area. In the Baltic states they moved with a courage and determination that did a service to all Europe.

In doing so they helped Lithuania, Latvia and Estonia to re-establish old links with the West down the Baltic, the links which built the lower, trading town of Tallinn in the Middle Ages. Tallinn still displays all the characteristics of a Hanseatic city, and though a multilingual notice on a bomb site details the damage done by a Soviet air attack, it was clearly next to nothing beside the devastation the Royal Air Force brought to Lübeck and Königsberg. Most of Tallinn's finest buildings are untouched by time and war: Fat Margaret's Gate leading to the harbour; the remains of a rambling Dominican monastery; the House of the Guild of Grain and Wine Merchants; the Church of The Holy Ghost with a glorious altarpiece by the Baltic genius, Bernt Notke; and the House of the Brotherhood of the Blackheads, where the younger merchants of the city gathered like a medieval Junior Chamber of Commerce.

Beyond the Hanseatic town extends the quietly dignified city which grew up under the Russians in the eighteenth and nineteenth centuries. The twentieth century has done its work too: on the one hand the monstrous concrete boxes of Stalinism and after; on the other an exquisite new national library built in the late 1980s, the quality of its construction distinguishing it from the mediocrity around it. It is as if the Estonians saw this new building as a symbol of better times they knew were coming, though no one could be quite sure when.

Arthur Ransome wrote of Tallinn in the 1920s: 'In Reval nothing is done for show, except, perhaps, an occasional march of troops or fire brigade. And that you must have in any capital. There is no single street in Reval given up to fine shops and the parades of fools. Everything is decent, homely and unflurried.' It remains an easygoing place seventy years later. When the folk-dancing exhibition that accompanied the song festival in 1994 was over, Estonia's president drove away unescorted in the most modest of Mercedes. The people waved, the car slowed to a crawl, the president stuck his head out of the window to chat to his friends. If Denmark and Sweden display the modesty of Baltic monarchies, that evening Estonia showed us the modesty of the Baltic republics.

Its position on the Gulf of Finland first attracted the Danes and Hanseatic seafarers to Tallinn, and it now welcomes cruise ships and ten ferries a day from Helsinki. For that matter, it was its position that first gave Tallinn its importance in Russian eyes, as part of the outlying defences of St Petersburg. Winter often closes it, like all the Gulf of Finland ports, but it comes to life in the long days of summer. And it is, surprisingly perhaps, a centre for yachtsmen.

Tallinn was a summer resort of the Russian aristocracy, and when in 1908 the Tsar of all the Russias planned a meeting with his cousin Edward VII, it was at Tallinn that they came together. The king and the royal family sailed up the Baltic in the royal yacht *Victoria and Albert* for a summer holiday with their cousins. It was only three years after the bloody suppression of the 1905 revolution in St Petersburg, and there were protests in the House of Commons about holidaymaking with a tyrant. German opinion was restive too: in the previous year Edward had visited Paris and the German press detected plans to encircle Germany. But the two royal families exchanged dinners and picnics and balls, and the whole visit seems to have been suffused with that summer light which, to judge by old mens' memories, filled those last years of peace. The British sailed away down the Baltic; the Russians went home to St Petersburg. Ten years later Nicholas and his family, denied asylum in Britain by the fear that their unpopularity would tarnish the brightness of the House of Windsor, were dead.

A few years later Arthur Ransome sailed into Tallinn harbour in a different kind of yacht. She was *Racundra*, on her maiden voyage to Tallinn from Riga, where Ransome had commissioned her. During the course of some extraordinary adventures around the Gulf of Finland, Ransome had got to know the people and the politics of the area in a way few Englishmen have done. We have seen him in the civil war shuttling between White and Red lines with his Bolshevik mistress in tow, and he himself acquired a reputation in British official circles as a dangerous Bolshevik. But his strongest sympathies lay with Estonia, and for a time he based himself in Tallinn. When he brought *Racundra* into Tallinn harbour he was coming home.

Ransome described his adventures in *Racundra's First Cruise*, which does for the Gulf of Riga and Gulf of Finland what *The Riddle of the Sands* does for sailing in Danish waters and the Heligoland Bight. Ransome's whimsical account of a half-finished boat, an ancient Estonian mariner as crew, his Bolshevik mistress as ship's cook and himself as master and owner had a charm that lured Englishmen to go sailing in the eastern Baltic. War put a stop to that, and for forty years afterwards the only small boats from the West that went prowling among the Estonian islands were probing Soviet defences or putting Baltic freedom fighters ashore on deserted beaches.

But in the 1960s sailing revived, with clubs carefully regulated to ensure that no one sailed away to Finland. Sailing was recognised as a Soviet sport, a fine yachting harbour was built beside the ruins of the old convent at Pirita outside Tallinn, and it was agreed that Estonia should play host to the Sailing Olympics in 1980. But the Soviet invasion of Afghanistan intervened, and with it the western boycott, with the result that the crews who came to Tallinn to challenge Russian sailors were from places such as Cuba and Upper Volta, and the Olympics failed to put East-West sailing rivalries to the test.

The German gentry who owned the houses in the upper town of Tallinn spent nine months of the year on their estates, and you can still find their manor houses – ruined or abandoned or restored – scattered around Estonia. They were never in the same league of grandeur as Biron's Rundale, but in their salons and dining rooms and vast greenhouses you can sense something of their charm, and among the ruins of the abandoned houses you can hear a whisper of the ghosts of the Baltic barons. In 1841 Lady Eastlake published *A Residence on the Shores of the Baltic*, a somewhat coy memoir of a visit to a married sister living in one of these manor houses. She describes houses devoid of all except essential furniture, sealed against the cold and heated by great Baltic stoves, swarming with tribes of children and nursery-maids and seamstresses and visitors, and men to stoke the stoves.

Her book does not much help us to judge the pros and cons of German rule in the Baltic provinces. Even seventy years after the Baltic barons were swept aside, opinions remain coloured by politics and nostalgia and bitterness. We have seen Raskolnikov's conviction that conditions on a German estate were like those on a slave plantation. The German philosopher Herder, himself a Prussian, wrote of the Baltic barons' crimes, and Estonian guides today will mutter to you lubriciously about their taste for the *jus primae noctis*. The notion that the Baltic barons dealt more harshly with their dependants than other overlords persists into our own times.

German aristocrats whom I used to know in the Federal Republic would invite their friends to espouse very different beliefs about the Baltic families from which they came. They would remember honour and justice and even tenderness, recollections that fly in the face of contrary evidence of oppression and exploitation. The whole business is like trying to take a view of settlers in Kenya or of the ascendancy in Ireland. Yet it is worth asking about German relations with their Estonian serfs or Latvian tenants, for such questions lie at the heart of much Baltic history.

A few things are clear. German masters and Baltic labour between them created Latvia and Estonia. The Germans brought standards of efficiency and probity that were rare in eastern Europe. They had a highly-developed sense of personal honour. They practised a passionate exclusivity of class and background. All this, to a greater or lesser degree, is the story of aristocracies all over Europe from the late Middle Ages almost to our own times. Where the Baltic barons were different was that blood and language set them apart from Estonians and Latvians.

The Russian and Polish aristocracies took pride in the instincts that linked them to their peasants and serfs. So did the Germans in Germany. Sometimes they were right; sometimes they deceived themselves. But the Baltic barons were colonists, among alien peoples. Lady Eastlake describes an exclusive society, absurdly conventional even to her eyes, sealed against all Estonians except coachmen and maids. She wrote about Estonia as privileged visitors wrote about the Ireland of the ascendancy. There too rulers and peasants lived in separate worlds. Conditions in Ireland, as in the Baltic provinces, horrified visitors who stood back from the charmed circle of the Anglo-Irish aristocracy.

At the end of the First World War the Baltic peasants at last got their chance to translate into action some of the poetic fantasies passed down the generations by word of mouth. They ransacked German manor houses, and sometimes murdered their owners. The world was in turmoil, at the end of a bloody, all-consuming war. They wanted land, and the landlords stood in their way. The Russian poor, whom the landowners had professed to understand, dealt just as harshly with their overlords. So had the French a century earlier. And everywhere there were exceptions, human affections bridging the divide, as much in ordinary times as in times of crisis. Latvians and Estonians rejoiced to be rid of their German masters. Today they want the material good things that German qualities can bring. But it will be generations yet before Estonians and Latvians wash from their subconscious their resentments against the Germans.

As you drive north through the Baltic states, you find that climate and landscape become more unforgiving. Lithuania is east European, Latvia a borderland between east and north, but Estonia is without question northern, a part of the Nordic world that happens to lie on the wrong side of the Baltic. Her northern coast falls just short of 60 degrees north, and that is a bleak latitude anywhere in the world. In Estonia the fields are littered with great boulders which geologists call granite erratics. Her crops are uncertain, her forests menacing. Even her flag is sombre, a tricolour of blue, black and white. Her people, Latvians and Lithuanians will tell you, are as solemn as Swedes.

The countryside belongs to the Estonians. The Germans are long since gone; the Russians by and large are confined to the towns. Estonians live by farming and forestry, with some fishing on the coast. The rare villages are pure Estonian: wooden huts and houses on foundations of granite boulders laboriously cleared from the fields; perhaps a shop; perhaps a church; almost certainly a great wooden swing the size of a gallows, on which young and old solemnly propel themselves backwards and forwards on summer evenings. Estonians today are beginning to offer bed and breakfast holidays on the farm: an uncomfortable idyll, probably, but a way to spend a Baltic summer in a countryside untouched by time.

Tartu, Estonia's second city and one-time capital, thinks of itself as particularly Estonian. It lies in the south-east, not far from Lake Peipus. In 1944 Russians and Germans slugged it out around Tartu and came close to destroying the city. But the damage has been patched up now, and within a ring of ugliness of the sort the twentieth century has thrown round cities all over the world, Tartu is a place of quiet charm, with a park rambling across a hilltop that was once a fortress, and a pretty classical square running down from the town hall to the river.

Tartu was Dorpat to the Germans, and it was the Treaty of Dorpat in February 1920 which concluded peace between Estonia and the Soviet Union. Lithuania and Latvia followed; and then, in a second

Treaty of Dorpat, the Finns also came to terms with the Bolsheviks. The Whites were still fighting in southern Russia and the Red Army was locked in battle with the Poles. The great powers were still intent on girdling the Soviet Union with a *cordon sanitaire* and they were not happy to see little Estonia break ranks. But for better or for worse, the first Treaty of Dorpat marked the beginnings of accommodation of Red Russia into the world, and the securing of independence for the Baltic states, if only for two decades.

Tartu has been a university city since the early seventeenth century, nearly as long as Vilnius. But whereas the Jesuits established Vilnius as an outpost of the Counter-Reformation, it was Lutheran Swedes who founded Tartu, their kingdom's second university. At the end of the Great Northern War which laid Estonia waste, the Swedes took the university away with them. It was not until the nineteenth century, after nearly 100 years of Russian rule, that Alexander II re-established a university in Tartu. It was a university not for Estonians but for Baltic Germans and Russians, and it produced many of the scholars who graced St Petersburg's Academy of Sciences. But in the paradoxical way that lightens tyrannies, it came to play a key role in the late nineteenth-century awakening of national sentiment in the Baltics.

Only in 1919 did Tartu become an Estonian-language university. Today it has the biggest library in Estonia and 8,000 students whose sailor caps on days of jollification turn the little city into what looks like a sea of Scandinavians. The library displays examples of the first faltering scraps of Baltic literacy: the first book in Estonian, a prayer book published in Germany in 1525; a book of sermons containing parallel native and German texts, so that German pastors could communicate after a fashion with their congregations; and the first, eighteenth-century, Old and New Testaments in Estonian. But there is nothing faltering today about Tartu University. It may be in a little country at the back of beyond but it takes itself with becoming seriousness. It reminds the supercilious visitor that living standards and political skills and experience may decline as you travel from west to east in Europe but that love of learning knows no frontiers. 'Send us books,' they say in Tartu university library; and in the reading-rooms lines of studious heads bend over them.

On the hill in Tartu stand the ruins of a great church in the familiar Baltic brick. It was once Tartu's cathedral, built in the thirteenth century, in its time the largest church in the eastern Baltic. But the demise of the Teutonic Knights brought Swedes, Poles and Russians pressing into the Baltic countries, and with them the long Livonian Wars. Tartu was fought over and the cathedral was destroyed. A century later its choir was restored and now houses the university's museum. But the nave and the west front remain as imposing in their ruins as any of the restored brick churches of the Baltic.

These ruins mark the eastern end of the world of Gothic brick that stretches across northern Europe from the English Channel to Estonia. Where exactly in the west it starts is anyone's guess: perhaps in the little town of Hesdin near St Pol in the département of the Somme. We have seen its cathedrals and churches in Lübeck and Wismar, Bad Doberan and Stralsund, Gdansk and Riga and Frombork. It comes to an end among the great empty arches and broken flying buttresses of the cathedral in Tartu. Further north, Estonia becomes a land of granite and limestone; further east, Russia is a land of wood and plaster.

We have reached the end of the Baltic states and our next stop is St Petersburg. Where do they stand, five years after their emancipation from a collapsing Soviet Union and admission to the United Nations, and what are their prospects?

All three still bristle with pride in their independent nationhood, a goal they kept in sight through half a century of Soviet rule. For most Lithuanians, Latvians and Estonians the right to identify themselves as such is the one thing that matters. Their passionate commitment to national identity exacerbates the problem of the Russian-speaking minorities. It treats Russians as outsiders, leaving them embittered and alienated from the countries in which they have made their homes. Prudence may keep this ethnic nationalism in check, for fear of infuriating the Russians or shocking the West. But Estonians, Latvians and Lithuanians believe that their ethnic identity is the essence of their nationhood. It is not negotiable.

Freedom means also the freedom to be impractical about politics. Political parties proliferate, much given to passionate advocacy of wild action. The three governments have to ride this whirlwind, slowly coaxing their countries to accept policies of unsatisfying reasonableness. They are in particular constrained by economic circumstances

The three newly-independent countries, and Latvia in particular, were caught up in the collapse of the Soviet economy precisely because they had been so thoroughly integrated into its military-industrial complex. Today you can see in Riga and Narva the consequences of that collapse: abandoned factories, industrial detritus, the unemployed idling on the streets. The answer, people in the Baltics will tell you, is economic reform, a reorientation of trade towards the west, and privatisation – the only way out from under the rubble Communism left behind. For others this programme only compounds the nations' difficulties. The middle-class woman picking fastidiously through the dustbins on a street corner in Tartu probably takes one view; the pushy young man in Riga with a hamburger stall and a Mercedes almost certainly takes the other.

Privatisation has already made the three republics surprisingly pleasant places for the visitor. Of course, he is cushioned by his western wealth: he can choose when to travel and where he goes. Privatisation has made no impact on the squalor of life in winter for a pensioner on one of Riga's vast housing estates, and the beggar is lucky if free-spending new businessmen throw him some small change. All the same, the Baltic states have what it takes to please the summer visitor, whether his interest is politics or historic cities or beachcombing, and he will find standards closer to those of the central European countries than those of the former Soviet Union.

In the countryside, the collective farms have been swept away and private farming has taken their place. Here in particular, political passion ran at cross-purposes with economic wisdom. Private farmers have recovered a motivation that the collectives stifled, but few can do more than scrape a living. Overall, yields are down and only a plan to harness private farming to the benefits of scale seems likely to restore them.

The Baltics turn resolutely to the west, where they feel they naturally belong. Russia is potentially dangerous, a power that could once again enslave them. Russia has no friends in the Baltics outside the Russian-speaking minorities. Economically she has had little to offer: collapsing markets, depreciating currency, nothing to sell except the energy on which Lithuania in particular depends. That may change, and is in some ways already changing. But to the Baltic states the west seems to offer much more: freedom and sophistication, political support, some degree of security protection, technological know-how, free markets and the goods which the Baltics crave.

So the Baltics are shooting for as much integration with the west as they can get: special links with Finland and Scandinavia; Partnership for Peace and association with the European Union today; full Union membership as soon as possible and perhaps even membership of NATO at the end of the road. But if they are eventually to take their place in these groupings they will need to learn to compromise and subordinate national to collective interest, a painful lesson which the West has been learning for forty years. As yet there is no recognition of the price that individualism has to pay for collective gain. The Baltic states are not yet ready to co-operate wholeheartedly even with one another.

But the heart of the matter is that, despite the hardship that grips the three Baltic countries, with inflated, free-market prices and high unemployment, low wages and even lower pensions, Lithuania, Latvia and Estonia seem in the main happy countries, rejoicing in their escape from the dead hand of Communism, and still euphoric about the recovery of nationhood and freedom. Each of them, and particularly Estonia, is picking her way out of the economic mire, confident that tomorrow will be better than today. They still fear the Russian Bear. But to me they seemed the happiest places around the Baltic.

9

Russia and St Petersburg

St Petersburg is unique among the cities of the Baltic. It is centuries younger than any of the others and by millions more populous. Where they grew out of huddles of old buildings and tangles of narrow streets, St Petersburg was planned from the start on a vast imperial scale. Only here did the Russian Orthodox faith plant itself enduringly on the Baltic. And today it faces problems and opportunities beside which those of other Baltic cities fade into insignificance.

The city was founded in 1703, the best part of a century after New York. Its founder's famous purpose was to give Russia a window on the west. Peter the Great planned a city to reflect his power and ambitions, worthy of the empire of which it was to be the capital. Throughout the eighteenth century his heirs added to St Petersburg's glories. The nineteenth century saw a bourgeois, industrial and artistic city grafted onto its imperial and aristocratic beginnings. In the twentieth, Leningrad lost its status as a capital but became a Soviet icon. Today St Petersburg is home to the best part of 5 million people, more populous than any other European city except Moscow, London and Istanbul. It is also home to extremes of wealth, poverty and crime, to ravishing beauty as well as corruption and pollution, to thinkers and workers, beggars and actors and organised criminals, and it nurtures the hope that its tenacity and vigour can yet sustain something worthy of the inspiration and sacrifice on which it was built.

The site Peter chose for his city lies on the very western edge of Russia, on the isthmus that separates Lake Ladoga from the Gulf of Finland. It straddles the Neva, which empties the waters of much of northern Russia into the Baltic. It is a city up to its knees in water. As Nigel Gosling puts it: 'Like Venice, Leningrad sits on a swamp, at the end of an inland sea. There is no tide. The brackish ripples lap against a shore where grass and trees grow down to the water's edge. The city is spread out only a few feet above sea-level, expanding inland in the crook of the Neva river and outwards over the estuary islands.' No place, in short, to build a capital; but the site promised to introduce Russia to the world.

Peter needed not only to open a window on the outside world, but to close the door to Russia against his enemies. The Swedes had established a fortress in the area, inhabited otherwise only by wolves, peasants and fishermen. Three years before he founded St Petersburg, Peter had seen his army melt away in battle against the Swedes at Narva, 100 miles away down the Gulf of Finland. It was only in 1709 that he finally disposed of the Swedish threat to his new creation, when he defeated Charles XII at Poltava in the Ukraine.

So St Petersburg has always been a Russian bastion as well as a point of entry into the western world. But it has been an exception in the Russian world as much as in the Baltic, remote in spirit from Moscow and Kiev and Novgorod, still more remote from the soul of rural Russia. Peter intended his city to be different and, by its example, to be an instrument of change. St Petersburg was to be modern, western, rational, a standing reproach to a traditional, superstitious Russia that looked inward for fulfilment. It would be a city of the Enlightenment, morally distancing itself from barbarous Moscow. It performed, if incompletely, the role which Peter assigned to it, but it did not change Russia. It remained a place that was with Russia but not of it, always at odds with other aspects of the empire. 'St Petersburg', said a later tsar, 'is Russian, but it is not Russia.' Tolstoy fills his pages with fulminations against the city. To him it was an alien place dominated by foreign ways, its glitter meretricious and its worldliness a betrayal of the Russian soul.

From the very beginning there were contradictions about Peter's creation. His new city was built by slave labour. It was developed by the exercise of the absolute authority of the tsars. Nobles were ordered, not invited, to build there. Building in stone elsewhere in the empire was forbidden, so that there would be enough stone for St Petersburg. A century after the city's first heroic days, serfs still laboured fifteen hours a day, seven days a week, on the construction of the cathedral of St Isaac. And the mid-nineteenth-century St Petersburg world that Dostoevsky describes is imbued with the ancient superstitions of an unchangeable Russia.

The fortress of SS Peter and Paul was one of the first of Peter's buildings, erected in haste to secure the new city against Swedish attack. It was meant to protect a modern, enlightened society, but almost at once its prison became a place of terror. Here Peter tortured his own son to death, and political prisoners languished in its cells. Even when Peter was dead and gone, the eighteenth-century empresses presided over a vicious court, brutal politics, and the crushing poverty of the serfs who sustained the autocratic system. Dostoevsky gives us insights into the casual cruelty of nineteenth-century St Petersburg. In Petrograd Lenin launched his fatal revolution that was to bring light and reason to the Russian empire, and many of its ensuing horrors were played out in Leningrad.

Writing of the city in 1964, Alexander Solzhenitsyn went back to its beginnings to explore these paradoxes. 'So alien to us,' he wrote, '– and yet our greatest glory – this magnificence. How delightful it is to stroll along these avenues! But other Russians, clenching their teeth and cursing, rotted in the sunless bog to build all this beauty.' But to retrospect he added Soviet reality: 'It is awesome to think that perhaps our own shapeless and wretched lives ... the groans of the executed and the tears of their wives, will all be clean forgotten. Will from this too come perfect and undying beauty?' All cities encompass such contradictions. Few carry them to such extremes as St Petersburg.

In St Petersburg we are in the world of the Cyrillic, which adds an extra dimension of difficulty to the problems of finding our way in its southern suburbs. But once you reach the city that the tsars' and the empresses' architects laid out, there is little need of directions. The great avenues of St Petersburg are straight, clear-cut, simple to identify, marching implacably towards the horizon, devouring the kilometres as they go.

The River Neva brings its own contribution to this city of superlatives. It flows from Lake Ladoga near Schlüsselburg, across the Karelian isthmus, and through the heart of St Petersburg on its way to the sea. It is immense, like pretty well everything else in the city, oily and turgid in the summer, frozen solid in winter, roaring with breaking ice and torrents of water in the spring. Close to its banks you find the monastery of Alexander Nevsky; the Smolny Cathedral and Convent and its Institute; the Finland Station and the Peter and Paul Fortress; and across the water from the fortress the Hermitage, the Admiralty, St Isaac's Cathedral and the heart of neo-classical St Petersburg.

Peter laid his first foundations at the point where the Neva divides, to continue on its way to the sea either side of Vasilevskiy island. The first houses were built on the landward point of the island, facing the earthen ramparts of the Peter and Paul Fortress across the river. Among the few survivors from the early years are the modest wooden house from which Peter supervised the beginning of the city; the palace of its first governor, Menshikov; the first administration building, known as the Twelve Colleges; the great fortress itself, where earth quickly gave way to brick, later to be reinforced with granite; and up-stream, far from the centre, the Alexander Nevsky Monastery. The court moved to St Petersburg in 1710 and in 1713 work started on Peter's first proper palace on the south bank of the Neva. By the time he died, in 1725, his city was a reality.

After him came four women, who between them ruled Russia for most of the rest of the century. Peter's widow outlived him for just two years. Next came Anne, whom we encountered in Latvia as the young widow of the duke of Courland, and who reigned for thirteen years. Her court was crude and brutal, and Biron – her favourite who built the glorious palace at Rundale – dealt viciously with his enemies. She was followed by the Empress Elizabeth, who after twenty years was in her turn succeeded by the Great Catherine, the last of this regiment of women, who ruled almost to the end of the century. Men came and went among these women: tsars and favourites, infants, pretenders and toyboys, lunatics and the impotent, regents and weaklings, males who were imprisoned, strangled, exiled – but after Peter it was these four empresses who shaped classical St Petersburg.

They built and rebuilt with passion and autocratic extravagance. Peter created the Nevskyi Prospekt, a great processional way comparable with the Champs Elysées. It runs from the heart of the city to the Alexander Nevsky Monastery, cutting straight across the chord of a great bend in the Neva. Empress Elizabeth built the startlingly blue Smolny Cathedral which stands at the very apex of that bend, with the Smolny Institute beside it to house and educate young noblewomen. The little river Fontanka, which curves round the old centre of the city, was walled and bridged and lined with buildings like a canal in Amsterdam. The Admiralty was built, and the Winter Palace created out of a succession of earlier palaces. Trezzini and Rastrelli the younger imposed the disciplined regularity of the eighteenth century on the city's vistas. Gold and icons warmed the interiors of cathedrals and churches, bringing the religious glow of holy Russia to the cold classicism outside. Stone replaced wood, empty sites were filled. Gradually Peter's sketch of a city became a completed masterpiece. By the time of Catherine's death in 1796, Russia had a capital worthy of its position as a great European power.

There followed under her son Paul one of those periods of inanition that punctuate Russian history. But in 1801 his son Alexander I succeeded to the throne, a man the equal of his grandmother. He was a complex, contradictory character, moderniser and mystic by turns. Throughout his reign Russia was preoccupied abroad, at first intermittently and later passionately involved in the struggle for mastery in Europe. Alexander fought Napoleon, made peace with him, fought him again, and met him on the famous raft on the Neman. When in 1812 Napoleon invaded Russia, Alexander fled before him from Vilnius. When Napoleon marched on Moscow, Alexander stayed in St Petersburg. But when Napoleon fled and the remnants of the Grande Armée limped into Poland, Alexander pursued the French all the way across Europe, to Paris itself. At the Congress of Vienna Russia's place on the European scene was given its diplomatic consecration.

To celebrate his victory, Alexander commissioned an unknown French architect to build a new St Isaac's Cathedral in the city. It took forty years to build, its exterior formal in its pillars and porticoes, its interior an explosion of colour and decoration. It stands in the middle of the city, and its gilded dome is still St Petersburg's most prominent landmark, rearing up above the neo-classicism of the Admiralty and the palaces. St Isaac's is a constant reminder of Russian Orthodoxy. And in its contrast with its neighbours it is a reminder too of the contradiction – between Russia and the West, old and new, faith and reason – that lies at the very heart of St Petersburg .

Alexander's success against Napoleon introduced ideas of reform alien to the principles on which the empire had been built. The reigns of the tsars who followed him are punctuated therefore, as those of the empresses were not, by plots, uprisings, repressions, assassinations and revolutions. Whereas the streets and squares of eighteenth-century St Petersburg had been a building site, they became in the nineteenth a stage-set for political theatre, and often for the theatre of the horrific, the macabre and the absurd.

The story starts with the death of Alexander I. At the very heart of St Petersburg, between St Isaac's and the Admiralty, lies Decembrists' Square. Visitors go there to admire the magnificent bronze equestrian statue of Peter the Great. In December 1825 a group of reform-

minded officers – the Decembrists – there assembled 3,000 men to
ensure that Alexander's heir, Nicholas, should succeed to the throne
on constitutional terms rather than as an absolute monarch. For
hours they faced units loyal to the tsar, who himself watched quietly
from a window in the Admiralty. Eventually the Decembrists were
overpowered. The outcome of their trial was inevitable: ringleaders
were hanged, many were exiled to Siberia, and some of the common
soldiers were condemned to the barbarity of the gauntlet. For more
than a quarter of a century thereafter, Nicholas imposed 'orthodoxy,
autocracy and nationality' on his empire.

He faced many challenges. The one that has made its mark on St
Petersburg was the plot of the Petrashevsky Circle – a group of
intellectuals, Dostoevsky among them, who believed they could bring
reform to Nicholas's Russia. Their meetings were betrayed and
twenty-one of them were sentenced to death. You can still see the
barracks parade ground, now an apology for a park, where they were
led out to execution. The first batch were blindfolded and led before
the firing squad, the others awaiting their turn. Then a horseman
rode across the parade ground waving a handkerchief. In a scene
Dostoevsky himself might have conceived, a general, perhaps hand-
picked by a sadistic official for his agonising stutter, stammered out
the reprieve. The conspirators were led away in chains to Siberia.

Nicholas was followed by a gentler tsar, Alexander II, the Liberator.
He succeeded to the throne during the Crimean War. A British fleet
was in the Gulf of Finland, threatening to put ashore a French army
to besiege St Petersburg. He brought the war to an end and set the
serfs free. But he failed to grapple with, still less fundamentally alter,
a system of government that was simultaneously authoritarian and
frivolous, inefficient and unjust. Beneath his ordered world, ferment
continued, surfacing from time to time in demonstration and conspiracy. In 1880 a group of nihilists, calling themselves the People's
Will, succeeded in detonating a bomb under his own dining table. He
survived that attempt on his life, but he met his death a year later while
driving beside the Griboedova Canal. As at Sarajevo thirty years later,
a first attempt at assassination succeeded only in killing a bystander
and mortally wounding the assassin. Ludicrously, Alexander got out of
his carriage to remonstrate with the dying man, and an accomplice
threw the second fatal bomb.

The next tsar, Alexander III, took refuge from the nihilists by
retreating into the St Petersburg countryside to his ramshackle palace

at Gatchina, where he lived like one of Tolstoy's visionary moujiks. But conspiracy continued, above all a plot hatched by a group of St Petersburg university students who thought they could change the world by assassinating the tsar. One of them was Lenin's elder brother. It was he who concocted the bomb; and when they were arrested it was he who insisted on taking responsibility. He was hanged, and his younger brother thereupon set his hand both against the autocracy and against the feeble, liberal associates who, he was convinced, had failed the brother he adored. So a St Petersburg plot that failed to change the nineteenth century gave Lenin the motive and the determination to make his ruthless mark upon the twentieth.

The 1890s brought a respite from plots, trials and executions, and for a decade it looked as if industry and prosperity might bring to the empire the changes which idealists and assassins had failed to achieve. But in February 1904 came war with Japan. A year later the Russian Baltic Fleet sailed away from Kronstadt on a voyage round the world that ended in its annihilation at Tsushima. But before then news of another military disaster, the surrender of Port Arthur to the Japanese on the first day of 1905, provoked a demonstration in St Petersburg that swiftly led to revolution.

The factory workers set out to present a petition to the tsar. The Narva Arch where they first clashed with the army stands today amid the shabby triumphalism of early Soviet Russia. They marched on, more than 100,000 of them, led by pious priests, patriotic banners and *agents provocateurs*, into the centre of the city. In Palace Square troops were drawn up to bar their way. In the manner of such crowds, they thought they were about to reason humbly with authority. The tsar, father of his people, remained criminally inaccessible. The crowds withstood a half-hearted cavalry charge, defying an order to disperse. The troops opened fire, killing 300 people, and the crowd streamed away in panic. The frivolity of Russia's nineteenth century was over; its unimaginably more brutal twentieth began.

While politically-minded intellectuals were thus locked in conflict with the nineteenth-century tsars, the majority of Russia's writers and artists chose another road. The eighteenth-century empresses had brought foreign ideas and foreign artists to St Petersburg, the foreigners whom Peter the Great meant to use until Russia could do without them. Then, in a few amazing decades in the nineteenth century, Russian writers created a national culture and bestowed on the nation an intellectual and artistic dowry that would sustain it through the political horrors that lay ahead. They worked mostly in St Petersburg. Until Tolstoy, no Russian writer voluntarily turned his back on the city. Pushkin lived and wrote there until his exile, and eventually died there in a duel. Lermontov went the same way, writing in St Petersburg, finding himself at cross-purposes with the court, and also dying in a duel. Gogol took the literature of protest further, with St Petersburg always providing the background, and Turgenev, who spent most of his life in the city, left it only when exiled because of an article he wrote about the death of Gogol. For them all, the city was an essential muse.

Tolstoy's association with St Petersburg is complex. He studied there, and embraced the sweet decadence of the life of the aristocracy. Then his revulsion against the frivolities of his youth became as compelling for him as his earlier life of dissipation. It turned into a revulsion against the city itself. St Petersburg emerges from his pages as shallow, insincere, a place of temptation which leads Anna Karenina astray, where German careerists such as Benningsen and Barclay de Tolly plot the undoing of honest, old, Russian Kutusov. Moscow by contrast breeds honest men and women, and the country even more so, until in the end Tolstoy could find virtue only among the peasantry. His hatred of St Petersburg is as telling as others' love. With Tolstoy's hostility, the city's central place in Russian literature comes of age.

Dostoevsky did for St Petersburg what Dickens did for London. He came to the capital to study, involved himself in politics, and, as we have seen, escaped execution by a whisker. Life in Siberian exile, a life which he captured in *Notes from the House of the Dead*, perhaps convinced him that politics was best left to the tsar. But *Crime and Punishment*, written on his return from exile, is in its way a profoundly political book, as filled with subversive thought as with the poverty-stricken desperation that besieges the Haymarket and tarnishes the glitter of the mid-nineteenth-century city.

Music followed the same course as literature: western imports began to give way to the first hesitant steps by Russian composers and then, in the second half of the century, to an explosion of Russian talent. Borodin, Moussorgsky and Rimsky-Korsakov claimed to defy the foreign influences that Russians of a nationalistic bent had tried unsuccessfully to root out of St Petersburg. Tchaikovsky started his career here, took himself off to Moscow, and returned to die in the capital – whether poisoned by Petersburg water, his enemies or his own hand being still a controversial issue.

The Russian composers fuelled the one art in which St Petersburg indisputably led the way. Peter the Great's widow introduced ballet to the Russians, Anne and Elizabeth developed it, and Catherine put its teaching and practice on a formal bureaucratic footing. Throughout the nineteenth century, the importance of ballet in St Petersburg rose and fell and rose again, its formality and discipline in accord with the formal hierarchy of court life as the work of writers could never be. Generations of dedicated children emerged from the Academy as great dancers. Dancers like Nijinsky, Pavlova and Karsavina achieved a personal fame that was new in hierarchical Russia.

Ballet, bringing reputation and fulfilment to composers, designers and choreographers as well as to dancers, runs like an unbroken thread through the history of St Petersburg from the eighteenth century into the twentieth. It was as central to the artistic and social life of Petrograd and then of Leningrad as it was and is again to St Petersburg. With literature, it is a field in which Russian artistic achievement holds an unchallengeably commanding place. And the ballet has been a relatively safe form of expression in a country where, from the time of Ivan the Terrible until the day before yesterday, it has been dangerous to reveal your thoughts.

The massacre in Palace Square in January 1905 triggered the first Russian revolution. It also marked the beginning of a process which was to stretch Russia on the rack for the best part of a century. If anywhere in St Petersburg can challenge the Kremlin for the honour, Palace Square can claim to have seen the beginning, the middle and the end of that dreadful Russian century. It lies in the very heart of the city, between the Neva and the end of the Nevskiy Prospekt. The Admiralty stands on one side, the Winter Palace on another, the General Staff building on a third. St Isaac's and Decembrists' Square are 500 yards away. In Palace Square the tsars would review their troops; it was from here that the Winter Palace was stormed in October 1917. During the siege of Leningrad German gunners set their sights on St Isaac's and on Palace Square. And here the crowds gathered in October 1991 to protest against the coup in Moscow whose defeat marked the end of Communism and the Soviet Union.

But in January 1905 Palace Square saw the 300 unarmed demonstrators shot dead. Trust between tsar and people died with them. After the killings, revolution spread throughout St Petersburg and much of Russia. It dragged on for months, with the murder of a grand duke, with concessions made and withdrawn, with mutiny on the battleship *Potemkin*, with demonstrations and assassinations, with a St Petersburg Soviet in which a young socialist named Lev Trotsky first made his name, and in the end with a constitution and a Duma. Finally uneasy compromises were struck between age-old autocracy and the demand for accountability, but from 1905 until its fall the monarchy lived on borrowed time.

The beginning of the end came in 1917, when once again defeat in war brought unrest to a head. As in 1905, workers from St Petersburg's great engineering works led the way. This time the troops who had been ordered to confront them mutinied, and soldiers and workers joined forces to take control of the city's streets and squares. The tsar, returning hurriedly from the front to his capital, uncomprehending as ever, was prevailed upon to abdicate. He retired to join his family at Tsarkoe Selo, one of the imperial palaces outside St Petersburg. House arrest imperceptibly became imprisonment, followed by deportation and eventually execution. Alexander Kerensky and his Provisional Government were left to struggle for control of the city and the country.

They based themselves at first in the Mariinskiy Palace, just across the Moyka river from St Isaac's, a building which later became the City Hall of Leningrad. But in July 1917, in a move that now seems to have been perversely calculated to play into the hands of their critics, they moved into the Winter Palace. There, amid the incongruous splendour of the Empress Alexandra's lustrous green Malachite Room, they tried for three months to govern an ungovernable Russia, until in October the Bolsheviks overthrew them.

The story of the Bolshevik seizure of power is another St Petersburg drama, but many of its events are strangely unheroic. A good starting-point is the Finland Station, on the far side of the Neva. Here Lenin arrived from Helsinki in April 1917, and from here, after receiving the plaudits of St Petersburg's few active Bolsheviks and of an excited crowd, he famously drove away in an armoured car. He took command of an ineffectual little group of tyro politicians, and turned their minds to the seizure of power.

Retrospect endows their success with an inevitability that the historical record belies. In fact they were barely more competent than their rivals, and in July Kerensky struck hard against them. Lenin panicked, went into ignominious hiding, and fled in disguise to Finland. He returned to St Petersburg and seized power only in the autumn. The diminutive steam engine which brought him not once but twice to St Petersburg is one of the sights of the city, likely in its innocent charm to survive the vagaries of the new politics more easily than many of the Bolshevik statues that still stand in the streets and squares.

There are other memorials of those famous days, most of them, like Lenin's engine, less dramatic than the legend that propaganda subsequently attached to them. The best is the cruiser *Aurora*, which fired the blank shots at the Winter Palace that precipitated the fall of the Provisional Government. Now she is moored in the river beside the Naval Academy, a couple of miles from the point at which she made her mark upon history.

While the *Aurora* was firing her fatal shots, troops stormed the Winter Palace from Palace Square. It was a disorganised assault, more of a scramble than a military operation, followed by a wild traipse through the corridors and rooms of the Palace in search of members of the Provisional Government. But for most purposes, Eisenstein's recreation of the seizure of the Winter Palace has usurped the historical record. Like his *Battleship Potemkin*, the storming of the Winter Palace has become an icon of the revolution, its status remaining unchallenged while Communism ruled the Soviet Union.

The magic of the events of October 1917 survives the myth that has been created around them. But after the glory days came the squalor and the bloodshed of war on four fronts: against the Germans; against the Whites; against the intervening troops of the western allies; and against the workers, soldiers and sailors who turned at last in despair against the Bolsheviks. From the end of 1917 to 1921 conflict raged around St Petersburg. Hundreds of thousands died: in battle, at the hands of commissars and disciplinarians of every political colour, and of starvation, disease and cold. Repeatedly the Whites came close to capturing the city. Terror consumed its citizens, and they endured horrors comparable with those of the great German siege twenty-five years later.

At the end of it all, in March 1921, the sailors of Kronstadt, who had been among the Bolsheviks' shock troops in 1917, had had enough. Kronstadt today is a husk of a place, open at last to the visitor after being embalmed for seventy years in Soviet military secrecy, the sad remnant of a great naval and military metropolis on an island fifteen miles offshore in the Baltic approaches to St Petersburg. Its sailors were waiting for the ice to melt. Once it did they had only to bring their ships up the Neva to dominate Leningrad. But the Bolsheviks struck first, mounting a wild infantry attack on Kronstadt across the ice, heroic and suicidal. The ice broke under the attackers' feet and thousands drowned. Those who reached the shore stormed the fortress, and thousands more died. The defenders who survived were shot out of hand or shipped off to Russia's penal camps. The last armed challenge to the Soviet Union's leaders was defeated. The revolution had begun to devour its children.

By 1921 the city on the Neva was no longer Russia's capital. From the Kremlin Lenin and his successors saw it as a potential focus of opposition. In time their suspicions brought terror to Leningrad, but in the early 1920s the city experienced a brief and intense cultural flowering. It owed much to the sense of infinite possibility which comes to the victors in political and social revolution, and much also to the achievements of St Petersburg during the last years of the tsars. Its strengths were music, ballet and its associated arts, and above all the new art of the cinema. For a few short years the revolution's well-wishers, if they were blessed with selective vision, could point to the prosperity that came with the New Economic Plan and to Soviet cultural and artistic achievements as the essence of a new order in which oppression and hardship were but ephemeral features.

Nevertheless, in Leningrad as throughout the Soviet Union reality broke through. The autocratic habits inherited from the old Russia joined forces with the ideology of the new and with the paranoia that the revolutionaries had brought out of the underground. To this was added Moscow's particular suspicions of its old rival. In 1934 the Smolny Institute, Catherine's school for noblewomen, saw the assassination of the Party Secretary of Leningrad, Sergey Kirov. Stalin, who had inspired the murder, used it as a pretext for a great purge. The people of Leningrad, demoralised, often terrorised, deprived of any prominence in the Soviet scheme of things, turned inward on themselves.

Even more terrible events rescued the city from the forgotten provincialism to which Moscow consigned it. In June 1941 Hitler invaded the Soviet Union. Unlike Napoleon, he advanced on Leningrad as well as Moscow. By September German tanks were in the southern suburbs. They severed the city's road and rail links with

Moscow and reached Lake Ladoga. The siege of Leningrad – the famous 900-day blockade – had begun.

It is said that Peter the Great spent more lives to build St Petersburg than were lost in the siege of Leningrad. The Civil War cost the city hundreds of thousands more. But comparisons cannot diminish the horrors of 1941–43. Nor can the visitor escape reminders of the siege. Today you see bemedalled heroes and crippled veterans taking their ease in the pale St Petersburg sunshine, and solemn children lay flowers on the grass-clad mass graves in the Piskarov Cemetery in the northern suburbs. The story of the siege has been absorbed into Russia's secular religion. The work of the Leningrad poets, and of Anna Akhmatova in particular, hauntingly recalls the experiences of those terrible days.

The Germans incessantly bombed and shelled the city, taking the dome of St Isaac as an aiming mark. The defenders camouflaged the gilding on the city's spires and buried its statues out of harm's way. The *Aurora* herself was scuttled in shallow water to save her from destruction. Each street had its safe side and its dangerous side, as in yesterday's Sarajevo. But the siege was less a battle than a test of endurance.

Leningrad was ill-prepared, its warehouses half-empty. The German advance closed all but one of the city's access routes, a winter track across the ice of Lake Ladoga. Rations were cut and cut again. Life shrank to a search for food and water. Hitler had talked of levelling Leningrad to the ground, but it was hunger, cold and disease that did the Germans' work. Whole families died. The living could not bury the dead. Around Dostoevsky's Haymarket there were rumours of cannibalism. Two long winters brought the worst of the horrors, but spring brought disease. In the end the exhausted Germans slipped quietly away. No one knows for certain how many died in the long siege of Leningrad, but 670,000 is the figure recorded in the history books.

When it was over the people of the city felt that the Soviet leadership did not give Leningrad the credit for what it had endured. Stalin wanted no heroes who might distract attention from Stalingrad. The Kremlin was jealous of any other centre of power. For two decades, St Petersburg was a suspect city, and suspect without a tangible cause.

And now, half a century after the siege, there are still tensions and antagonisms. St Petersburg remains Russian, but it is still not Russia.

You are left wondering whether, if things were to turn sour in tomorrow's Russia, St Petersburg might not be tempted to try to go its own way, to become another free city of the Baltic. There is no precedent in Russian history for such a move, with the whole weight of Russia's experience crying out above all else for unity. Today St Petersburg shares Russia's hopes and problems. It has its poverty, violence, corruption, the interlocking mafias from the southern republics and from the city's own underworld. There is corruption and lack of resources, sloth and ignorance.

But there is also, and perhaps more manifestly in St Petersburg than elsewhere in Russia, the beginnings of a new hope. Amid the moral and material squalor you can find a passion for democracy, a search for accountability, the assertion of personal freedom and the vigorous strivings of private businessmen. There are still people in St Petersburg who recall its dynamism before the First World War. They talk about recapturing the hope of those years, building the city into a great Baltic port and a real window on the world. Like cities further west, St Petersburg is rediscovering the Baltic. A Russia that turned to nationalism and the bad old ways would encounter resistance here, as it would not in Kaliningrad. It is still a city of two worlds, of Russia and of the Baltic. It will not lightly turn its back on Russia, but nor will it surrender its Baltic heritage.

IO

Finland

The road to Finland leaves St Petersburg through an industrial wilderness, emerging eventually into the fields and forests of southern Karelia. Some Finns will tell you that Karelia embodies the historical essence of Finland, but it is a vast, ill-defined area, extending northwards for 400 miles to the Arctic Circle, much of it lying to the east of the long Russian-Finnish border. Southern Karelia is geographically more specific, filling the wedge-shaped isthmus to the north-west of St Petersburg between Lake Ladoga and the Gulf of Finland.

Southern Karelia today is as Russian as St Petersburg itself, but it was not always so. In the first twenty years of Finnish independence, the border with the Soviet Union ran close to the suburbs of Leningrad. Viipuri – Vyborg today – was the centre of a thriving Finnish province and itself one of Finland's more substantial cities. In two brave but ultimately unsuccessful wars in 1939–40 and 1941–44, the Finns lost southern Karelia to the Russians. Four hundred thousand Finns left the province and Russian settlers moved in. Today, some Finns talk about reclaiming what was lost in Karelia half a century ago; more see the wisdom of leaving things as they are.

Yet there is still something Finnish about this part of Russia. Before Peter the Great came to the site of St Petersburg the marshes were known only to fishermen and hunters speaking something close to Finnish. Farmers and fishermen from Karelia fed the early inhabitants of the new city, and Finnish porters carried their bags. Finns will tell you that they built the Finland Station; Finnish businessmen still know the Leningrad *oblast* better than other westerners; and you can see evidence today of Finnish investment and joint ventures around the city.

Vyborg has gone to the dogs since its golden days as Viipuri: fought-over, broken, neglected, in most respects now just another Russian provincial town. But there are still remnants of the old

Hanseatic city to be discerned and the city library is a neglected masterpiece of cubism. Alvar Aalto, the Finnish architectural genius, designed the library at Viipuri in the early 1930s, and sixty years later it stands in the alien wilderness as a lone example of Finnish architectural elegance. Now the Aalto design office in Helsinki is helping the Russians with its restoration, but it will need even greater upheavals in Russia to restore the library to its makers and transform Vyborg back into Viipuri.

The border with Finland lies thirty miles beyond Vyborg. Vaalimaa is a classic frontier post, much as Checkpoint Charlie used to be. In Berlin, Soviet and American troops faced one another eye-to-eye; at Vaalimaa and along the Finnish border, as nowhere else except in the Norwegian Arctic, the Soviet Union looked onto the western world without the benefit of satellite intermediaries.

Now the Finns have an even greater interest than the Russians in frontier control. This is not one of those European borders that you have crossed before you notice it. Rather, it is a painstaking, suspicious, hard-eyed kind of place. For the Finns, the Russian border troops and customs officers are their first line of defence against drug smugglers or the Russian mafia or refugees. But their own frontier service is a highly professional organisation, guarding 700 miles of frontier with Russia. Foreigners are excluded from a five-kilometre strip of wilderness just behind the border itself; and, winter and summer, frontier patrols move quietly through the woods. Disaster in Russia – starvation, say – could face the Finns with critical problems, perhaps even a mass exodus from St Petersburg. Russians don't walk, the Finns will tell you, especially in winter when such a disaster is most likely. They would get relief into Russia before Russians tried to break out. All the same, nowhere else in Europe do the problems of chaotic, poverty-stricken Russia abut so brutally on prosperity and order. 'Good fences make good neighbours' has a special resonance here.

As you leave the frontier, you are entering the western world. For all her necessary equivocation during the cold war, Finland was a democracy, socially and emotionally – if not politically – at one with western values. In the Conference on Security and Co-operation in Europe and in the European Free Trade Area she did what she could to build relationships that underpinned those values. Now membership of the European Union takes Finland a giant step further,

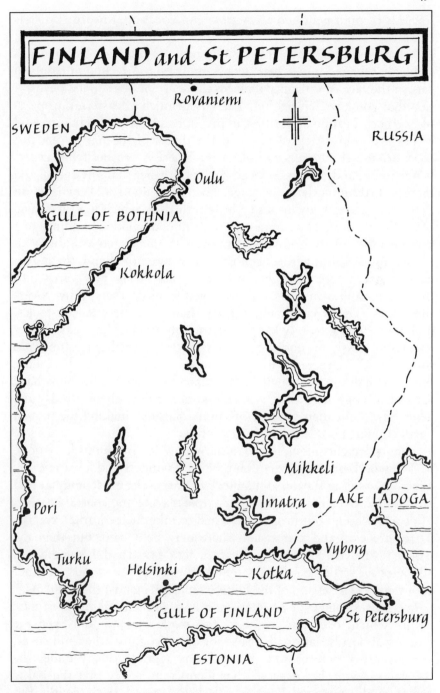

FINLAND and St PETERSBURG

Rovaniemi

SWEDEN

RUSSIA

Oulu

GULF OF BOTHNIA

Kokkola

Mikkeli

Imatra   LAKE LADOGA

Pori

Vyborg

Turku

Helsinki   Kotka

GULF OF FINLAND   St Petersburg

ESTONIA

towards commitment and away from equivocation, towards Brussels and away from Moscow.

But as you drive down your first Finnish road you are by no means suddenly plunged into a sparkling Scandinavia. A feeling of troubled care in the face of difficulty replaces the sense of abandoned devastation that you have left behind. There is as much of eastern Europe as of northern Europe about first impressions of Finland. Hamina and Kotka are uninspiring places, and the traces of the past along this coast are mostly the relics of old wars. There is prosperity, as everywhere in Finland, but its roots go back no further than the 1960s, and there is little underlying heritage, no patina upon it. Porvoo is an exception, a small city around a little cathedral, which has the charm of an older world. The simple oxblood-stained wooden buildings of a seventeenth-century ironworks run up with unaffected Scandinavian art are another. But here as almost everywhere in Finland, the harshness of nature presses right up to the road. Walk fifty yards into the woods and you slip and slide on the moss that thinly covers the stones. The trees somehow force their roots between obstacles, grabbing a living from what passes for soil among the rocks. Water trickles aimlessly around the boulders. Even in northern Estonia nature is kind compared with the Finnish wilderness, which reaches from this Baltic roadside all the way into the Arctic. The Finns have learned to cope with their wilderness, but it does them no favours. They have built their civilisation on its margins, making the best of harsh climate, poor soil and cruel winters.

The settlements along the road show how today's Finns have done it. The woods give way to a pond, beyond which stand a warehouse, a factory, a filling station and a block of flats – clean, rectangular and quietly assertive. This is a world of triple glazing and central heating, of people who go out properly-clothed to take their Nordic exercise. There are cars and shops, and there may be a café, but then the woods resume their brooding presence beside the road. Five miles on, and another settlement breaks the monotony of the woods, another coolly clinical assertion of the Finns' campaign against the elements.

It is this struggle of resolute men and women against obstinate nature which, over the centuries, has made Finland. But even the Finns, stubbornly nationalistic as they are, recognise other influences. For a century before 1917, Finland was a grand duchy under the Russian crown. She preserved her identity in a way that the Baltic provinces did not, and Russian rule here was relatively gentle. But

the Russian century put its stamp on Finland, which we will find
wherever we go in the country but which is at its most striking here in
the south-east and in the capital.

It is a stamp at least as deep as the earlier Swedish impress. To the
Russians, as to the Swedes before them, the Finns were a peasant
people, without culture or literature, and benighted by an incomprehensible language; but Russian disdain was mingled with affection. When Nicholas I banned the foreign travel that brought back
dangerous ideas, the aristocracy of St Petersburg discovered holidays
in Finland instead. Later they would take the train from the Finland
Station to Imatra on the Finnish lakes when they wanted to breathe
country air. Russian businessmen made tentative but profitable in-
vestments here. There was cautious political recognition that Finland formed a distinct entity within the Russian empire, with aspirations and qualities of her own. But the idea that Finland's little capital might one day overtake St Petersburg in material sophistication
would have been as unimaginable to Finns as to Russians.

We have seen that the Finns, like the Estonians, speak a Finno-Ugrian
language. There were human settlements here in the Stone Age, and a
new influx into the country 3,500 years ago. Where the Lapps in
the north came from, and when, is uncertain. But the forebears of
the Finns came relatively recently, probably less than 2,000 years
ago, trying to establish a settled life as far to the north as soil and
climate permit anywhere on the globe. For most of recorded history
they scratched a living from hunting, fishing, forestry and subsistence
farming, isolated from their neighbours by geography and language.

In the twelfth century Swedes ventured across the Gulf of Bothnia
into Finland. Like the Germans further south, they came to trade,
settle and convert. With Finns who joined them, they established a
Christian foothold centred on Åbo, now Turku, in the south-west,
which they slowly extended eastwards and northwards. Over the
centuries they integrated their possessions in Finland into the Swedish
kingdom. Finland became Swedish, but she was always an outpost
of the Swedish Baltic empire. By the sixteenth century, expansion
brought Russia to the Baltic, and in the seventeenth she was locked in
suspicious rivalry and sporadic wars with Sweden. This rivalry was
played out in what became the Russian Baltic provinces – and in
Finland.

Today's Finns exhibit national characteristics that it would be

convenient to ascribe to their experience at the hands of Swedes and
Russians over the centuries. These characteristics are eloquent of a
people who have for too long been discounted and exploited. The
Finns are stubborn, introspective and self-reliant. Sometimes they
seem grudgingly to accept others' assessment of their inferiority, at
other times they bristle with self-assertion.

But Finnish qualities reach back beyond Christianity and conquest.
The Finns have a mystic identity with nature and with the tribe. They
cherish their language not as a means of communication with outsiders but as a reaffirmation of hidden virtues and as a vehicle of
Finland's legend and history. We have heard a similar story from the
Estonians and the Balts, peoples hemmed in like the Finns by larger
races. But Finland's national characteristics subsist beside qualities
that have made her a dynamic, go-ahead country and which today's
Finns display in full measure: sophistication and subtlety; an artistic sense that has given them a proud place in modern architecture
and design; and the tough-minded pursuit of success as foresters,
businessmen and seafarers.

All these influences, Swedish, Russian and Finnish, have played their
part in shaping Helsinki, after Reykjavik the world's most northerly
capital and, Finns will tell you, the Athens of the North. To the
Swedes, who centred their rule in Finland on Åbo, Helsinki was no
more than a fishing settlement in the back of beyond. They decided to
make more of the place in the sixteenth century, but only as an
obstacle to Russian expansion. Two centuries later, with the Russians still pressing, they built the fortress of Sveaborg to protect Helsinki's natural harbour. But even when the Russians, having conquered southern Finland, decided to move the capital here from Åbo
in 1812, Helsinki was still home to no more than 4,000 people.

You can still find a Swedish flavour in parts of Helsinki, but it is
not a Scandinavian city. It stands by the water in the same way as
Stockholm, and has the same pale northern light. Like Stockholm it
has an air of making the most of the summer before hunkering
down for the winter. The old harbour with its thriving fish market,
overlooked by classical merchants' palaces, is quintessentially Scandinavian. So is the view down the bay, where the great ferries
nudge their way to their moorings through flocks of sailing boats.
Esplanadi, a broad peaceful avenue under the trees, might have
been imported from Copenhagen. So might the cool interior of the

classical Lutheran cathedral. But all these aspects of Helsinki are set in a context which is east European and central European by turns. This is a Baltic city which has much of St Petersburg about it, but a St Petersburg cut down to human size. It is different from the capitals we shall find further west, Stockholm, Oslo and Copenhagen, and different again from the Hanseatic cities along the southern and eastern shores of the Baltic.

Helsinki became a real city in the Russian years. The Lutheran cathedral in the city's heart, just above the harbour, dates from the 1840s. It stands at the top of a massive flight of steps which is as wide as the cathedral's facade, dangerously, even theatrically steep, like the Odessa steps in Eisenstein's *Battleship Potemkin*. With its domes and its columns it is an opulent *grande dame* of a building. Looking out over its flight of steps it dominates a square such as you might find in any capital in eastern Europe, framed by administrative and civic buildings in the creamy stucco we saw in Vilnius. Turn towards the harbour and 500 yards away a very different kind of cathedral breaks the skyline: the Uspenski, ornate, Orthodox, onion-domed, bringing a feeling of Kiev to this northern city.

But turn another corner and you are somewhere else again. Mannerheimintie is the spine of central Helsinki, with its shops and the National Museum and the old Swedish theatre at one end and the brand new opera house at the other. To start with at least, it has a precisely central-European air to it, as if the shops in a street in the old, Communist East Berlin had miraculously been filled with Scandinavian prosperity and good taste. Just off it is Eliel Saarinen's railway station. Admirers of a heavy, Baltic variant of Art Nouveau worship this massive rock of a building, which becomes almost intimate as you enter and then, at the back, positively unpretentious, even diffident, with platforms open to the elements like a south London suburban station. Further up, on the other side of Mannerheimintie, stands another great granite temple, Parliament, a product of the 1930s whose pillared splendour might have appealed to Mussolini, and which bewilders the casual eye by hiding its entrance around a corner.

On the other side of Mannerheimintie from Parliament you find yourself back in nineteenth-century Russia. Here in the heart of Helsinki linger the remains of an old goods station, faded paint on cracked timber walls, in a way not much more than huts, but with a careful architect's hand revealed in the proportions of doors and windows and columns and pediments. Inside you find next week's modern art exhibition being painstakingly assembled, the offices of a cultural charity trying to get by on a shoestring, and a young lady who wants to sell you batik or an arrangement of dried flowers.

But there is more of Helsinki's eclecticism to discover. A little to the west of Mannerheimintie is a modern church-in-the-round in the middle of a quiet little square of discreet apartment houses. Where other churches stand, this church crouches below ground level, carved out of the living granite, topped by a low copper dome. It is not a church whose transcendence seizes you by the throat, and it seems to offer more in the way of concerts than religious services. But its raw stone walls capture, here in the middle of the city, the genius for fusing the natural with the divine that we observed in Estonia.

Back across Mannerheimintie, at the Finlandia Hall, you find nature fused with music. The Finlandia, designed by Alvar Aalto in the 1960s, is like a long white ship. On the far side it looks over a lake, whose fluidity it reflects. Here the Finns congregate to worship Sibelius among Aalto's concrete waves.

But to a whole generation of diplomats the Finlandia Hall came to be associated not with the musically sublime but with the Conference on Security and Co-operation in Europe. CSCE, like the Ostpolitik, grew from the belief that diplomacy could do something to blunt the sharp edges of the division of Europe, even if an end of the division remained unimaginable. While the Ostpolitik addressed itself to Germany's relations with its old enemies and victims in eastern Europe, the CSCE brought all the European states together. It aspired to rise above a bloc-to-bloc approach, and to give the neutrals a voice.

The Helsinki process wound its weary way through the 1970s and the early 1980s, with conferences in one European capital after another. The idea of process, of a peripatetic effort pursuing first one aspect of European security and co-operation and then another, was indeed its gift to diplomacy. But the heavy, ground-breaking work was done in Helsinki, and the Finns played a big part in it. In the end the long meetings in the Finlandia Hall brought a surprising amount of benefit to Europe, and helped prepare the way for the vast changes which came about when, at last, the end of the division of the continent no longer seemed unimaginable. And the CSCE brought also a welcome touch of the cosmopolitan to Helsinki, with diplomats and visiting ministers and black limousines, and call-girls in the city's newly prosperous hotels.

Yet Helsinki still stands apart from the world. There are Swedish and Russian strains in its ancestry and there are ships coming into its harbour from all over the Baltic and the seas of the world. Finland's leaders are internationalists, and the country has committed herself even more firmly than Sweden to the European Union. But in the end that gruff sense of distinct identity, of a Finland that has suffered at the hands of foreigners and, like an Irish nationalist, trusts herself alone, makes Helsinki different from its neighbours and sustains the Finns in their suspicion of outsiders. Their twentieth-century history tells us why.

At Mikkeli in Finland's lakeland, 120 miles from Helsinki, you can see an exhibition of Finland's military past. There is a museum of weapons from the civil war after Finland achieved its independence, and from the two wars with the Russians in 1939–40 and 1941–44. You can see the modest headquarters from which Marshal Mannerheim, architect and defender of Finland's independence, autocrat and national hero, directed the battles with the Russians. You can even see the records of Finland's peacekeeping work for the United Nations. These exhibits, which in other countries might be dust-laden and neglected, bring Finns to the lakeland with quite as much enthusiasm as the music festival attracts them to Savonlinna fifty miles away. For Finns take pride in the wars they fought to protect their independence. They rightly see them as their country's greatest formative experiences in the twentieth century.

It all started very quietly. Towards the end of the nineteenth century, the easy-going tolerance that had characterised Russian rule in Finland began to fray. There came an assertion of conflicting wills: centralisers in Russia demanding Finland's subordination, the Finnish intellectuals' discovery of their country's peasant culture and identity provoking demands for further recognition of her distinctiveness. The *Kalevala*, a national epic of the 1840s based on the oral traditions of Finland and Karelia, became a focus of self-assertion. Conflict between Swedish and Finnish speakers became embittered, with nationalists demanding wider acceptance of the Finnish language from Russians and Swedes alike. Sibelius wrote his *Finlandia* as a definitive statement of the Finnish spirit, and the Russians banned its performance in any patriotic context. The tsar appointed a tough new governor-general and a Finnish patriot shot him. The relationship festered. Finland, like Ireland, was deeply divided within herself. But a group of powerfully motivated Finns looked to independence.

The 1917 revolution in St Petersburg gave them their opportunity. To Finnish constitutionalists, the fall of the tsar broke the allegiance which alone held Russia and Finland together. Finnish sovereignty, the nationalists asserted, reverted to the National Assembly; and in Moscow and St Petersburg the Russians had bigger issues to concern them than Finnish independence. It was at first an easy escape from the bloodshed which overtook the Russian empire. But there were bitter differences between left and right within Finland, and a lack of the political experience that might have resolved them. Finland was caught up in the vaster struggle for power in Russia. Finns in Germany and 12,000 German soldiers came to the support of the right, a few Russian Bolsheviks to the aid of their opponents. The Social Democrats split into constitutionalist and revolutionary factions. The country found herself divided on social and geographical lines. Gradually she drifted into civil war.

The left, backed by the Red Guards, held the south of the country. The greatest strength of the right was in the west, on the Gulf of Bothnia, where the Civil Guards were turned into an army, the White Guards. The war was conducted with an almost naïve ferocity, with political and social animosities intensified by the identification of the other side with external enemies. In scrappy, scattered and bitter battles the Germans and the White Guards gradually drove back the Reds, until finally they held Helsinki. They took 70,000 of the Red Guards prisoner. Hunger, cold and the great flu epidemic of 1918 took a terrible toll of the prisoners. But in a cold frenzy of righteous ruthlessness the Whites brought 8,000 of them before firing squads. This was political killing on a scale unimaginable in a small country in those innocent days, mayhem proportionately greater than anything produced by the Civil War in Russia or in Bosnia today. For twenty years afterwards Finland was divided by memories of the horrors of her civil war.

Even when independence had been won, Finland, like the Baltic republics, found herself lonely and vulnerable. Germany, Finland's friend, was weak; Britain and France remote. Finland attracted American sympathy as the plucky little nation which, alone among the United States' debtors, repaid her wartime bills; but an isolationist America was no factor in the European balance. The

Finns harboured historic resentments of the Swedes and visceral fears of the Soviet Union. The new republic cautiously built up a successful society and economy, but with a constant fear, intensifying throughout the 1930s, that it could not last.

In 1939 Stalin, with the Molotov-Ribbentrop pact safely dividing eastern Europe, demanded concessions of little Finland. In great-power terms, his needs were understandable: a defensible belt in Karelia to protect Leningrad, and the lease of a base at Hangö in the Finnish south-west to control access into the Gulf of Finland. But he muddled matters by seeking to instal a puppet government in Finland. It was a demand that united the Finns in a passion of solidarity as absolute as the passions which had divided them in the civil war. With absurd over-confidence, they determined to defy the Russians. On 30 November the Red Army advanced into Finland.

You have to be old indeed to remember the impact on world opinion of this war between David and Goliath. The Polish campaign was over and the Phoney War had begun. British and French opinion was consumed by guilt at the failure to help Poland and by a fearful frustration at the quiet that reigned on the western front. Suddenly the Finns provided a release from both. They were fighting a war for their very existence against impossible odds. The West must come to their rescue.

In Finland too emotions were exalted. In southern Karelia Finnish troops held a frail string of pill boxes which came to be known as the Mannerheim Line. Small units of determined men succeeded in holding back mass attacks by untrained Russians. Further north, from Lake Ladoga all the way to the Arctic, they were fighting in a forest wilderness, where a few locals who knew the woods were more than a match for the clumsy Russian columns. The world was regaled with accounts of ghostly skiers swathed in white slipping silently through the winter woods. Euphoria seized the Finns and their sympathisers. The Swedish government refused to come to the help of the Finns but Scandinavian volunteers set off for Finland. Britain and France sent equipment and, as things began inevitably to turn against the outnumbered Finns, began to talk in terms of an expeditionary force.

There was a terrible fecklessness about the way Britain and France, faced early in 1940 by the might of Hitler, contemplated declaring war against Stalin. Emotions were running high; the French wanted to fight this war anywhere but where they had fought the last, in

their own northern and eastern provinces; Britain hatched complicated schemes whereby the expeditionary force on its way to Finland would simultaneously close off the supply of Scandinavian iron
ore to Germany. Harold Macmillan was despatched to Helsinki and
returned with exalted ideas about the Finns, clutching the white fur
hat that he was to wear on his Moscow visits twenty years later. It
was a romantic time, with the Finns providing the heroism and the
rest of the world the fantasy.

Gradually, reality obtruded. The Scandinavians refused to be
drawn into the West's wars, whether with Hitler or with Stalin. The
Russians learned from their mistakes and brought up fresh troops.
The Finns' resources were nearing exhaustion. On 12 March Finland
came to terms with the Soviet Union. A month later Germany
attacked Denmark and Norway. By the early summer Britain and
France were fighting for their own existence and had forgotten
plucky little Finland.

The Finns surrendered southern Karelia to the Russians and leased
to them the base at Hangö. They looked around for arms to re-equip
their forces, and found themselves more or less entirely dependent on
Germany. Some wanted revenge, others feared that before long the
Russians would come back for more; and as Germany and the Soviet
Union moved towards war the Finns prepared themselves to win
back the soil they had surrendered to the Russians. Their chance
came in 1941. As the Germans advanced towards Leningrad, the
Finns moved into Karelia. Mannerheim resisted German pressure and
held back from the siege of Leningrad; and in the west at least Finland's restraint was noted to her credit. But she had committed herself to Hitler's war, and at the end of it the Soviet Union had her
revenge. The Finns were ordered to drive out their German allies; to
surrender the lands they had recovered and more; and to lease a
second Baltic base to the Russians. They had fought their last war with
their eastern neighbour. A cautious respect for Soviet wishes would
inform their policy ever afterwards.

That respect held Finland in a kind of suspended animation for
over forty years. She had the institutions and instincts of a western
democracy but she found herself not in the benign light of NATO but
on the Soviet Union's dark doorstep. To Sweden's cautious neutrality
she added a self-discipline very different from the bellicose over-confidence which had cost her so much. This caution affected policy in
every field, domestic as well as foreign. Westerners who should have

known better criticised it as unheroic, as an unprincipled yielding to Soviet pressure. They talked about Finlandisation.

But Finnish policy was quietly successful. In the post-war years it kept the Soviet Union satisfied while she was consuming eastern Europe and might have chosen to consume Finland too. The Finns built their own particular inhibitions into a Nordic balance which they shared with Sweden's neutrality and with Norwegian and Danish membership of the Atlantic Alliance. As the years passed Finland gradually won herself elbow-room through the CSCE and EFTA, while never presuming on Soviet benevolence. All the while she continued to build Finnish prosperity, brilliantly exploiting her relationship with Moscow to develop Soviet markets, to the point where a little country on the edge of the Arctic came to enjoy the sixth highest GDP per head in the world.

In the early 1990s came Finland's opportunity. Gorbachev redefined the Soviet Union's relationships with the countries of eastern Europe and, by implication, what she required of Finland. As East-West tensions eased, the constraints of neutrality relaxed also. At the same time, Soviet economic and political power was ebbing away. Finland found herself losing a familiar, undemanding market on her doorstep. She must find western markets to replace it. But at last she was at liberty, as she had never been since 1945, to redefine her relationship with the western markets to which she would have to turn. She advanced from EFTA membership, through negotiations to create the European Economic Area, to an application for membership of the European Community. Sweden and Norway moved with her.

The shock of change ran through every Finnish institution. For decades eyes had been fixed on Moscow; now they had to refocus on Brussels, a very different city with very different attitudes. Finland had brought her diplomatic skills to political debate, at the United Nations and in the CSCE; now they were turned to economic bargaining. Above all, she had looked to her own separateness, holding back from commitment and alignment; suddenly she was in business with an organisation that wanted to unite Europe.

All three Nordic candidates' bids to join the Community were controversial. Norway had applied before and then, after her 1972 referendum, decided not to join. Sweden and Finland had been held back by fears that the Community would demand of them steps that would test their neutrality and Soviet tolerance. That inhibition was now removed, but domestic doubts remained. Finns, particularly Finns from the countryside, felt themselves remote from Brussels and were suspicious of the requirements of integration. Concerns for sovereignty, tradition, religion and the environment came into play. So did fears of what would become of Finland's economy, exposed to competition within the Community, yet geographically so far from its natural centre of gravity.

But the political arguments, rarely stated openly, were what really mattered. It might look as if Finland was moving away from the world of politics into economics, away from her old obsession with the Russian Bear to a new interest in European integration. But the real issues were still Russia – and politics. Finland could not transplant herself from Russia's doorstep; she could not persuade herself that the threat from the east was gone for good; but she could, by joining the Community, cloak herself in the security of association with the major European powers. Community membership was not on the face of it about security or defence, but in practice it offered solid protection against any renewal of Russian ill-will of which Finns never speak, but which, if they are wise, they never forget.

Of the three Nordic applicants to join the European Union, Finland always seemed to be the one most likely to vote in favour. She was the first of the three to hold her referendum, on 16 October 1994. On that day fifty-seven per cent of the voters committed the Finns to even closer union with foreign partners in an organisation moving towards an unknown destination. By doing so they increased the chances that the Swedes might also vote in favour in their referendum a month later – and there was wry satisfaction in Helsinki at the thought of Sweden following Finland's lead. But above all, the vote marked the end of an era in which Finland had so skilfully held the balance between her western predilections and her fear of Moscow. Finland had joined the West; her years of ambivalence were over.

Driving from Helsinki towards the south-west of the country, you find that nature relents a little. There are meadows between the woods and at least a show of farming; and where the woods retreat you can see small hills in the middle distance. The oppressiveness that dominates the eastern Finnish countryside is lifted here, at least for a little space. It is almost welcoming country. You are approaching the part to which medieval Swedish settlers first came.

Swedish-speakers amount to no more than six per cent of the
Finnish population. Most are farmers and fishermen, but until recent
times a small Swedish-speaking élite dominated Finnish life, and they
still play a more important part in it than their numbers would
suggest. There is still a mild animus against Sweden and Swedish-
speakers in Finland, a kind of common man's resentment, but it is
combined with an impeccable – perhaps over-generous – concern for
Swedish rights. As a language, Swedish at least in theory enjoys equal
rights with Finnish. There is Swedish on the road signs, even in parts
of the country where you never hear Swedish spoken, but like
Flemings in Belgium the Finns will make unhappy noises if a foreigner calls a place by its Swedish name.

Swedish urban settlement started at Turku, in the extreme south-
west, and Swedish-speaking Finns still call it Åbo. It stands on a little
river running down to the sea. Beyond it innumerable islands stretch
to the horizon and most of the way to Sweden, over 100 miles away.
Most of the people of Turku today are Finnish speakers, but it keeps
its Swedish memories. At one end of the city stands the cathedral.
Swedish crusaders led by a bishop from England, Henry of Uppsala,
built their first church here. The cathedral's interest and beauty have
survived fires and reconstructions, and it brings to a country that
otherwise conspicuously lacks it a brooding sense of the northern
medieval world, part genuine, part laborious reconstruction. Its exterior mixes stone and Baltic brick, and the interior is rendered in a
cold Nordic grey. But a jumble of chapels and tombs and monuments
and other impedimenta of Swedish supremacy in Finland give it life
and interest.

At the other end of the city, down by the river mouth, is Turku
Castle. It was in turn a fortress against attack from the sea, the centre
of Swedish power in Finland and the home of the Swedish viceroys.
But unlike the cathedral it conveys little sense of history. The restorers have earnestly produced a soulless place from which the past
has been expunged. Perhaps its cleanliness, the spanking paint, the
bright modern lighting, the concealed tape recorder and its period
music are the Finns' revenge on the Swedes who built it.

Between the cathedral and the castle lies the centre of Turku. On
one side a hill is crowned by an art gallery. On the other there are
seductive walks beside the river. But the centre of Turku is otherwise a rectilinear, proper, tedious place, with none of the boldness of
the best Finnish buildings about it, and only the open space of a

market square to lift the spirit. Rain adds to the gloom. But there is another Turku away from the rain, an indoor city within and beneath the city blocks. Like Montreal but on a more intimate scale, Turku has bound itself together with underground, weatherproof walkways, with subterranean malls of shops and cafés, a way of life insulated from the elements outside.

In the seventeenth century the Swedes founded a university in Turku – Åbo Academy, the only Swedish-language university in Finland. Turku University's Finnish students heavily outnumber the Academy's Swedes. There could be material for trouble here, as if Oxford and Cambridge were practising their rivalries within a single city. But to the casual eye the students of Turku University and Åbo Academy seem to co-exist in a happily Nordic kind of way, chasing each other's girls with sensible impartiality.

So far we have looked only at the southern coast of Finland, and before long the ferry from Turku to Stockholm will take us through the delectable seascapes of the Åland Islands. But you cannot ignore the Gulf of Bothnia: it makes up a third of the whole Baltic, and there are 400 miles of Finnish coast between Turku and the fringe of the Arctic.

This is a different coast from that which lines the Gulf of Finland, and it is full of surprises. Faced with its dauntingly empty distances I wondered whether a book about the Baltic really demanded intensive treatment of the Gulf of Bothnia. But if you venture northwards you find a new aspect of the Nordic world. Sand takes the place of rocks, there are long, accommodating beaches, and the sea water is warm enough to attract Norwegians for the summer bathing. The Ostrobothnian countryside is more open than anything we have seen in Finland, and it yields wheat in the short bright summers. This is conservative, farmers' Finland, and there is about it something of the rural calm we found in Estonia.

Pori, on the southern edge of this Ostrobothnian world, is a generous place. Its summer jazz festival pulls in thousands of young people from all over the Baltic. Even out of season it works hard to beguile its citizens. When I was there the municipal art gallery was advertising an autumnal diversion. A local artist announced that he would dismantle a house, shingle by shingle, beam by beam, make a happening of the process and a work of art of the components; and the lady in charge, like the lady in Rostock, was urging her visitors to keep an open mind about this deeply suspect form of self-expression.

Two other towns up the Gulf of Bothnia offer their own surprises, even if neither *vaut le détour*. Oulu in the last century depended on the filthiest of trades, the making of tar, and shipped it to the cities of the world. Oulu grew rich, like a blackened Klondyke, but in this century it has replaced tar by something else, and something cleaner. Now it makes microchips, and the whole place glistens in the Arctic air like an air-conditioned laboratory.

In Kokkola the Finns will show you a local treasure, and their pleasure will be greater if you reveal that you are British. The treasure is rare indeed, a vessel of the Royal Navy captured by the enemy and still in alien hands. She met her fate in the Crimean War, which brought ships of the fleet prowling along this coast in search of Russian property. A landing was made; the Finns, fighting sturdily on the Russians' side, ambushed the expedition; and the navy fled, leaving a boat behind and wildly exaggerating the strength of the opposition. It was an affair which like the whole campaign in the Gulf of Bothnia reflected little credit on the Royal Navy, but 150 years later it still gives Finns wry amusement.

To the visitor, it looks as if the Finns need all the diversion they can get if they are to lead contented lives at the northern end of the Gulf of Bothnia. There is little here but enormous, empty distances between them and the Arctic itself. Winters are interminable, dark and harsh. But this is country for walkers, hunters and cross-country skiers – the sort of people Finns pride themselves on being. It is a place for the self-assured, the loner, the seeker after solitude. Foreigners come here for these things, for ethnographical research among the Lapps, or for a sentimental encounter with Father Christmas and his reindeer. Rovaniemi, just five miles short of the Arctic Circle, is the point of departure for every kind of excursion into Lapland. For us, it marks the northernmost point of our Baltic journey.

The Islands

The Baltic world is bound together by ferries. Little ships shuttle incessantly between little islands. Bigger ones plough imperturbably between Helsinki and Travemünde. The ferries that link Helsinki and Turku with Stockholm are the size of liners, with restaurants and cabins, swimming pools and saunas; and the latest, the *Silja Europa*, is at 60,000 tons almost the size of the *Queen Elizabeth 2*. Ferries are a part of the texture of Baltic life: for business, for pleasure, for sea-borne seminars and duty-free drinking. In ports all around the Baltic people look up expectantly when they know the ferry is due. The ferry is part of the family. When the *Estonia* went down in 1994, whole groups of colleagues and friends went with her, and scarcely a community was unaffected in Estonia, where she was registered, or in Sweden, her destination.

The ferry from Turku to Stockholm takes you through some of the most delectable scenery the world has to offer. She sails serenely through the Åland archipelago, 6,000 islands strung between Finland and Sweden across the mouth of the Gulf of Bothnia. Most of these islands are small, uninhabited except by a handful of summer visitors. Many are nothing more than rocky outcrops, barely rising above the surface of the sea, with one or two black pines anchored in the cracks between the rocks. The blacks, greys and sombre greens of the islands contrast with the silver of the sea, the relationship between water and land constantly shifting as the ferry moves on. The vista is one of horizontals, yet strangely reminiscent of the dramatic verticals of the western Norwegian fiords in its changing counterpoint of land and water. If you are lucky there will be a rival ferry in sight for much of the journey, her gleaming superstructure towering above the islands a mile away. And this living cinema film unwinds unbroken for nearly 100 miles, from Turku to Mariehamn, the capital of the Åland islands.

This panorama of land and water is a vivid reminder of the part that islands play in the Baltic world. If you include every rock and sandbar and skerry, the Baltic has as many islands as there are lakes around its shores, and they, as we have seen, are innumerable. Many of them, like most of the Åland islands, are uninhabited, visited only by fishermen and summer yachtsmen. Some, like the main Danish islands, are an intrinsic part of the country to which they belong. But a few are places of historical and geographical individuality, apologising to no man. The Åland islands themselves, the islands of Estonia, Gotland midway between Sweden and Latvia, the long low strip of Öland just off south-eastern Sweden, Bornholm and Christiansø 100 miles east of the Denmark to which they belong, German Rügen and Fehmarn, each has a character of its own to offer the visitor.

Fehmarn is the smallest, no more than fifty miles around, lying only 1,000 yards off shore from Holstein. A bridge already links it to the mainland, and the bridge that may one day join Denmark and Germany would come down to earth here, having spanned the ten miles of water that separate Fehmarn from Danish Lolland. Already the main road across Fehmarn carries a great weight of traffic from the mainland to its ferry port at Puttgarden, and thence to Copenhagen. Its farms have mostly become holiday homes, its harbours berths for pleasure craft and its great old barns winter storage-space for yachts.

And yet Fehmarn retains its individuality, a character that distinguishes it from the German mainland. Puttgarden is dominated by its ferry responsibilities, but an older way of life peeps out around it. Winding roads, choked with Mercedes and yacht trailers and campers and Volkswagens in summer, lead from Burg in the centre to two little towns in the west and one in the east of the island. These roads twist their way between fertile wheat fields, past prosperous farms subverted to serve tourism's purposes, and reveal occasional dazzling glimpses of the sea around unexpected corners.

Fehmarn is less than two hours drive from Hamburg. It lies in the middle of superb sailing grounds. Kiel Bay stretches away on one side, Mecklenburg Bay, free now from the obsessive prowling of East German patrol boats, on the other. German yachtsmen bring their boats to Fehmarn into more homely harbours than can be found in Kiel Bay. The feeling in summer is one of saturation, an island overrun by holidaymakers. In winter the tide recedes, revealing traces of the old Fehmarn.

Rügen, 100 miles to the east of Fehmarn, transmits very different messages. It is Germany's biggest island, forty miles from north to south and perhaps 200 miles around, with strong historical roots, a record of visitors that goes back far beyond the flood tide of the 1960s, and a recent history in which time stood still as it did throughout East Germany.

Rügen juts out into the mid-Baltic from the coast of Mecklenburg-Vorpommern. Less than half a mile of water, bridged by an embankment, separates it from Stralsund. Unlike the spits that line most of the coast of the old East Germany, Rügen has a bone structure that shapes its hills and breaks the surface as chalk cliffs where the land meets the sea. Unlike Fehmarn its coast is deeply fretted, with bays piercing deep inland, Danish fashion. It has lakes of its own, beech forests, wheat fields and pastures. Its 600 square miles take time to explore. Bergen, the principal town, has 12,000 permanent residents, and there are other little towns and villages dotted all over the island. Rügen in its small space offers geographical complexity.

It displays historical complexity also. There are traces of very early societies, who established a lakeside site of human sacrifice to the Goddess Hertha; Slavonic tribes settled here, and Danes came raiding from the sea in the twelfth century. The Germans pushed in from the land a century later, and fishermen from the Hansa cities cured their herring on Rügen's beaches. It was caught up in the seventeenth-century sieges of Stralsund, and became part of Swedish Pomerania. In the nineteenth century a local prince took it into the modern world of sea bathing and summer visitors, and in the 1960s and 1970s it attracted 1 million East German holidaymakers each summer.

Today there is a new and nostalgic German interest in Rügen. But the island has always tended to slide back into the rustic obscurity of a quiet corner of north Germany, and it seems to treasure its remoteness. It has its bathing beaches, its little resorts, there are excursion buses on country roads, and in one of its bays a vast Russian river boat is moored, offering the extra hotel space for summer visitors which the towns cannot provide. But, at least for a little while, most of Rügen will remain as it were stranded in the 1930s, half a century behind Fehmarn.

In the last century Rügen received three literary visitors. The first was Marianne North. Miss North was to become an indefatigable traveller, whose tropical botanical paintings are one of the hidden delights of Kew Gardens, but she was a girl travelling with her family when she visited Rügen in 1849. In *Recollections of a Happy Life*, published nearly forty years afterwards, she describes her visit with breathless innocence.

Her family travelled to the Baltic from Berlin, and came down the Oder from Stettin to Swinemünde. A coasting steamer brought them to Rügen, where they settled themselves in Putbus, on the south-east coast of the island. The Prince of Putbus was said to be one of the richest noblemen of Germany and had established his credentials with the English when he represented Prussia at Queen Victoria's coronation. He and his wife were kind to strangers: 'Of course the newly-arrived English family were asked at once to dine at the Palace at four o'clock.'

The Norths went on to explore Rügen. Marianne recorded that its shores were never straight for half a mile in any direction; its chalk heights were 'all sprinkled over with granite boulders'; the bathing was delicious; Prince Putbus's Kapellmeister introduced her to the music of Handel; and Hertha's temple beside its funereal lake 'seemed most wonderful'. Eventually they drove in a procession of carts along the strand to catch the ferry to Stralsund, and the family of Victorian explorers went on their way to Hamburg and home.

Theodor Fontane brought Effi Briest and her husband to Rügen from their home in Kessin thirty years later. They had intended to go further afield, to Oberammergau in Bavaria, but Instetten's duties stood in their way. So they came to Sassnitz, some way beyond Marianne North's Putbus, in August, late in the Rügen season. They too explored Lake Hertha, and went up the coast to Stubbenkammer, and admired the views, and looked for pebble-free beaches from which to bathe. But Effi could not relax in Rügen. For once, Instetten bent to her whim and they caught a steamer to continue their holiday in Copenhagen.

The third literary visitor was Elizabeth von Arnim, who turned her exploration of Rügen into a coy but at times astringent little novel, *The Adventures of Elizabeth in Rügen*. The manifestly autobiographical English wife of a Pomeranian landowner longs to get away from her husband for a time. In her library she comes across Marianne North's memoirs, which inspire her to explore Rügen. She and her stoic maid set off with the family coachman. A long-lost cousin running away from her professorial husband appears; Elizabeth resolves to help them save their marriage; the adventure takes the little party all over a Rügen apparently little changed from the island that Marianne North recorded half a century earlier. In its more contrived way, the novel captures the innocence which permeated Miss North's impressions of this innocent island.

Bornholm lies sixty miles north-east of Rügen. It is as close to the Polish coast as it is to Rügen, and on a clear day you can see it from the southernmost tip of Sweden. But Bornholm, with its 50,000 people, five little towns, unique fortified round churches, and sparkling beaches which, it is claimed, are composed of the finest sand in the world, is Danish. It is a tidy little island, roughly rectangular, with its towns distributed evenly about it. The cliffs come as a surprise. So does the forest on rising ground in its centre. But most of it is agricultural land, sloping gently to the sea. It could stand – summer visitors apart – as a model of timeless Baltic tranquillity. The guidebook calls it The Baltic Hideaway .

But Bornholm has its own history. From within the castle of Hamershus, whose massive, fractured ruins still attract visitors, a succession of princes, bishops, barons and governors ruled the island with history's usual heavy hand. In 1658 the island passed to Swedish control, along with Denmark's old provinces in southern Sweden. But the islanders revolted, the Swedish governor was assassinated, and in 1660 the Bornholmers – perhaps preferring distant masters to nearer ones – bound themselves to Copenhagen.

Danish it remained; and on the island of Christiansø, fifteen miles off the north-eastern coast of Bornholm, the Danish kings built a naval base and forbidding fortifications to defend their easternmost possession. Christiansø is about as remote from Copenhagen as you can get in Denmark, with its 150 inhabitants, a single inn, huts and cottages for summer visitors, and a reputation for spiced herring. A governor who doubles as the lighthouse-keeper runs Christiansø. He enjoys an official garden, planted with all the exotic flora which Bornholm's sea-captains brought back to Christiansø. But in the first half of the nineteenth century, when the Danish monarchs were still, and in retrospect surprisingly absolute, the governor was responsible for something more serious than anything you will find in Christiansø today: the safe custody of political troublemakers.

The Germans occupied Bornholm and Christiansø when they invaded Denmark in 1940, and a stubborn officer refused to surrender them to the Russians in 1945, provoking a bombing raid that the inhabitants remember as Bornholm's great catastrophe. Russian occupation followed, and there were fears that it might become permanent. But by the end of 1945 the Russians had left and the Danes gradually developed Bornholm into a western listening post in the middle of the Baltic, with Danish Air Force antennae sprouting from the island's low hills. Now the Bornholmers worry about the damage pollution has done to the Baltic fisheries, and the fluctuation in the tourist trade, with the special fear that German holidaymakers will neglect Bornholm and turn to their own east German Baltic bathing stations instead.

But Bornholm remains idyllic, as long as the sun shines on its beaches and the little houses of its five towns. It displays the same gentle and egalitarian prosperity that you find all over Scandinavia. Yet not so long ago the spirit of the place was quite different and infinitely harsher. The Danish novelist Martin Andersen Nexø set the early chapters of his novel *Pelle the Conqueror* on a Bornholm farm. He was writing in the early years of this century with a fierce socialist purpose. In *Pelle the Conqueror* he describes a life of virtual serfdom in Bornholm not much more than 100 years ago. The novel starts with a bang, as the boat from Sweden bringing labourers looking for work enters Rønne harbour. 'Well, you see,' says an upright citizen, 'we're expecting the steamer from Ystad today with a big cargo of slaves – cheap Swedish labourers, that's to say, who live on black bread and salt herrings, and do the work of three. They ought to be flogged with red-hot icicles, that sort, and the brutes of farmers, too.'

Nexø was writing of a time when poverty at home drove one Swedish family in four into emigration. His characters were at the mercy of the farmers and their overseers. Pelle's father swears to deal with the young apprentice bailiff who thrashes his son, but he crumbles as he recognises his own powerlessness. A Midsummer's eve outing to a fair is a treat for which the labourers save up for months. When they finally set out, it is with the innocent timidity of Tolstoy's serfs or of slaves in the ante-bellum South. In the end Pelle escapes by running away to the squalor of the slums of Copenhagen. But Nexø's book documents the starting point of a process through which Bornholm, like all Scandinavia, achieved a peaceful, un-remarked miracle, replacing something near serfdom by egalitarian Social Democracy within half a century.

Öland lies another 100 miles up the Baltic. Like Bornholm, it attracts summer visitors in droves, but it is a bleak sort of place, a flat, drab stretch of treeless steppe moored off the east coast of Sweden, with nothing of Bornholm's intimacy and with no trace of Scandinavian muscle. It is eighty miles long, never more than ten miles wide, or more than fifteen miles off-shore. Two roads link its long chain of anonymous villages. A bridge – the longest if perhaps the least dramatic bridge in Europe – joins it to the mainland at Kalmar.

Öland greets the visitor with a sense of timeless desolation and of geographical displacement. Traces of early history abound. The remains of a fifth-century village have been carefully restored and give a forbidding impression of the bleakness of subsistence in the Dark Ages. You can explore the ruins of a fortress from the same period: a huge space protected by walls twenty-five feet thick. The Vikings came 400 years later, leaving innumerable runes behind them. The ruins of Borgholm Castle, medieval in origin, modernised in the age of the enlightenment, burnt out in 1806, seem almost contemporary by contrast. So do the 400 windmills which once whirled in the wind down the length of the island.

But Öland is not entirely grim. The Swedish royal family have a summer home, the palace of Solliden, on the west coast, half hidden down a quiet road from Borgholm Castle. Here a nineteenth-century Queen of Sweden came to fight tuberculosis with fresh sea air, and in the summer the palace shines white and cheerful, in contrast to the quiet gloom of so much of Öland, looking out on a sea that glows like burnished steel. And in the spring and autumn, they say, legions of birds take a break in Öland as they migrate up and down the globe.

We surveyed the outlying Åland islands at the beginning of this chapter, but they deserve more than a glance from the deck of a ferry picking her way between them. On its western edge, facing towards Sweden, the fragmentary islets of the archipelago give way to something bigger, a cluster of islands around the capital, Mariehamn. This is where most of the islands' 20,000 inhabitants live: farmers, fishermen, hoteliers, and a remarkable clan of seafarers. The islands are Finnish, but the inhabitants are Swedish-speaking, and they make much of their hard-won autonomy with a very Nordic mixture of passion and restraint.

Mariehamn sits between two inlets. Ferries and tourist buses come and go, there are museums to visit and clock-golf down by the water's edge, souvenir shops and parking spaces, all the paraphernalia of a Scandinavian holiday resort. Yet less than a century ago,

Mariehamn was a far-flung outpost of the Russian empire, as much the tsar's as Baku or Tashkent. Swedish-speaking they may have been, but the Åland Islands passed to Russia along with Finland in 1809. There, as in Finland and throughout the empire to Vladivostok, the tsar's officials set about establishing imperial uniformity. They built a post road across the main Åland islands and, in a village at their western extremity, an incongruously vast post office to receive the mail entering the empire from Sweden and the west. They impressed the islanders to work as imperial postmen. And at Bomarsund, a little to the north of Mariehamn, they started to build a great imperial fortress.

It is not too fanciful to see in nineteenth-century Bomarsund what Kaliningrad represents today and Soviet military bases in Germany represented the day before yesterday: the perennial quest for security that drives Russia westward into Europe as far as the facts of power permit. You can see the remains of the fortress today, great interlocking blocks of stone forming inter-connecting bastions, sprawled across fields and a gentle hillside, commanding what looks like an unimportant channel between two of the Ålands' innumerable islands. Wandering among them it is hard to believe that Bomarsund ever had any real military importance. But to the Russians it was a strongpoint commanding the entrance to the Gulf of Bothnia, reaching out to the west beyond the Finnish mainland, and glowering if need be across the water towards Stockholm. Completed and properly defended, Bomarsund would have been an important factor in the geopolitics of the Baltic.

Incomplete and with an inadequate garrison, it attracted enemies intent on its destruction. When war with Russia broke out in 1854, the British and the French turned first to the shores of the Black Sea. But Britannia ruled the waves, and the Baltic offered a second front and a direct route to St Petersburg, the heart of the Russian empire. If the Royal Navy could force a way past Bomarsund, Sveaborg, Reval and Kronstadt, its presence off St Petersburg alone might bring the Russians to terms. Add to this naval presence a French army disembarking near the city before Russian troops could march back the length of Russia from the Crimea, and success would be certain. From these sound strategic calculations came the Royal Navy's Baltic campaigns of 1854–55.

To turn these calculations into successful reality tested the Victorian navy and its French allies to the limit. The campaign was hampered from the beginning by fantasy: the fear that a Russian fleet emerging from the Baltic might land an army on the undefended east coast of England. The first task of the British commanders in the Baltic was to ensure that whatever happened the Russians did not succeed in capturing Lowestoft. The second handicap was the lack of shallow draught vessels that could get in among the Baltic skerries and attack Russian coastal fortifications. The third was the character of the commander-in-chief. Admiral Sir Charles Napier seems to have made himself an early Victorian naval hero by a combination of courage, self-promotion, indiscipline and luck. By the time he took the fleet to the Baltic in 1854 he had added to these characteristics timidity, sloth and a deep if justified suspicion of others' ill-will towards him. After the fighting was over there appeared *The History of the Baltic Campaign of 1854*, filled with hysterical attacks on his superiors and almost all of his associates. It is worth reading even today as an example of how self-justification can finally destroy an already damaged reputation.

The fact is that Napier faced real difficulties in the Baltic, which his own timidity and indecision magnified. He established a base in neutral Gotland. From there he blockaded the Gulf of Finland and sent ships and squadrons on half-hearted expeditions to the east and north. He failed to attack a Russian fleet trapped in the ice off Helsinki when his officers believed it was at his mercy. And he acquiesced when subordinates, eager for fame, action or bounty money, set themselves to seize or destroy enemy property which usually belonged to inoffensive Finnish farmers or shipowners. This ineffectual and seedy business led to the loss of men and the ship's boat that we have seen on display at Kokkola in the Gulf of Bothnia. It took the Royal Navy to Liepaja in Courland and on expeditions into the Estonian countryside. The first Victoria Cross was awarded for gallantry in the Baltic campaign, and two more were won, in our eyes very easily, by men who kidnapped an unarmed enemy postman in peculiar circumstances on the Åland Islands' post road. More purposefully, the navy succeeded in attacking Sveaborg and Kotka and Vyborg, and with French support it turned its attention to Bomarsund.

The Reverend Edgar Hughes, Fellow of Magdalene College, Cambridge, has given us an account of the action. In 1855 this scholar and man of God published *Two Summer Cruises with the Baltic Fleet*. Subtitled *The Log of the Pet*, it tells the story of his adventures on an eight-ton yacht, in which he followed the fleet into the Baltic as far as Bomarsund. It has something of the same callous naiveté that took the beaux and belles of Washington society out in their carriages to observe the first battle of Bull Run. Hughes interfered wherever he could, fraternising with the fleet's officers and abusing the Russians' conduct; and he has left us a fascinating, but also rather chilling account of this strange campaign and the curious camp-followers it attracted.

Hughes watched the fleet close in on the great fortress in the back of beyond, its guns thundering across the quiet water. French troops swarmed ashore and dug trenches in the green meadows. Excursion steamers brought tourists from Gotland to join Hughes in observing the proceedings. The Russians, their numbers quite inadequate to hold the defences, surrendered. Disease descended on victors and vanquished alike. When peace came, the Russians were confirmed in their possession of the Åland Islands and of all Finland. They would remain Russian for another half century.

But in every sense except the political, the Åland Islands were Swedish. The Ålanders devoted themselves to Swedish-style agriculture; to fishing; and to trade. With fishing and trade came a commitment to seafaring, around the Baltic and further afield. At first they built their own ships in Mariehamn. When steam propulsion came in, the Ålanders clung stubbornly to sail, and by the early twentieth century Åland captains and ships had come to monopolise what remained of the clipper trade with the Antipodes. Eventually the Ålanders shifted to steam, and they continued to navigate the seven seas. Today Åland companies dominate the ferry business of the Baltic, still based in Mariehamn, watching their big ships glide into the little harbour on their daily voyages between Stockholm and Helsinki.

When Finland won her independence in 1917, the Åland Islands wanted to go their own way. The islanders spoke Swedish and thought of themselves as Swedish; and stable Sweden looked a more attractive mother country than a Finland on the brink of civil war. Politicians in Helsinki reacted with the shrill exaggeration of people themselves new to independence, threatening the Åland leaders with charges of high treason. In the end, and with the help of the League of Nations, moderation triumphed. The islands remained Finnish, but with guarantees of their autonomy. Finland, Sweden and the Soviet Union entered into desultory talks about demilitarisation. Today, no one disputes the manifest fact that the Åland Islands, secure in their own flag and special status, are different. Argentine statesmen point to them as an improbable model for the Falklands, and they made their own decision to join the European Union. It seems unlikely, despite their strategic position at the mouth of the Gulf of Bothnia, that foreign fleets will come again to bombard the Åland Islands or foreign troops to kidnap postmen among their woods and fields.

Bornholm, Rügen and the Åland Islands are pearls of the Baltic, and Fehmarn and Öland have their particular fascinations. But Gotland is perhaps the brightest jewel of them all. It blends history and beauty, winter roses and medieval architecture, heath and dark woods and starkly beautiful village churches, a walled medieval city and the glories of Baltic sunsets.

Gotland is unquestioningly Swedish, but Swedish with a difference. It is the largest Baltic island, with a complex history that has distinguished it over the centuries. It has been ruled by Danes, by Germans, and by pirates who were naval victuallers, rather as if the NAAFI were to go privateering. Today Gotland has a pride of place, a sense of community, and its own distinct identity.

The island lies in the middle of the fairway between Sweden and the coast of Latvia, straddling the trade and war routes of the eastern Baltic. The Vikings called there as they nosed their way eastward, and it became a base for them as they pressed on through Russia to Constantinople. The Gotlanders themselves were travellers and merchants, and when they became Christians in the eleventh century, a chronicle records that they carried goods to 'all countries, whether Christian or heathen'. They waxed fat on trade with the Orient, whose goods reached them through Kiev, Smolensk and Novgorod, where they had a base long before the Hansa, as Russian merchants had in Gotland. But they also traded in the west, and archaeologists working in the island today occasionally unearth the English groats they brought home with them.

In the twelfth century German merchants pushing into the eastern Baltic from Lübeck found the Gotlanders barring their way. Their ships were better than the Gotlanders', and they had the might of the Holy Roman Empire behind them. The Lübeckers formed a society of merchants of the empire visiting Gotland. It developed by uncertain and hesitant steps into the Hanseatic League. Visby, the island's capital, was among the earliest Hansa cities, and in the early days among the most important. German merchants settled there, the 'Germans dwelling in Gotland' competing with the Lübeckers' society of visitors. The earthworks around the city gave way to the walls that still encircle it, walls intended as much to keep foreign merchants within bounds as for defence. Churches, merchants' palaces and warehouses multiplied. Visby became one of the great entrepôt cities of the Middle Ages, its trade as important as that of Bruges or London.

There were farmer-merchants and farmer-shipbuilders all over Gotland. Rivalry with the citizens of Visby intensified. The pride and wealth of the smaller towns and villages expressed itself in church building, and nearly 100 of their churches remain. They are stark, white-rendered buildings in which verticals predominate, easily as tall as they are long. You pass them on the way to Gotland's beaches, to its Viking ship burials and to the remains of prehistoric forts.

But Visby is the pride of Gotland. The old city has an untouched completeness you will not find anywhere else in northern Europe. Its walls are scarcely breached. Most of its sixteen medieval churches are in ruins, but the twelfth-century cathedral has been restored to aseptic Scandinavian ecclesiastical standards. It stands at the foot of a precipitous hill that divides the city in two. The upper town used to be poor man's Visby. Today its cottages have been restored in a Scandinavian version of gentrification, or, where they were beyond saving, replaced by discreet modern flats and houses. Most of them enjoy views over the cathedral and the roofs of the lower city towards the harbour and Gotland's famous sunsets. The lower town was the merchants'. Now the ruined churches are given over in summer to artistic happenings, but the rest of the medieval city remains a practical, businesslike place, its buildings crowding the squares and the narrow streets and lanes. Lübeck must have been like this before the bombers and the rebuilders and the traffic took the heart out of the medieval city.

There is another side to Gotland, which is revealed in summer. Swedes who visit Gotland feel something of the release of going abroad. Some hope to catch a glimpse of Ingmar Bergman's cinematic vision, and more long for a sighting of his actresses. All revel in Gotland's short warm summers. For two short months it is a place of jazz and rock and heavy metal, of nudist beaches and beer cans and camp sites among the stunted pines, of twenty-hour days and noisy nights, where Swedes can unbend and forget themselves.

But Gotland takes its mid-Baltic position seriously. Fehmarn and Rügen are German with a difference, Öland a strange off-shore Swedish island. Bornholm's distance from the metropolis gives it a stronger identity, but it is still essentially Danish. The Åland Islands have their special status, not fully Finnish, not fully Swedish, and are commercially the most successful of the Baltic islands. Gotland is something more, loyally Swedish but a distinct community with a will of its own. It has ambitions to exploit change in the Baltic, and tries to reach out to every corner of it. The recently-established ferry link to Latvia evokes recollections of Gotland's pivotal position in a Hansa which penetrated throughout northern Europe, and prompts ideas of reinterpreting that position in modern terms. In 1996 Visby played host to a summit conference of the Baltic Sea countries, looking at ways to tackle the region's problems co-operatively. When I visited the city, it was given over to an immense display of modern art and sculpture from all around the Baltic, seeking – if perhaps not finding – artistic expression of regional unity. More than anywhere else, Visby is a Baltic city.

Off the coast of Estonia, almost closing the mouth of the Gulf of Riga, lie the magical islands of Saaremaa, Hiiumaa, Muhu and 500 others, the last mysteries of the Baltic. These islands have been held in turn by Danes, the Livonian Order, Swedes, Russians and Soviets, and have now returned to their original Estonian distinctiveness. When Arthur Ransome, who called the main islands by their Swedish names of Oesel and Dagö and Moon, visited them in *Racundra*, he found people more isolated than any others around the Baltic except the Lapps, and yet among them there were fishermen who took their catch to Stockholm in open boats and retired seamen who knew all the oceans and half the seaports of the world. Most of the islands' inhabitants were Swedish speakers, and when the Russians seized Estonia in 1940, many of them fled to Sweden.

The Soviet rule that so transformed the Estonian mainland had the opposite effect in the islands. For forty years they were kept in a state of virtual isolation, closed to foreigners and to most Estonians and Russians. In Estonia's years of independence in the 1920s and 1930s the islands were still content with the conditions of the last century. Soviet occupation kept those simplicities unchanged into the early 1990s. In the same way as the British army claims its training areas protect the wildlife of Northumberland and Salisbury Plain, so

Soviet military occupation preserved the life of Saaremaa, Hiiumaa and Muhu. Estonians and those few foreigners who set out today to discover the islands are transported back into the Baltic world of Marianne North or Effi Briest. Anyone who loves the Baltic must before long make the pilgrimage to these islands. Like the prisoner of Reading Gaol, visitors will kill the thing they love, and their weapon will be the banal demands of the twentieth century. But for the moment the Estonian islands offer beaches and fishing harbours and causeways between the islands, dark woods and clear waters, lighthouses and water mills and windmills, fat eels and local beers, juniper bushes and Midsummer's eve rituals, the same sort of devotion to folk-song and folk-dancing that you find on the mainland, and the same sense of peace that Arthur Ransome found here seventy years ago.

12

Sweden

Many people will tell you that Stockholm is the most beautiful of the
Baltic's cities. Others argue for St Petersburg or Lübeck, Copenhagen
or Tallinn. But few will challenge Stockholm's setting, at the heart of
a maze of lakes and bays and islands, surrounded by the cool greens,
blacks and greys of the Swedish countryside.

The ferry threads its way from Mariehamn into Stockholm
through a wilderness of islands as beautiful and apparently as
deserted as the Åland archipelago. But these hundreds of islands are
almost part of Stockholm's suburbs – its summer suburbs at least –
and on a Friday evening the yachts of Stockholm are outward bound
for a weekend among the city's own islands as the ferry slides
through the fortified narrows that guard the approaches to the city.
Beyond the narrows lies a long spear of water thrusting right into the
city's heart, and as the ferry noses into its berth all the splendours of
the capital are revealed across the harbour.

The approaches from the sea are only one aspect of Stockholm's
topographical wonders. From the west other waterways thread their
way into the city from Lake Malaren, which stretches sixty miles into
Stockholm's hinterland. The waters from the sea and the lake meet in
the centre of Stockholm, around the island on which the original city,
the old town, stands. This island, and two smaller islands beside it,
contain the essence of old Sweden: a fourteenth-century cathedral,
the crooked alleys of the old town, the royal palace, Parliament, the
arrogant elegance of the House of the Nobility, and the eccentric
beauty of the Riddarholm church, in which the kings of Sweden are
buried.

Stockholm old and new tells better than anywhere else in Sweden
the story of the country's miraculous rise from abject northern
poverty to an enviable level of social and private prosperity. By most
worldly measures, the Swedes are among the most fortunate people
in the world. Their story sets people searching for the formula which
has brought them such success. But the tomb in the Riddarholm

church of a general who died in 1652 testifies to reasons for Sweden's failure. It bears a curious and didactic statement listing six causes of Swedish misfortune: 'self-interest, instinctive hatred, contempt for law, indifference to the public welfare, the thoughtless extension of favours to foreigners, and obstinate envy between Swedes'. Swedish visitors still stand before the tomb, perhaps lost in prayer for the general's soul, or searching their conscience for these vices, or wondering whether they still characterise Swedish society .

The back streets of the old town have much the same flavour we have found in other old Baltic cities. There are houses that might have been Hansa merchants', and Gothic brick makes its reappearance in the old churches. But Parliament and palace, looking out over the water towards the north and east, conjure up a different world. The palace in all its expansive glory was built in the eighteenth century by Tessin the younger, who did for Stockholm what Rastrelli did for St Petersburg. Parliament is much younger, a turn of the century building. But from across the water they complement one another, and this in a strangely non-Baltic way. The palace in particular has an almost Mediterranean air to it, and its renaissance solemnity and dusty pink stucco would grace a city such as Genoa.

This air of southern European urbanity is continued on the other side of the water that separates the old city from the business and social heart of Stockholm. There government offices, museums and the Opera House line a curving waterfront. Behind them stretch the monuments to the city's nineteenth-century prosperity, and the shopping street which was so precious to the privileged classes 100 years ago that peasants and the poor were excluded from it. Today's prosperity is more democratic, but the north side of Stockholm is still the preserve of the well-to-do: a world first of bankers and ambassadors and then of spanking new suburbs gradually yielding to old villages set among woods and ponds and meadowland. Southern Stockholm is more interesting if less perfect: a heartland of Social Democratic values, displaying a working-class prosperity as reassuring in its own way as the world of the plutocrats on the other side of the harbour.

Stockholm's City Hall serves as a symbol of those values. It stands at the water's edge, facing across Lake Malaren towards Staden. Ragnar Ostberg built it in the 1920s for a city council that wanted a civic headquarters whose dignity and quality would equal that of the royal palace. Its position gives it dignity, and you can see its quality precisely expressed in the building's massive brickwork. This is no Gothic brick, weathered and worn by age, but engineering brick, expressing national romanticism with a typically Scandinavian concern for detail. From across the water the City Hall looks like a Venetian palace; close up it is the obsessive perfectionism of its brickwork which overwhelms you; go inside and you find the Golden Hall and the vast Blue Hall where the Nobel Prize banquets are held.

Stockholm was not always the bastion of social prosperity which it is today. Nor was Sweden one of the richest countries in the world. A century ago more than half the population still depended on agriculture for a living, and this on land and at latitudes which reduced farming to a harsh struggle for subsistence. In the previous chapter we saw Swedish farm labourers selling themselves into slavery in Bornholm. In the second half of the last century, one in four Swedes emigrated, most of them to the New World, where some made themselves prosperous in the bleakest states of the American mid-west along the Canadian border.

But those who stayed behind did even better, creating in the last 100 years a very special Swedish miracle. It provided a standard for all Scandinavia, and a model for many elsewhere who wanted to emulate it. Now it has encountered problems as grave in their way as those that struck down a very different model on the other side of the Baltic. How they are resolved will be a test of Social Democracy, with a significance extending well beyond Sweden.

Nineteenth-century Sweden had a few – very few – advantages. One was an inheritance of rural industry based on timber and iron ore. Another was a national hardihood bred out of climatic and agricultural disadvantage. Self-discipline was a third, evoked in the main by the influence of the Lutheran Church, which you can see documented in Ingmar Bergman's film *The Ox*. A passion for education and self-improvement also played its part. But none of these explains the relative ease with which Sweden made the transition from a harsh society of master and man to the dignity – some would say complacency – of Social Democracy.

There is nothing idyllic about Swedish history. Sixteenth-century civil conflict was resolved by a mass execution known to history as the Stockholm Blood Bath. The long wars with Denmark produced vicious soldiers and guerrilla fighters. The nineteenth century is filled with the harsh struggle between unbending authority and the first stirrings of popular self-assertion. The First World War saw popular demonstrations against starvation wages and in support of the Bolsheviks. Universal adult suffrage was achieved in 1919, but right through the 1920s the country remained politically and socially divided. Unemployment and wage cuts led to strikes, riots and violent deaths. Sweden was still far from the left-of-centre consensus which has monopolised its politics for most of our lifetimes.

But the underpinnings of Swedish life were changing. The second half of the last century and the first half of this saw economic growth at a rate equalled only in Japan. Waterways and then railways opened up hitherto isolated provinces. Iron ore led to a steel industry, timber to paper and then furniture. In many fields Swedish industry began to set standards for Europe. By 1950 it was employing twice as many Swedes as were employed in agriculture. What was at first limited prosperity spread to the whole population.

Prosperity was harnessed to political restraint. A constructive – some would say clinical – approach came to monopolise Swedish politics. The obsessive perfectionism that built Stockholm's City Hall went to work also on all the institutions of a welfare state, uninterrupted by war, revolution or occupation. By the 1950s Sweden had achieved her economic miracle, quiet and little-celebrated by comparison with Germany's post-war achievement, but in its way quite as remarkable. Together with national consensus on political ends and means, it formed the basis for a social prosperity that made Sweden a model in the eyes of much of the world.

The Swedish model has always attracted mockery. The Swedes have been called smug, complacent, mind-deadeningly dull. They have been charged with pursuing equality and social justice at the expense of liberty. Certainly their ubiquitous system of social welfare demanded crippling taxation, which eroded interest in wealth creation. But the model delivered real benefits to the Swedes, in the eyes of most of them well worth the price of mockery and taxes. For decades Sweden could lay a claim to be Europe's most successful society.

Things look rather different in the 1990s. The industrialisation which brought so much wealth to Sweden has peaked. Like the rest of the developed world, Sweden has to find post-industrial fields to conquer. The obsessive filling of one social need after another has imposed burdens on the Swedish economy which it is not broad-shouldered enough to bear. The country faces economic difficulties which spill over into social and political uncertainty. And the complacency bred by past success has turned into an inflexibility which is costing Sweden dear.

In the last decade the smugness has been beaten out of Sweden's social scientists and economists. Governments are torn between the need to tell the electorate hard truths and the need to win elections. In the early 1990s the country experimented with right-of-centre government under a young prime minister, Carl Bildt, who delighted in saying the unthinkable. In the autumn of 1994 the country turned him out and brought back the familiar Social Democrats. Now Sweden is searching for a way forward. Hence the agony of rethinking old verities. Hence above all the turning to a European Union which calls so many of those old verities into question.

Sweden's Bothnian coastline stretches northwards for 500 miles from the capital to the Finnish frontier, at first punctuated every fifty miles or so by unexpectedly substantial towns, each with its church and harbour and town square and hinterland. Looking at the map, I found its distances as daunting as those across the Gulf of Bothnia along the Finnish coast. This time I decided I would do no more than sample it. I went to Gävle, which used to ship Swedish timber for the navies of the world; to Söderhamn, with its magnificent church above a churchyard overrun with roses and its extraordinary white lookout tower; and to Hudiksvall, which cherishes simple wooden houses with the same classical architecture about them as we saw in the old railway station in Helsinki. None of these towns gives an impression of a beleaguered community perched on the edge of a northern wilderness, and there are more little towns, each of them comfortable, relatively prosperous places, at steadily increasing distances all the way to the Finnish border. But at Hudiksvall I turned back towards Uppsala, leaving the rest of Bothnia for another expedition at another time.

Uppsala has a better claim than Stockholm to be the cradle of the Swedish nation. There was a pagan temple and pilgrimage centre there in the Dark Ages. It was at Uppsala that the Swedish kings first accepted Christianity; by the middle of the twelfth century it was the seat of an archbishop; and in the thirteenth the people of Uppsala started work on the cathedral which towers over their city today. They conceived it on a grand scale to outdo its Norwegian rival in Trondheim and built the largest church in Scandinavia: its red brick is powerful still, but any very strong sense of age or of faith has been knocked out of it by over-zealous restoration. The little church of the Holy Trinity, standing in its lee like St Margaret's beside Westminster Abbey, has kept its heart in a way that the cathedral has not.

Up a quiet road beyond the cathedral stands the university library. It bears the splendid name Carolina Rediviva, houses a stock of 4 million books and displays a rare example of the famous Carta Marina, which was the first printed map to depict the whole Baltic with reasonable accuracy. In the 1530s, Sweden along with most of northern Europe broke away from Rome. Olaus Magnus, the last Catholic archbishop of Sweden, went into exile in Italy. In 1539 he published his Carta Marina. It extends westwards from Lake Ladoga to the north of Scotland and from northern Germany to the North Cape. Whales frolic beside the Faroes and sea dragons surface off the coast of Norway. Horses draw sledges across the frozen Gulf of Bothnia, men ski across the ice of the Gulf of Finland, and in Lithuania a bear who has been after honey is assailed by a swarm of bees.

As well as his great map, Olaus Magnus also produced his *Historia de Omnibus Gothorum Sueonumque Regibus* – a history of the Scandinavian kings. Between them they are touching examples of the civilisation which the universal church brought to the Baltic. Olaus Magnus went into exile 500 years after the appointment of Adalbert of Bremen as the pope's first representative in northern Europe. In those centuries Catholicism converted kings and chieftains and their peoples, launched crusades into the eastern Baltic, established bishoprics, built abbeys and cathedrals, and made of the Baltic a Catholic world. At the height of Rome's ascendancy the whole Baltic, divided as it might be by wars and dynastic and commercial rivalries, nevertheless worshipped at the same altars. But finally the Reformation overtook north Germany and Scandinavia, sending Olaus Magnus into his sad exile in Italy, and Muscovy broke through to the sea and established the Orthodox Church on the eastern Baltic.

As I left the Carolina Rediviva I was stopped by a man obsessed, and held with his glittering eye. 'Why bother with a dead map?' he asked me, eyes boring into mine. 'Let me show you something live.' He set off, down the little hill, across the river, in a loping half-walk, half-run; and behind a forbidding fence we very much found something alive. The botanical gardens, named after Carl Linnaeus, the botanical pioneer who is perhaps Uppsala's best-remembered scholar, are the city's best-kept secret. They are no Kew Gardens; a retiring little rectangle rather, no more than 150 yards square, where the specimens in their muted colours stand rooted in disciplined ranks. Indeed, nature in the Linnaeus Gardens is even more muted than the elegant little pavilion which forms its backdrop.

The geometrical order of these gardens reflects the principal concern that Carl Linnaeus brought to botany. He was imbued with the eighteenth-century passion to categorise, and he pursued it with a particularly Swedish intensity. He also pioneered a new interpretation of the plant kingdom in sexual terms. In his time flowers had just been recognised as plant life's sexual organs. Linnaeus saw them as the key to an understanding of botany. His sexual system of botanical categorisation swept through the western world, just at the time when biologists were discovering and perhaps exaggerating the importance of human sexual differentiation.

So Linnaeus had a hand in shaping the modern world's attitude to matters sexual. He also shaped its attitude to Sweden. Before his time Sweden was little regarded in European intellectual circles. Now those circles found themselves enchanted by the idea of genius flowering in such unpromising soil. Swedes enjoyed Linnaeus's reflected glory, and rewarded him as a favourite son. His students worshipped him, the king honoured him with a knighthood and the people christened him the King of Flowers. His name is still one to conjure with in Sweden. In the hidden Linnaeus Gardens he has an exquisite living memorial.

He has also an artistic memorial. The interest in flora which Linnaeus evoked in Sweden spread throughout Scandinavia. In Denmark it led to a project to record in colour plates every one of the 3,000 plants to be found within the Danish kingdom. They proved to be things of beauty as well as scientific interest, and the Royal Copenhagen Company reproduced them in porcelain. The first Flora Danica dinner service was intended to be a gift for Catherine the Great. She died before it was completed and it remained in Copenhagen, where it is still brought out to grace the table at Danish royal banquets. Flora Danica has continued in production ever since, to delight the connoisseur and those few porcelain collectors who can afford to buy it.

In my tentative foray up the coast of the Gulf of Bothnia, I discovered the power of Sweden's distances. Outside Södertalje, only twenty-five miles south-west of Stockholm, I discovered the space that goes with such distances and which is one of Sweden's greatest untapped resources.

Södertalje itself lies in the most developed heartland of Sweden. Like Stockholm, it stands at a point where Lake Malaren and an inlet from the Baltic meet. But it has none of Stockholm's glamour and is ignored by the guidebooks. It is a clean, civilised city, facing serenely onto its harbour and ship canal. There is an air of respectability about it, of a place where prosperity comes easily. But the key to its prosperity, the Saab-Scania plant, lies on its outskirts and beyond, where acre after acre of factory sheds, workshops, warehouses and office buildings stretch away from Södertalje. This is Swedish industry at its most powerful, the industry that gives Sweden a gross domestic product approaching that of the Netherlands with just over half her population.

Yet if you take the road out of town past the plant, the Swedish countryside quickly closes in on you again. There are woods, sporadic fields, gentle grey woodland lakes, the occasional farmhouse and little village. Beyond these, Swedish space stretches into the Swedish distance, a great emptiness such as you can find in Europe today only in Russia and Finland. Beside the road that runs south from Södertalje there is room for a dozen more Saab-Scanias – and all this within commuting distance of Stockholm.

For the fact is that Sweden has nearly as great a capacity as Canada to absorb human beings and economic activity into its empty spaces. In the agricultural age, soil and climate set strict limits to population, and when they were exceeded only emigration provided an escape. In the industrial era Sweden achieved its economic miracle through careful targeting of what it could do well, and Saab-Scania's trucks, motor-cars and aeroplanes were among them. Today it has what it takes to build a successful post-industrial society: human skills, a strong infrastructure, space and unspoiled countryside. Sweden could absorb a further 50 million people without overloading its natural endowment.

Of course, in today's circumstances that will not happen. Sweden's own population is stable, its empty spaces a precious element of the Swedishness its people cherish. Nor are the peoples of the Third World yet clamouring for admission to the Swedes' cold climate. But if the world stands on the brink of a new era of migration, we shall see old assumptions challenged and undermined. Russians fleeing chaos at home could look to Sweden for refuge. So could central and western Europeans, using their common citizenship, settle where the woods are emptier and the lakes are cleaner. The very thought would horrify Swedes today, but they have the resources of space, infrastructure and skills to make a success of what may become tomorrow's reality.

If you continue southwards down Sweden's long Baltic shore, three hours' easy driving brings you to Kalmar, a classical, rectangular town pretty well surrounded by water. On the way I experienced something that the Swedes' neighbours, the Danes, tell you does not exist – the Swedish sense of fantasy. In a field between woods were stacked gigantic sausages of hay wrapped in black plastic against the elements. On the circular end of each bale a caricaturist had been at work. Here, instantly recognisable at 200 paces, was Grumpy; here was Sleepy, there was Happy with a lop-sided grin, and away at the far end of the field the other four dwarfs, each of them bold, white-painted fantasies in the wilderness.

The centre of Kalmar is dominated by a baroque cathedral that looks more like a town hall than a church. The sixteenth-century castle, which is what brings visitors to Kalmar, is interesting in an understated kind of way, strangely set apart from the town at the end of a quiet suburban street. But the most interesting thing about Kalmar is the Kalmar Union, which, had it endured, might have changed the face of Scandinavia and the Baltic.

Throughout the Middle Ages, Sweden and Denmark were locked in wars as perennial and in retrospect as futile as those between Britain and France. The issue was Baltic pre-eminence. But there were always others to claim that pre-eminence: the Lübeckers, the Teutonic Knights, the kings of Poland and the princes of north Germany. There came a time when the rulers of Sweden, Denmark and Norway decided to put their differences behind them. They signed the treaty that created the Kalmar Union and on Trinity Sunday, 1397, Eric of Pomerania, great-nephew of Queen Margareta of Denmark, was crowned king of each of the Scandinavian nations. A draft constitution provided that each and every successor should be king of all three countries; that each country should continue to manage its internal affairs; that foreign policy should be handled by the Union; and that an armed attack on any member of the Union should be treated as an attack on all.

The Kalmar Union persisted as an idea through the next century of Baltic history, but in practice it never secured the broad and sustained support which might have built a united kingdom in Scandinavia. Gradually the centralising ambitions of the Renaissance monarchs of Denmark and Sweden crushed disorder and indiscipline within their realms. But their rivalries gave them and their neighbours no peace. In the late sixteenth century it seemed at times as if the Danes might succeed in imposing themselves on the Swedes, but within half a century fortunes were reversed and it was Gustavus Adolfus of Sweden whose military prowess predominated. Throughout, Norway and Finland were treated as colonies, not free participants in a union of equals.

The idea of a Scandinavian Union was an anachronism, coming perhaps a century too soon: there probably was never any real chance of its effectively uniting Scandinavia. Yet if it had succeeded in rallying support around Eric and his successors as kings of Sweden,

Denmark and Norway, the story of the Scandinavian renaissance would have been very different. Christian IV and Gustavus Adolfus each showed what an able and ambitious Renaissance monarch could do in northern Europe. A successful Kalmar Union would have put all of Scandinavia at the disposal of one man, imposing Christian's architectural genius throughout all four countries, or placing their combined military strength behind Gustavus Adolfus in his battles with Wallenstein.

An effective Union might have sustained later Swedish kings in their struggles in Poland and against the Russians. A united seventeenth-century Scandinavia would have had the muscle to challenge the Netherlands at sea, and in the eighteenth century to acquire colonial possessions. In the nineteenth it could have built Sweden's primitive industrial strength into an economic capacity to rival Britain's. In the twentieth we might have seen in Scandinavia a single nation of 25 million people, strong enough to deter Hitler and Stalin from Nordic excursions, and a real power for good in the Baltic.

Whether such a state could have cultivated the qualities of Social Democracy that we see today in Finland, Sweden, Norway and Denmark beside the cruder, realpolitik assets of a major European power is, like everything else to do with the Kalmar Union, a might-have-been kind of question. It might not have made Scandinavia a better place or a happier one, but it would have given it, today and perhaps tomorrow, a more central place in European affairs.

Instead, the Kalmar Union remained unrealised, and within two centuries Sweden made her lone bid for European prominence. It was sustained for a century, on the basis of naval and military strength, and a phenomenal exercise of will-power far exceeding the national capacity that lay behind it.

In a museum in Stockholm you can see an extraordinary example of Sweden's war machine. In 1628 the royal shipyards completed the *Vasa*, the greatest warship of the age. She was huge: 150 feet long with a 35 foot beam, carrying 14,000 square foot of sails. With her crew of 145 sailors, 64 guns and 300 soldiers, she was designed to dominate the Baltic. On 10 August the admiring people of Stockholm watched her leave her moorings for the first time. She edged out into the middle of the harbour and there, catching a gentle breeze, she capsized and sank. The king suspected treachery, but the *Vasa* was the victim of no more than over-ambition and miscalculation. She was salvaged 300 years later and painstakingly restored. In the semi-darkness of the museum, berthed, roofed over and tamed, she still displays the terrifying face of seventeenth-century naval power.

Even without the *Vasa*, Gustavus Adolfus committed himself to European war. We have seen the omens that accompanied his landing at Peenemünde on the German Pomeranian coast in 1630. For two years he led his Swedes and Finns against the Emperor's troops all over Germany, and after his death in action his chancellor, Axel Oxenstierna, kept up the fight until the Treaty of Westphalia. It confirmed Sweden in possession of the mouths of the Oder, the Elbe and the Weser: a major Protestant weight in the European balance.

There was more to be fought for further east, and by 1655 Charles X of Sweden was leading his German allies in an invasion that Polish history calls the Deluge. War with Russia followed, and at the end of the century Sweden held more of the Baltic coastline than any of her rivals: her own and the Finnish coasts, the eastern Baltic, and most of the German Baltic coast. Riga was Sweden's second city; Tartu her second university. In the end it took the mad ambition of Charles XII, and above all his invasion of Russia, to put an end to Swedish predominance in the Baltic, and when he was gone Sweden ceded most of her Baltic possessions to Hanover, Prussia and Russia in turn. But she continued to hold Finland against the Russians for another century. The sustained naval and military achievement of this poor and under-populated Nordic nation was astonishing, in improbable contrast with the careful neutrality of Swedish policy in the last two centuries.

The city which best represents this aspect of Sweden's history is Karlskrona, established by Charles XI in the 1670s. It is a handsome city, still distinguished by evidence of its military and naval purposes. Old fortresses guard the harbour entrances. There is a naval academy, a naval church, a maritime museum and statues of Sweden's naval heroes. There is the usual Scandinavian fishing and yacht harbour. Offshore lie the islands and rocks and reefs among which the Swedish navy hunted clandestine Soviet visitors for so long and to such ridicule, until an unfortunate Soviet submarine commander stranded his Whisky Class boat among them in 1981.

This affair of Whisky on the Rocks brought to symbolic prominence many concerns about the role of defence in peace-loving Sweden. Hers is in principle an armed neutrality, prepared to take on all comers if attacked. But twice in the Second World War Sweden disappointed her neighbours and shocked many of her own people: she refused to go to the aid of the Finns in the Winter War; and she allowed German troops to use the Swedish rail system to enter Finland during Hitler's attack on the Soviet Union. We have seen that Finland still harbours resentment towards Sweden, and Sweden's quite reasonable refusal to intervene in the Winter War is one of its causes. Nor is it too hard to unearth similar resentments in Norway.

As long as tension in the Baltic lasted, there was ambivalence about defence within Swedish society too. Sweden was spending 6 billion dollars a year on defence, almost as much as the Netherlands. She could in theory mobilise 700,000 men and women, 900 tanks, 40 warships, and 200 Swedish-built fighter aircraft. With her space and terrain and climate she could have put up a formidable defence.

But somehow the story of Sweden's twentieth-century neutrality and the social attitudes of her people called in question the nation's readiness to fight if she had to. Right up to the end of the cold war the Finns knew that they would fight if the Russians attacked them. Experience had taught them not to expect Swedish support, and they doubted whether the Swedes would fight if attacked themselves. NATO asked itself the same questions about the Swedes: would they try and could they succeed in stopping a Soviet attack in the Baltic or across northern Scandinavia? These questions were crucial to NATO's own chances of holding its northern flank.

Europe is different now, and European Union membership brings new security to Sweden and Finland. The Partnership for Peace extends some of the promise of the NATO system deep into eastern Europe. The north's immediate concern is that trouble in the Baltic states could provoke the Russians to protect their interests in this part of their 'near abroad'. The northern countries offer the three republics training and equipment for their armies. Swedish leaders speak with little equivocation about their security interests in the eastern Baltic and their concern for the integrity of the Baltic states. But the questions posed by a century's neutrality still erode the conviction with which they speak. Karlskrona represents a glorious, bloodthirsty, eventually futile military and naval past. You have to look elsewhere for clues to Sweden's future.

You may find such clues far to the west of Karlskrona. As you drive westwards you are entering the old Danish provinces. Halland, Skåne and Blekinge were fought over one way and another for four centuries, always disputed by the Swedes, but Danish in law and instinct until the last half of the seventeenth century. If Stockholm and central Sweden have traditionally faced eastwards onto the upper Baltic, this south-western part of Sweden looks to the west and south.

Malmö, on the eastern shore of the Sound opposite Copenhagen, was for centuries Denmark's second city. Today it looks towards Copenhagen, and a bridge across the Sound will bind both cities, and the whole of Sjaelland and southern Sweden, into a single economic area. Lund's twelfth-century cathedral is older than anything in Stockholm or Uppsala, and was once the see of a proud Danish bishop. The provinces' manor houses were built for the delectation of Danish owners. And Christian IV's wonderful church at Kristianstad in the southern tip of Sweden is perhaps the finest example of seventeenth-century Danish architecture anywhere, more perfect than any of the churches in his own capital.

The Danish-Swedish wars were vicious affairs, fought across the three provinces and the Danish islands and at sea from spring to autumn; and in winter on land and on the sea ice whenever it was thick enough to bear the weight of fighting men. They were fought by regular armies and levies and armed farmers. Guerrilla attacks and reprisals and executions dragged on well into the eighteenth century. This troubled history has left behind it a subdued animosity between Denmark and Sweden quite different from Finland's and Norway's colonial resentments, and somewhat incongruous between these two gentle and smiling sister-monarchies.

The Swedes and Danes were fighting about territory, and in particular Skåne, Halland and Blekinge. They were fighting to control the Sound and exercise the right to levy dues on shipping passing through the narrows between Helsingør and Hälsingborg. Each sought supremacy in the Baltic. And, subconsciously, each sought to represent to all Europe the fact of power in Scandinavia. Neither won outright, but Sweden emerged the more powerful. In 1660 Denmark lost Skåne and Blekinge to Sweden, and in his grief Christian V of Denmark is said to have bricked up the windows of Kronborg Castle that faced his lost provinces across the Sound.

Thereafter Sweden and Denmark went their separate ways, and for the next three centuries Sweden seemed to make a better fist of it. Through skill, good fortune and geographical position she avoided the repeated hammerings Denmark suffered during the Napoleonic Wars. She lost Finland to Russia in 1809, but acquired Norway from

Denmark five years later. The nineteenth century left her in peaceful isolation, nurturing her own development, while Denmark was locked in dispute with Germany over Schleswig-Holstein and then preoccupied with coming to terms with the loss of those provinces. Above all, Sweden managed to cling to her neutrality and avoid German occupation in the Second World War. She has today a population and a gross domestic product more than half as big again as her old rival.

When, after the Second World War, an attempt at building a Scandinavian defence system failed, Denmark and Norway, scarred by enemy occupation, committed themselves to NATO. Sweden, still instinctively neutral and concerned for the Nordic balance, stood aloof. And Denmark, uninhibited by the requirements of neutrality, felt free to enter the European Community with Britain at its first enlargement in 1973. Despite her continuing anxieties about Brussels, she has maintained her position and influence in the organisation for over twenty years.

Sweden, by contrast, was inhibited throughout the cold war from joining a European Community whose basic political and economic characteristics were close to her own but whose ambitions in the field of security seemed likely to call her neutrality in question. So Sweden has come to the European Union only at its fourth enlargement, facing a great body of principle and practice built up by others over more than three decades. She is entering a new phase in her relationship with continental Europe, without the benefit of the experience Denmark has acquired.

The Swedes typify most of the attitudes that Scandinavian newcomers bring to the European Community. They see no domestic need to subordinate their nationhood to a federal or fully-integrated union. Their belief in Sweden, for herself and as a part of the European whole, has persisted throughout recorded history. The Union is for them a way of benefiting national interests, reconciling national concerns. They look to it for economic advantage, while acknowledging its political role and even – now the Soviet Union is gone and the old pressing concerns about neutrality gone with it – its role in security .

We have seen that the Swedes are rich, as individuals and as a society. They are accustomed to taking the benefits of their wealth largely in social dividends. And they are used, up to a point, to sharing their wealth with non-Swedish but deserving poor. Sweden's creditable contribution to Third World development and relief illustrates this very substantial aspect of Swedish merit. There is therefore in the Swedish mind a predisposition to listen to the Commission's wealth-sharing propositions, through solidarity with its southern members, through regional development, and through interventionist social and economic policies across the Union.

But the Swedes and the Scandinavians believe in doing things right, in proper bureaucratic order, and with due respect for law and regulation. They bring to the Union a watchful and sceptical eye for others' fulfilment of rules and regulations, and an intolerance of Mediterranean disarray and disregard for obligation. And they are not grandiloquent people, ready at the drop of a hat to put their names to windy declarations. They judge the European Union more by its deeds than by its words; they question integration for its own sake; and they judge proposals for further enlargement towards the east with strict regard to the stability it can bring to Europe.

As the Swedes complete their commitment, however wary, to the European Union, they follow in Danish footsteps. Compared with them, the Danes are fully-qualified, experienced Europeans. The Swedes bring the Danes reinforcement and co-operate with them on most issues. But Swedes who ponder their history on their journeys to Brussels and Strasbourg may reflect that the Danes, whom they drove out of Skåne, Halland and Blekinge three centuries ago and whom most Swedes even today think of as not entirely serious people, have in the last twenty years stolen a march on them. In today's Brussels, the Swedes are coming from behind in their unremitting struggle with the Danes as to which nation better represents Scandinavia to continental Europeans.

The Swedes and other Scandinavians do not see Europe as sufficient in itself. They look to a European Union open to the rest of the world, and if politicians and officials in Stockholm ever seemed likely to go along with Fortress Europe conceptions the people of Gothenburg, Sweden's second city, would oppose them every inch of the way.

Gothenburg lies on the west coast of Sweden, less than 100 miles from the Norwegian frontier. The completion of the Gota Canal in the early nineteenth century gave it a link across the waist of Sweden to Stockholm and the eastern Baltic. Now it trades by sea, air and overland with the rest of the Baltic world. But it is not a Baltic city; it is the first place that we have visited that looks to the ocean rather than to northern Europe's inland sea. Its ferries sail to Harwich and Hull, its ships to North America and South Asia and the Far East. In the last thirty years of the nineteenth century the emigrants sailed from Gothenburg on the ships of the Gothenburg-America Line. Today, 2,400 tons of bananas arrive here from Central America every week, to feed a gargantuan Swedish appetite for the fruit. And 6,000 Volvos at a time are exported from Gothenburg in special transporters to the United States.

Gothenburg has always looked beyond the Baltic. Gustavus Adolfus II founded it as a means of getting Swedish goods away to the west without paying dues for passage through the Sound at Helsingør. Dutch engineers developed its canals and Dutch, German and British merchants its trading contacts. In 1664 Samuel Pepys placed an order in Gothenburg for a thousand masts, 'the biggest that ever was made in the Navy and wholly of my composing, and a good one I hope it is for the King.' Like Hamburg, it still looks more to the west than to the Baltic. Like Hamburg it values its links with London, where its merchants were granted the status almost of honorary Englishmen on the Baltic Exchange.

So Gothenburg is for Sweden a reminder of the wider world with which it is so forcefully and on the whole so constructively engaged. Sweden has troops on UN service in Angola, Croatia, Cyprus, El Salvador, the subcontinent, Kuwait, Korea, the Lebanon and Yugoslavia. For years she has been one of the very few members of the United Nations to fulfil their development assistance commitments. Swedish diplomats take United Nations business seriously, and strive to find ways to make it efficient. Swedish good deeds have not gone unpunished. Just as twenty-five years ago what looks in retrospect like principled and sensible Swedish opposition to American policy in Vietnam infuriated Washington, so Sweden's special interest in places like Tanzania still provokes the cynicism of hard men everywhere. But in the world outside Europe, Sweden continues to display an admirable moral seriousness that is backed by commercial interest.

So Sweden looks outwards: east towards the Baltic republics and Russia, south towards the continent, west towards the oceans and the world. But she also looks in on herself with sound Scandinavian introspection, content in the main with what she sees but anxious about her chances of holding on to what she has.

Swedes seem more ambivalent than most about the past, about what went before the establishment of broad social and political consensus early this century. They cherish their natural inheritance of woods, lakes and wilderness. They value the peasant skills that created their traditional buildings, farm implements and machinery, and which suffuse so much of Swedish art. If you take a narrow-boat along the Gota Canal, you see the care that has gone into preserving the old Sweden. But Sweden is also a country in successful search of tomorrow's world. Modern houses, empty highways, glass and steel offices and warehouses and factories half-hidden in the woods remind you of some of the emptier corners of the industrial United States, of parts of New England, Michigan or Minnesota.

There is the same ambivalence in social attitudes. Leave aside the choking snobbery and social rigidity of a small number of Swedes with pretensions and you still have fundamental social contradictions. The do-gooding authoritarianism of Social Democracy has bitten deep. There is an acceptance of authority, of the demands of society. This in some ways is a benevolent police state tempered by impeccable democracy, and the inmates are happy in their prison. But beside this is the individualism of the Swedes, the cult of loneliness, of solitary pursuits. They escape into the wilderness from their aseptic cities. They sail, ski, fish, gather berries in the woods. They go to their country huts, each with its sauna cabin on the edge of some unspoiled piece of water. In their domestic interiors they enjoy the simple forms and subdued colours of their peasant past. These are not the characteristics of people who readily resign themselves to the communal will.

This ambivalence is reflected in politics. A new political wind has blown through Swedish life in recent years: a youthful, right-of-centre eagerness to draw lines under past practice, set individualism free, embrace efficiency and call equality in question. It is an attitude that appeals to Thatcherites everywhere but it seems, so far, to have none of the shrillness of English Thatcherism. The Social Democrats came storming back on the eve of the European Union referendum, in the autumn of 1994, but the struggle between right-of-centre convictions and left-of-centre Swedish tradition looks likely to persist. At the moment tradition looks the more powerful force, the ideas of a radical change a flash in the pan by contrast. But powerful arguments

stand behind each approach, and the struggle between them will be
fought out in novel circumstances, in a Sweden at last committed to
union with the continent. The outcome of the struggle will shape
Sweden, and with it Scandinavia.

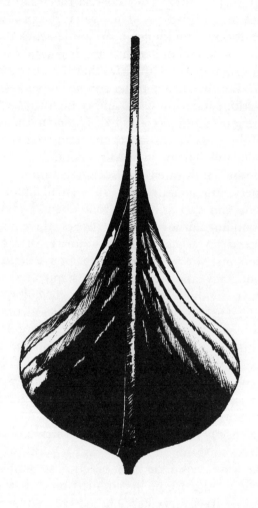

13
Norway

Norway is a country of the Atlantic rather than the Baltic: 1200 miles of her coastline face towards the Atlantic and the Arctic, less than 300 towards the Skagerrak and the Baltic approaches. Yet she has her place in the Baltic by virtue of affinity, in particular her affinity with Denmark and Sweden, which persists despite Norway's decision to stay out of the European Union. And Norwegians bring qualities of their own to Scandinavia, and so to the Baltic world.

The Norwegians were the first people since the Athenians to build an essentially maritime empire. They first erupted across the sea in the Viking age, whose sudden explosion of energy in the north in the ninth and tenth centuries sent its explorers and raiders out into the world. From Sweden the Vikings went east to Russia. From Denmark they sailed south-west. But the Norwegians' position condemned them to the most hazardous route, west into the Atlantic, to the Faroes and Iceland and the Orkneys and Shetlands. A few sailed even further west, to Greenland and the New World. More swung south, to the Hebrides and the Irish Sea. They founded Dublin and established a Viking kingdom in the Isle of Man. From there they invaded northern England from the west and joined hands with other Viking conquerors coming from Yorkshire and Northumberland; and they say that dialect-fanciers can detect in northern English speech today the point at which the two groups met. But the Norwegians in England and those at home remained dependent on the oceans and the islands of their maritime empire for any cohesion between them.

The Vikings first came to England as raiders to terrorise honest Christians, but they settled there to build lasting kingdoms of their own. They also achieved a unity that had eluded them at home, scattered as they were along the vast distances of the Norwegian fiords. So it was Norsemen returning from England at the end of the eleventh century who first brought to Norway the beginnings of a sense of national cohesion. The same century saw the coming of Christianity.

The history of twelfth-century Norway is a story of rivalries and cross-purposes, nation-building and bloodshed, the spread of Christianity and of permanent settlements. Danish kings were involved in these struggles for power, but the focus of activity was not in the south, where Norway faces Denmark, but in the west, at Trondheim and later at Bergen. Eventually the Norwegians lost the Hebrides and the Isle of Man to the Scots; but they held on to the Faroes and Iceland. By the thirteenth century Norway was recognised as a nation, and the great cathedral at Trondheim became a place of pilgrimage for all Scandinavia. But she was still emphatically a nation of the Atlantic.

A shift of emphasis was in the making. South-eastern Norway, adjoining the Swedish frontier and facing south towards Denmark, was richer than the west, and the king moved his capital to Oslo. Hanseatic traders from Lübeck established themselves in the country. In 1294 a treaty gave them a monopoly of Norwegian commerce, completing the process of drawing Norway into the Hansa's North Sea and Baltic trading world. Dynastic links pulled in the same direction, and in 1380 Olav of Denmark, who had already succeeded his maternal grandfather on the Danish throne, inherited the Norwegian monarchy from his father, King Håkon. A Norway poorer by far than Denmark was thus united with her southern neighbour. The political links that make Norway relevant to our Baltic story had been established, to persist in their different ways into our own times.

For 400 years the country was joined with Denmark under monarchs who thought of themselves as Danes, in a union dominated by Copenhagen. The Norwegians are a proud and individualistic people, shaped by the harshness of their country and the perils of their maritime adventures. They seem to have stood emotionally alone all through history, but they did not escape from Danish rule until the beginning of the nineteenth century, and then only into the arms of the Swedes, and it was only in 1905 that they recovered the independence and nationhood they lost in 1380. Today, after nearly a century of independence, they still bear the marks of their years of subordination, and there is an edge of bitterness to their Scandinavian relationships to this day. In 1994, Norwegians campaigning for a Yes vote in the referendum about the European Union found the very word Union an embarrassment; in the valleys and along the fiords of western Norway it still reminded voters of Norway's old union with Sweden. If you want to understand today's Norway you have to understand her past subordination, like Finland's, to more powerful and sophisticated neighbours.

Norway's 400 years of association with Denmark took her from the high Middle Ages through the Kalmar Union and the achievements and failures of Denmark's Renaissance kings, to the eighteenth century and the Napoleonic Wars. In those centuries she developed side by side with Denmark, though always lagging behind her in wealth, influence and material achievement. Most Norwegians lived hard lives in fishing and agricultural communities on the very edge of a sustainable existence. Their memorials are to be found in little fields scraped out of the wilderness, bleak villages, and occasional stave churches. The urban centres, such as Trondheim, Bergen and Oslo, display more evidence of the Danish-dominated past. So, very particularly, do Frederikstad and Kristiansand.

Frederikstad is a bustling country town to the east of Oslo Fiord, forty miles south of the capital. Across a broad stretch of water served by an indignantly fussy little ferry lies the old town. It was built in the seventeenth century as a military settlement to block the approach to Oslo and has survived almost unchanged to this day. Frederikstad was conceived and laid out like a Roman legionaries' camp: four-square, symmetrical, protected by earthen ramparts. There are four gates, from which streets quarter the little town. The army still has a presence here, with a military police Jeep parked beside the old guard house. An old manor house just within the ramparts houses a school of anti-aircraft artillery, and there is a barracks for the local infantry regiment across a quiet road from the church, where the ladies of the garrison go to morning service. You can find the necessities of civilian life in Frederikstad – it has its bank, grocer and restaurants – but a gun adorns the front gate of one of its barracks; and in all essentials it remains a garrison town of 300 years ago.

Away to the west, on the southern cape of Norway, lies Kristiansand. It owes its name to King Christian IV of Denmark, whose wonderful church we saw at Kristianstad in Sweden. Christian built the two towns at opposite ends of his empire on the same careful rectangular plan. Norwegian Kristiansand is the busier of the two: a holiday resort, a terminal for ferries from England and Denmark, and a fishing port. It never had a church to rival Kristianstad's, and its streets have lost their seventeenth-century regularity. But away from the ferry port, facing down the yacht harbour between the islands towards the sea, Christian's little fortress stands behind its grass-covered ramparts and granite walls, with a low round keep within. Kristiansand held southern Norway for the Danes, just as Kristianstad held southern Sweden. They are 250 miles apart as the crow flies, 500 by water, a reminder of the extent of the empire controlled by Nordic renaissance kings.

Christian IV also had a hand in the reshaping of Oslo. Indeed, he shifted it from its old site to where it stands today, surrounding Akershus Castle at the head of Oslo fiord. Predictably he renamed it Christiania; and he rebuilt Akershus. For 200 years the castle was the centre of Danish administration in Norway. When, three centuries later, the Norwegians felt the time had come to reassert themselves, they rechristened their capital Oslo. Today Christian's name lives on in different forms in many Scandinavian places; and Christiania survives as the name of a tax-free, police-free, bourgeois-free haven for hippies and dropouts and the homeless on the unfashionable side of Copenhagen harbour.

In 1814, by the Treaty of Kiel, Denmark lost Norway to Swedish suzerainty. The Danes, as we shall see in the next chapter, had made a series of disastrous miscalculations during the Napoleonic Wars. Sweden, having adopted one of Napoleon's marshals as her Crown Prince, and aided by the fact that Bernadotte had the gumption to distance his new country from his old master, lost Finland to Russia but gained Norway in compensation. The Norwegians, their trade even more comprehensively ruined than the Danes' by the British blockade, were transferred without consultation from the care of their bankrupt landlord to that of his more prosperous neighbour.

Swedish rule in Norway lasted for ninety-one years. Like Sweden, Norway benefited from the long nineteenth-century years of peace, in which Lutheran virtues of hard work and social discipline, education and church-going brought material dividends. Like Sweden, Norway grew, if not rich then less poor. She developed her fisheries and farming, and her merchant fleet expanded to become the third largest in the world. Gradually the Norwegians took into their own hands most functions of government except foreign policy and defence. But even into the twentieth century Norway remained relatively backward, neglected by Stockholm and mildly despised by the Swedes.

The centre of today's Oslo was created in those Swedish years. Its setting is superb, with the waters of the fiord stretching away before it in front and a mountainous backdrop behind. And Oslo can claim, despite its changes of site and name, to be the oldest of the Nordic capitals. But it lacks the qualities that Copenhagen and Stockholm proclaim in such full measure: urbanity, grace and an air of the cosmopolitan. Oslo, a bit Germanic, remains provincial and heavy-in-the-hand.

You see these defects at Frogner, in a showpiece that ought to be sublime. Gustav Vigeland is an early twentieth-century Norwegian cultural hero. He started life as a wood-carver and then took to working in stone. His ambition was to represent every stage in the cycle of human life, from birth through childhood to maturity, senescence and death. He offered to fill a park in the city with his sculptures, and Frogner, a steeply sloping open space containing more than 600 statues, is the result.

Vigeland devoted a lifetime to their production. The statues writhe under the artist's hand. There is a fountain borne up by human figures to represent the burden of life, and a massive monolith to give focus to it all. The commitment that this achievement represents is enormous, and the Norwegians proudly claim that Vigeland's work stands comparison with Rodin, with whom he studied in the early 1890s. Perhaps individual pieces do, but to my eye the effect of the whole is grotesque, as if the ornaments with which Hitler might have graced an imperial Berlin were gathered together on one absurdly overcrowded site. Frogner is an odd showpiece for the simple capital of an unpretentious country. It is overbearing in a provincial kind of way, and totally at odds with the cool understatement that characterises the best of Scandinavian life and art.

To me, most of the heart of Oslo is disappointing in its varying ways. Away from the water's edge it is sombre and cramped, constantly urging you back to the waterfront and the long views down the fiord. Oslo is small – you can walk with a suitcase from one end of the centre to the other with no more than one change of carrying hand and no need to hail a taxi – and its buildings seem dingy even on a clear day. There is a claustrophobic air about the city centre; and when you reflect upon the spiritual oppression of a conventional, conservative society 100 years ago you understand better the suppressed hysteria with which Edvard Munch filled so many of his canvases.

Remark gently to a Norwegian upon these characteristics, and he will tell you about the open views in the suburb where he lives, or the merits of Oslo's museums, like Thor Heyerdahl's *Kon Tiki* and the exhibition of Viking ships beside the fiord. He will also tell you that like all Norwegians he has a hut on a fiord or a lake or a mountain to which to escape. And the city has its cultural delights. An example? The National Theatre. What are they playing? *Hedda Gabler*.

Oil wealth may be changing Oslo for the better, but the fact remains that it is a capital which cannot live up to the country for which it stands – its fiords, mountains and islands, its great headlands, and its distances stretching away to eternity.

In 1905 the deadlock between Norway's insistence on separate representation abroad and an intransigent Swedish king was brought to its inevitable end by Scandinavian good sense. While the Finns, a few years later, opted for a president, the Norwegians turned to the Danes for a king when they won their independence, and Prince Karl of Denmark sailed up Oslo Fiord to become Håkon VII of Norway. His line has given Norway the continuity of honest, simple, Scandinavian monarchy ever since, through a century punctuated by two events which fundamentally changed the country: German occupation in the 1940s and the development of the country's oil and gas resources thirty years later.

The Norwegian resistance to Hitler is a fine story of a small and stubborn people using the vast spaces of its country to frustrate the invader and occupier. But it takes us far from our Baltic theme, so the story of a gun battery must suffice instead. The battery guards the narrows at Oscarsborg on the Oslo Fiord, where you can still see fortifications which date back, like so much else in southern Norway, to the ubiquitous Christian IV. Here, in 1940, Colonel Birger Erikson of the Norwegian coastal artillery commanded a battery of three guns. They were named Aaron, Joshua and Moses.

On 9 April 1940, Erikson found himself confronted with an apparition. Out of the shadows of the fiord a ship materialised. She was the German battle-cruiser *Blücher*, and she carried the complete military, administrative and security team despatched by the Führer to take control of Oslo.

To send a capital ship into the narrow waters of Oslo Fiord was typical of Nazi audacity. The Germans relied on surprise, on the awe in which they were held, on the hopelessness of resistance, and if all else failed on the damage which *Blücher*'s big guns could inflict on

Oslo, as *Schleswig-Holstein*'s had on Danzig eight months earlier. They had not reckoned with Colonel Erikson's three Old Testament heroes. He knew that he would only have time to fire each gun once, so he waited until *Blücher* was at point-blank range. Then he fired Moses. The shell penetrated *Blücher*'s magazine, and the explosion that followed sent her down into the depths of Oslo Fiord, taking with her 1,000 Nazi victims of a good Jewish gun. Half a century later, an occasional oil slick still seeps to the tranquil surface of the fiord.

The Norwegians learned much from their wartime experiences. They conceived a hatred of Germany which, in an infinitely milder form, survives today. They learned an affection for Britain, which came boldly if unsuccessfully to their support and armed and sustained their resistance; and not even the damage done to Norwegian forests by acid rain from Britain has entirely eroded that friendship. Resentment of the Swedes, who allowed German troop trains to pass through Sweden on their way to Norway, feeds a conviction, as in Finland, that their neighbours will always look first to their own selfish interests. There is a gentle, almost whimsical disdain for Denmark, which so readily came to terms with the Germans. Above all, invasion and occupation convinced the Norwegians that they must henceforth find safety in collective defence, and they committed their country, otherwise so strongly inclined to go her own way in the world, wholeheartedly to NATO.

But suddenly the world's oil men and the wealth of a Klondike were visited on a puritanically ascetic country. Since the 1970s, oil and gas wealth has modified many of the attitudes which Norway has derived from her history. It has not altered Norway's basic characteristics, but it has added colour to what has traditionally been a monochrome society, and has brought a touch of vulgarity to its habitual restraint. And this change in the country's domestic circumstances has influenced Norway's relationship with the European Community.

Norway first opened negotiations for Community membership in the early 1970s, along with Denmark, Britain and Ireland. At that time gas was just beginning to impinge on the country's fortunes, and the oil fields were still in their development phase. Fishing and whaling and religion and the preservation of Norway's traditional rural life still dominated Norwegian thinking. Finally, the negotiators reached agreement in Brussels. But the electorate turned the deal down, leaving Denmark alone in Scandinavia to join a European Community which pulled, or seemed to pull her, in a direction quite different from her Nordic neighbours.

For the next twenty years Norway grew rich, richer than Denmark and nearly as rich as Sweden. But with wealth and an appreciating currency, her dependence on energy resources increased. Her economy had always been poor but balanced; now she was rich beyond imagination but acutely vulnerable. And the disjunctions between the energy-based prosperity of a port such as Stavanger and the primitive poverty of agricultural Norway brought new social strains to this essentially cohesive, egalitarian country. Norway joined her Nordic neighbours in the European Economic Area, which linked them, though without membership and a vote, to the European Union. But she was growing more dissimilar from them.

As we have seen, change in the Soviet Union and its eventual collapse gave Finland and Sweden the opportunity to commit themselves to European Union membership. The Norwegians remained sceptical. In November 1994 they went to the polls in their second referendum in twenty-two years.

Advocates of Union membership pointed to opportunities, and to the dangers of isolation. Its opponents appealed to Norway's deep conservatism, arguing that its fishing, whaling and agriculture, its very way of life and even its religion would be at risk in a Union dominated by Brussels. Norway, safely a member of NATO, did not need the security Union membership might bring. And it was clear that her energy wealth gave her an option that Finland and Sweden did not have. The Norwegians voted No by a small but clear majority, putting their faith not in age-old Scandinavian affinities or in union with a complicated continent but in the simple values of isolation.

14
Denmark

You can fly from Oslo to Copenhagen in under an hour, but the overnight ferry offers a more rewarding experience. The ship sails out of Oslo harbour in the evening, winds her way down the fiord as the sun goes down, and brings you to the mouth of the Sound at Kronborg in the early morning. The rest of the journey, about an hour's sail from Kronborg to Copenhagen, takes you past much of the documentation of Danish history.

The Danish monarchy is the oldest in Europe. Today's Queen presides elegantly over 5 million Danes to their general satisfaction. The Danes see themselves as homogeneous, certainly distinct from their German neighbours but distinct also from their Scandinavian cousins. Yet the outsider cannot help wondering why throughout their history in their archipelago and peninsula they have been such a clearly separate nation.

As so often, geography supplies the answer. Denmark's position across the mouth of what Hilaire Belloc called the river of the Baltic gave her the means and the will to maintain her own identity. Her story is one of a long struggle to control the narrows, to keep the Baltic open or closed, and to profit from the fact that maritime trade between east and west through the Baltic passes through Danish waters. The story unfolds before your eyes as the ferry from Oslo sails down the Sound.

Kronborg, the fortress at Helsingør that commands the narrows between Sweden and Denmark, makes a powerful statement even today. When Frederick II built it in the late sixteenth century in time for Shakespeare to make it immortal as Hamlet's Elsinore twenty years later, it was one of the great fortresses of Europe. Its guns enforced payment of the dues which the Danish monarchy levied for passage through the Sound. Helsingør grew prosperous at Kronborg's feet. Its guns struck fear even into the battle-hardened crews of Admiral Hyde Parker's squadron as they prepared to enter the Sound on their way to Copenhagen in 1801; but when the moment of truth

came they were ineffective. It was left to the scratch Danish fleet, as
little prepared for battle as the gunners of Kronborg but brimming
with fighting spirit, to give Hyde Parker's deputy, Nelson, the fight of
his life when the British fleet arrived off Copenhagen.

An endless procession of ships still enters and leaves the Baltic
through the narrows at Helsingør; but now its harbour is crowded
only with the ferries that serve the short crossing to Sweden. They
nuzzle in and out between the bulk of Kronborg Castle on the one
hand and on the other a railway station whose nineteenth-century
splendour vies with the castle in vainglory.

The Sound grows steadily wider south of Kronborg, and Sweden
gradually recedes while the ferry hugs the Danish coast all the way to
Copenhagen. At Humlebaek you pass an inlet where Danish oar-
powered gunboats used to lurk, trying to control passage through the
Sound even after the British had stolen the sailing fleet away; but if
you go searching for this inlet overland you find that it lies within the
grounds of Louisiana, most exquisite of modern art galleries, and
only a vivid imagination can conjure up the ghosts of men-of-war
behind the African sculptures and the Henry Moore in Louisiana's
gardens.

As the Oslo ferry approaches Copenhagen, history crowds in upon
you. The position at which the Danes drew up their line of battle
to receive Nelson's assault is away to the left, lost beneath land
reclaimed to extend the city; but the remains of a land battery are to
be seen to the right, surrounded by the houses of an expensive
suburb. Further out to sea is Middelgrund, the great fortress that the
Danes built in the first years of this century to protect the seaward
approaches to Copenhagen, reputedly as powerful as the First World
War fortresses at Verdun and Liège, but never tested in war. In
front of you, as you approach Copenhagen's waterfront, is a little
eighteenth-century island castello. On the mainland, almost on the
waterfront, is the much larger Castellet, built like the Tower of
London to ensure royal control of the city, but in Danish fashion
green and dreamy, with the sails of its own windmill peeping above
the ramparts. In April 1940 the Germans brought into Copenhagen a
collier packed with troops hidden below decks. When the moment
came to attack, they swarmed over the ramparts of Castellet, seizing
control of fortress, capital and kingdom almost simultaneously.

The ferry is in narrow waters now, easing slowly past the old
warehouses that line the quay. Across the water is the historic naval

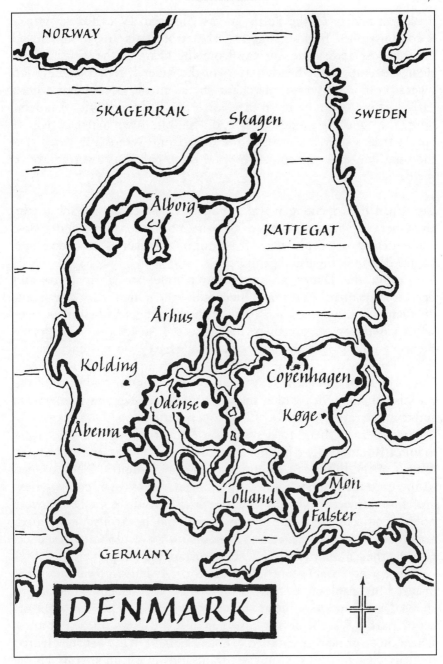

NORWAY

SKAGERRAK

Skagen

SWEDEN

Ålborg

KATTEGAT

Århus

Kolding

Copenhagen

Odense

Køge

Åbenrå

Møn

Lolland

Falster

GERMANY

DENMARK

dockyard and base, the fleet's lair as Christian IV called it, with a decommissioned frigate, sinister fast patrol boats and a submarine moored just across the fairway from the heart of the city. On the right, close up, is the headquarters of the Maersk group, Denmark's biggest company, whose merchant ships sail the oceans but whose early fortunes were made in the North Sea and the Baltic. Amalienborg, the Queen's modest collection of four town palaces, whose back gardens stretch almost to the waterfront, stands 200 yards further on. The ship ties up just beyond these palaces, towering above them.

To return to Copenhagen was for me a home-coming, back to the city where I spent three years as British ambassador in the mid-1980s, encountering there pleasure, frustration, friendships, paradox and contradiction in the usual proportions.

I found the Danes an intriguing people, straightforward and perverse by turns. Sentiment persuades them that they are Scandinavians, but Denmark has none of the bleakness and empty spaces which condition her northern neighbours. Instead, the Danes pride themselves on smallness, on social homogeneity, on intimacy, lacing these things with a passion to keep ambition and assertion in check. They think of themselves as relaxed and humour-loving, but the astonished stare with which they so often greet everyday statements spoke to me rather of well-controlled insecurity.

Long before their 1993 vote on Maastricht, the Danes were manifestly ambivalent about their place in Europe and about the impact of the European Community on their country. They seemed to me quite as reserved, as confused even, as my own countrymen, and more introverted by far than the British. And yet the Danes were polyglot citizens of Europe and the world, much travelled, cultivated, good judges of red wine, and a people with a global conscience, pouring their money into the relief of distant hardship.

There were other contradictions too. A statist, levelling spirit inspired by deeply-ingrained Social Democratic principles seemed to shape Danish politics, even under rainbow coalitions of right-of-centre parties; yet the people railed against the heavy burden of taxes which those principles entailed. They resented NATO yet they feared the Russians and enlisted in their thousands in a Dad's Army Home Guard. After six months I found that I had failed to discern any guiding organising principle in Denmark.

If geography is the clue to history, history is the key to national psychology. The Danes, I found, were no exception to this rule. They cherish 1,000 years of continuity. They remember that their kings' writ used to run to the gates of Hamburg, as far as the North Cape and across the Sound deep into southern Sweden. Gradually they lost their empire, and its loss, along with wars with Sweden and Prussia and high-handed British arrogance, has left its mark on the national psyche. Similarly, the Danes' passionate egalitarianism is a peasant nation's response to memories of royal absolutism and a harsh, German aristocracy. Their taste for education and self-improvement springs from the bitter years of the 1860s, when the Danes determined to recover in bleak Jutland the wealth stolen from them in Schleswig-Holstein. It was clear that, if I were to begin to understand the Danes, I must grapple with the complexities and confusions of Danish history.

But how to make sense of all those historical complications? I returned to geography. What we are and what we do is conditioned by where we live. The Danes have always lived on islands and sandbars and a bleak peninsula across the mouth of the Baltic. Their history is in a sense the story of an unending struggle to control its maritime entrances.

Denmark's position implies control of the three channels that link the Baltic to the North Sea and the oceans beyond. In Frederiksborg Castle you can see the slit through which the Danish kings used to drop into safe custody in the cellar the dues which seafarers paid for passage through the Sound into the Baltic. For centuries Denmark fought Sweden for supremacy in the Baltic, and when she lost the last battle her mastery of the Sound began to slip away. Nelson descended upon Copenhagen to ensure that the Danes and their allies should not close the Baltic and markets of northern Europe against England's trade.

This is not just a tale lost in the mists of time. It shapes this century quite as much as earlier ones. At the start of both World Wars, Germany was determined to ensure that Denmark should not admit the Royal Navy into the Baltic. For the last fifty years Denmark's importance to NATO has been that of the stopper in the bottle. Even in the 1980s, the Chief of Danish Defence would talk to me of the threat that could suddenly come out of the Baltic and of what the Danes could do to hold the Baltic approaches. Danish history, I saw, was filled with Denmark's attempts over the centuries to exploit her

control of the Sound and the Belts and with others' attempts to force
the Danes to open them or close them.

As our ferry entered Copenhagen harbour we passed Denmark's
most famous monument, the statue of Hans Andersen's Little Mermaid on the rocks at the water's edge. The Little Mermaid is almost
self-consciously small, just as Denmark hugs to herself the fact that
she is little. The psychology of this emphasis on smallness is worth
exploring before we embark on our tour of Denmark. It tells us a
good deal about the Danes.

Denmark is little because in the course of history she lost so much.
In the seventeenth century she was shorn of the southern Swedish
provinces across the Sound from Copenhagen. In 1814 she ceded
Norway to Sweden. In 1864 she lost Schleswig, Holstein and Lauenburg to Germany. In the Second World War she lost Iceland. She is
left with Greenland and the Faroes, both largely self-governing; with
Bornholm in the Baltic; and remains little Denmark today.

The Danish psyche seems to have come to terms with this long
history of loss with admirable equanimity. Animosity towards
Sweden, for example, runs no deeper than the Oxford versus
Cambridge variety. But with Denmark's readiness to face reality
came passivity, a sense that she lies exposed to the mercy of her
neighbours and of superior force.

One consequence was Denmark's refusal to fight the invader in
1940: a sensible enough policy in a hopeless situation, but its memory
still festers in some Danish minds. Another was Denmark's refusal
throughout the long years of the cold war to carry her fair share
of NATO's burdens, something which festered in the minds of her
allies. A fringe political party led by a charlatan who went to gaol for
tax evasion announced twenty years ago that the best instrument for
Denmark's defence would be an answering machine to respond 'We
surrender' when the Soviet embassy telephoned. Denmark disowned
this dubious citizen, but his parody contained a germ of truth.

Even so, Denmark has done her bit in NATO, if only on a shoestring. She has sent peacekeepers to Cyprus, to the Middle East and
to Kashmir. But there has always been a reserve about Danish involvement in military matters, in any activity that smacked of assertion. When the great European changes came, openings in the east
and unification in Germany, they provoked a new, quite different
Danish commitment to the tasks that change demanded. Denmark

sent a warship to the Gulf in 1991, and troops to Bosnia. Main battle tanks went with them, and when the need arose, they opened fire. In my time in Denmark that Danish fire would have brought the government down; now Danes take pride in their new-found temerity. And Denmark is reaching out to Poland and the three republics in the eastern Baltic; her troops train with the Poles who once seemed to threaten them, and a Danish battalion is twinned with a Lithuanian company. To this new commitment the Danes bring an attractive, laid-back grace in which efficiency and informality are combined.

This recent Danish self-assertion reminds one that their emphasis on the littleness of Denmark has always had something self-consciously whimsical about it, almost Yiddish in its self-deprecation. For the Danes are rightly a proud people, with a proud history. They number among their ancestors the Vikings who conquered England. At Jelling in Jutland a seventy-year-old doctor just back from tending Moslem freedom fighters in Afghanistan showed me the village's tenth-century runic stone. It was erected by Harald Bluetooth in honour of his father Gorm the Old, who 'united all Denmark and Norway under himself and made the Danes Christians'. Further south, in what since 1864 has been German Schleswig, you can see the remains of the Danevirke, a defensive rampart across the neck of land between North Sea and Baltic to keep the German tribes out of Jutland. The ghost of Holger Dansk sleeps in the bowels of Kronborg castle, ready like Francis Drake to arise when his country needs him. Odense in Fyn, Hans Andersen's city, can trace its origins back 1,000 years. We shall see that in Køge Bay, south of Copenhagen, the Danes fought a series of great naval battles against the Swedes, and that in 1864 at Dybbøl in southern Jutland they withstood a siege against the Prussians. Far away in the eastern Baltic, Gotland and Tallinn trace their histories back to Danish kings and merchant venturers, and there are Danish Jews alive today thanks to the Pimpernels who smuggled them to safety across the Sound in 1943. Many Danes find that their self-deprecating whimsicality sits uneasily with their proud past.

Yet the modern history of little Denmark is a triumphant success story. When the Danish crown ceded its richest provinces to Germany in 1864, the Danes set themselves to develop the bleak heathland of Jutland and to create wealth there to replace the lost riches of Schleswig-Holstein. At the same time they began to lay the educational and socially egalitarian foundations of today's Denmark. But the country remained a poor and simple society, and though some Danes profited from neutrality in the First World War, simplicity and relative poverty still characterised it right up to the Second. So prosperity, public and private well-being, the quality of private homes and old people's homes alike, are recent, hard-won societal strengths, nurtured by hard work, careful identification of the things the Danes do well, political stability and the strong sense of social cohesion that pervades the whole of Danish society.

To Danes, and to many foreign observers, Denmark is an ideal society. No one is very poor; few are very rich. There are few of the classic social tensions. Immigrants, refugees and asylum seekers may be resented as carbuncles on the face of a homogeneous society, but they are accommodated, cared for and incorporated into Danish life. The state and its police are surprisingly intrusive, but their intrusions are accepted as necessary to that fairness and order which the Danes prize so highly. The uncertainties and delays of complicated coalitions and consensus politics are accepted for the same reason. No commentator poured scorn on the minister who wrote a book a few years ago proclaiming that 'there is something wonderful in the state of Denmark'.

So Denmark is at peace with herself. But she has difficulty in finding a satisfactory place for herself in Europe. For the Danes are torn between the manifest necessity to involve themselves in the continent on whose edge they precariously sit, and their own deep longing to make sure that no outsider upsets their utopia. The Danes do not know what they are: their emotions make them Scandinavians or isolationists; their calculations would have them continentals, indeed partners in the European Union. Emotion drives them to put their interests at risk in dangerous referenda, reason reminds them that it would be nonsense to detach themselves from the affairs of the European Union. Sturm und Drang rages beneath the fixed placidity of the Danish countenance.

'The thing to understand about the Danes', a woman in Copenhagen said to me, 'is that at bottom we are Germans trying to be British.' She would not have said this to her compatriots, for the Danes fear the Germans with a visceral dread, the more particularly now that Germany is unified and assertive. The Danes like to think of themselves as Scandinavians but with a sense of humour. They like the British, but despair at the fact that we are as ambivalent about our place in the world as they are. Sometimes they wish that the world would go away. As it will not, they bend their minds to the hopeless task of preventing the winds of the world from blowing through their Danish Eden.

As we have seen, Denmark's Nordic neighbours are on the march, and two out of the three have committed themselves to the European Union. There is a danger that the Finns and Swedes will overtake the Danes in their dedication to the schemes and ideals that Brussels generates. The Danes find this faintly embarrassing, but it serves their interests. It gives them Nordic allies in Brussels, and shifts the Union's centre of gravity a few degrees in their direction.

Engineering works also bring Denmark closer to the continent. Bridge and tunnel links between the ferry ports of Halskov and Nyborg are almost complete. These link Sjaelland to Fyn and hence to Jutland and the continent. Work has started on another fixed link, across the Sound between Copenhagen and Malmö in southern Sweden, which will transform the two cities into a single metropolitan area of 2.5 million people. There is talk of yet another link, a great bridge between the southernmost Danish islands and Fehmarn in Germany. These projects will together fundamentally alter the economic geography of the western Baltic and bring Sweden and Denmark much closer to the commercial heart of Europe. With their heads the Danes welcome this; in their hearts some dread the juggernauts that the tunnels and bridges will bring thundering across their Eden.

Copenhagen, Scandinavia's largest city, huge out of all proportion to Denmark yet tranquil and serenely beautiful, needs the shot in the arm that changing economic geography can bring. When Denmark ruled southern Sweden, Copenhagen lay at the heart of the Danish realm. But modern history finds it at its very edge, its interests divergent from those of the rest of the country. At the beginning of this century different views about defence priorities – should the capital or the land frontier in Jutland be the first line of defence? – reshaped Danish politics in the same way as the repeal of the Corn Laws reshaped the British. Jutlanders today complain that they make the money and that Copenhagen spends it – on teachers and social workers and the unemployed of the over-populous capital of a welfare state.

But it would be hard even for sceptical Jutlanders not to be proud of
Copenhagen. The city has lost its merchant shipping and is about to
lose its naval base; yet the harbour still brings reflected light and
colour to the heart of the city, lapping close to the garden wall of the
Queen's palace, glittering between the seventeenth-century Stock Exchange and the Foreign Ministry, sending its tributary canals probing
through the city all the way to the Royal Theatre and Parliament.
The water reflects gaunt brick warehouses, an ancient wooden crane
in the naval dockyard, eighteenth-century houses, a few remaining
merchant sloops and brigs, and visiting yachts in the summer time.
Copenhagen has the tawny brick and the steep red roofs we have seen
along the southern shore of the Baltic. But the sea runs through it as it
does not through Lübeck. It has the size Tallinn lacks. It gleams
where Gdansk glowers. The smooth granite and glass modernity of
the National Bank beside the harbour counterpoints the old brick.
In contrast to St Petersburg and Stralsund, Copenhagen is spanking
clean. Only Stockholm rivals it as a great modern city of the Baltic.

Copenhagen also has a splendid hinterland, worth exploring
before we travel south down the coast towards Sjaelland's own
offshore islands. Northern Sjaelland contains three great palaces:
Kronborg on the sound, rural Fredensborg, and Frederiksborg on its
lake. It has beech woods where you can walk in solitude for hours,
and beaches backed by the summer houses of Copenhagen's rich.
Denmark's coastline wears a fringe of yacht harbours, at its most
luxuriant just north of Copenhagen. The rich and middling people of
Denmark may be taxed out of their minds, even taxed to the bone,
but they are not yet taxed to extinction.

If you go west from Copenhagen you come to Roskilde, formerly a
royal residence and a bishopric since the time of Bishop Absalon,
who built the cathedral before he went on to transform Copenhagen
from a fishing village into a merchant city. His cathedral is another of
the red brick churches of the Baltic, small by the standards of Stralsund or Lübeck, but with a precise elegance of its own. Most of
Denmark's kings and queens are buried here. It sits serenely above
the little city and its fiord. On the water's edge can be found one of
the most impressive of the Baltic ship museums that house vessels of
the Viking period, in this case merchant ships, scuttled to block the
fiord against attackers, then laboriously recovered and restored, and
now brilliantly displayed behind huge picture windows facing out
over the fiord.

Before we leave the environs of Copenhagen we must make one more expedition. Two bridges, and two bridges only, take you across the harbour from the centre of Copenhagen into Christianshavn, where elegant eighteenth-century houses stand juxtaposed to the naval dockyard and to Christiania, the old barracks taken over twenty years ago by the alternative culture of drugs and hippies, and now beginning to show its age. On your way out of the city to the south-east you pass the old ramparts, a seventeenth-century toll booth like a doll's-house, and an urban windmill. Beyond the ramparts you are plunged unceremoniously into the twentieth century. The coastal suburbs north of Copenhagen which we saw from the Oslo ferry are the expensive ones. Here to the south on the island of Amager they are very ordinary, stretching out towards market gardens created by Dutch immigrants 300 years ago, towards Copenhagen airport, and towards neglected wasteland, oddly empty within five miles of the centre of a major city. You feel that here you are on the road to nowhere, unless you want to fly to Tokyo or New York. But suddenly you find yourself in Dragør.

Dragør calls itself a fishing village, but there is more to it than that: colour-washed cottages step back from the water's edge in tidy rows; there are pubs, and a museum of odds and ends. Minor ferries run to Sweden from Dragør, but they are eclipsed by the speed and the noise of the airport's hovercraft connection to Malmö. The whole town will be forgotten when the bridge to Sweden is completed. In Britain, even more in Germany, a community under that kind of threat would be edgy, placarded, already blighted. Dragør by contrast preserves its soul in contentment and in patient resignation.

To drive southwards down the coast of Sjaelland you have to double back across the western entrance to Copenhagen harbour. As you leave the city behind, a dreary road takes you round the long curve of Køge Bay. When NATO practised defending Copenhagen against threats that might emerge from the Baltic, it envisaged a Polish brigade storming ashore at Køge. It all seemed very plausible a few years ago. The East German coast was only a hundred miles away, and troops coming ashore in Køge Bay would be a mere fifteen miles from the capital. Danish defence spokesmen described Copenhagen as the most exposed of all NATO's capitals to a sudden blow from the east, in the hope rather than the expectation of stirring their countrymen to put more money into defence.

NATO exercises and talk of Polish brigades seem infinitely remote today, but Køge Bay has seen real rather than make-believe battles fought against Denmark's enemies. In 1677 Denmark and Sweden were locked in particularly vicious warfare, the endgame of a struggle that had dragged on for thirty years. The issues between them were supremacy in the Baltic, control of the Sound, and ownership of Denmark's Swedish provinces. Earlier campaigns had been fought in Jutland; on the Danish islands and across the ice between them; and far out in the Baltic. Now the fighting raged across Skåne and Blekinge, with Christian V of Denmark at first triumphant. At Køge the Danish naval hero, Niels Juel, pounded the Swedish fleet to pieces. But gradually the Swedish army overwhelmed the Danes and in 1679, in Fontainebleau of all places, Denmark surrendered the last of her southern Swedish provinces to her old rival. It was the start of the retreat that led step by step to today's little Denmark.

One hundred and thirty years later, in 1807, another enemy, Arthur Wellesley, later Duke of Wellington, brought an army to Køge. In British history books, Wellesley's bombardment of Copenhagen is recalled less vividly than Nelson's descent upon the city six years earlier, but it made an even more terrible impact upon the Danes. As before, concern about the Baltic and the Danish fleet brought the British to Sjaelland. Denmark found herself caught up in the clash of the great European powers. She sympathised with Britain but feared Napoleon. For her part Britain feared a Danish surrender to the French. Diplomatic cross-purposes abounded.

You can interpret what followed as British brutality in dealing with a weak country, or as the necessary ruthlessness of a country fighting alone against a continent. But whatever the interpretation, the price paid by the Danes was high: 30,000 British soldiers landed around Copenhagen, to the north of the city and in Køge Bay. The invaders set themselves to bombard the capital into surrendering the Danish fleet. For three days in early September British guns battered an almost defenceless Copenhagen.

They killed nearly 2,000 of the city's 100,000 people. The Danes were appalled by the slaughter and grief-stricken when the British seized the Danish fleet and sailed away with it up the Sound. Even British opinion was scandalised, recalling the chicanery with which Nelson had induced the Danes to surrender six years earlier. In retrospect the best one can say of both affairs is that they show neither of Britain's great heroes at his best. The Danes seem to bear no manifest grievance, and remind you with pride that Wellington rode a horse called Copenhagen throughout his Spanish campaign and on the field of Waterloo.

Beyond Køge stands one of Denmark's few cliffs, and beyond the cliff lies Fakse Bay. Praestø is unknown to the guide books, but it is one of those small Danish towns which seem to have captured a tranquil moment and set it in an amber miniature. No traffic goes through Praestø; there are one or two yachts among the fishing-boats in the harbour but none of the gin palaces you find along the Sound north of Copenhagen; this is Denmark totally without pretension. And the beer in the pink-washed inn on the harbour comes from Fakse up the road, not from the great Carlsberg-and-Tuborg monopoly in Copenhagen.

After Praestø the roads go island-hopping. A little bridge takes you into Møn, a remote island tipped at its easternmost point by a great cliff, Møns Klint, by comparison with Denmark's flatnesses a monster of white chalk above the blue Baltic. Behind it, Møn is a quiet little island, scarcely more than a string of small towns, each with its simple brick church, several of them adorned with the thirteenth-century wall paintings which are an almost secret pride of Denmark. They tell bible stories with the skilled but apparently artless craftsmanship of simple lines and cool colours. A British ambassador and his wife church-crawled their way round Denmark, and round Møn in particular. They captured these paintings in photography and made an attractive book of them. The Danes looked on in pleased surprise: pleased that their wall paintings should be noticed and surprised that foreigners should take the trouble to photograph and reproduce them.

The German novelist Günter Grass is a more famous visitor to Møn, coming every summer to a rented cottage by the sea. He says he finds there qualities of sweetness and simplicity which he extrapolates to all Denmark, qualities he believes that Germany lacks. 'The Danes are a special kind of civilised people,' he once told a British journalist. 'They lost everything, all their empire, and they accepted it.' His own people, by contrast, are dangerous still. They lack simplicity and the ability to accept misfortune. His novels tell the story of what happened when the Danzig Germans refused to accept the loss of dominance. The same spirit, Grass believes, is alive in Germany today. Whether he is right or wrong about the Germans, there is something in what he says about the Danes: endurance of the unheroic, the stamina to accept what comes, these are perhaps to be seen at their best in quiet corners like Møn.

But you cannot escape the influence of Germany in Denmark for long. If you go south from Sjaelland you are on the highway to Germany. A great bridge carries the road high over a broad belt of water into the island of Falster. The Danes succumbed late to the idea of the autobahn, but a motorway now runs unbroken from Copenhagen, through Falster and on into Lolland, all the way to Rødbyhavn. From there ferries sail to Puttgarden in Fehmarn, opening the way to mainland Germany and all Europe. If the bridge to Fehmarn comes, as it may do early in the twenty-first century, it will bring still more traffic to this road and pose another threat to Denmark's special sense of isolation. Even now, the motorway has ripped much of the heart out of Falster and Lolland, unoffending islands that deserve to be left to themselves at the back of beyond.

Rødbyhavn stands at the very end of one Danish axis, but there are others to be explored. Denmark is the smallest of the Baltic countries but its islands and its indented coasts give it 4,000 miles of coastline. There is no obvious and logical best way to explore them; you are faced with choices at every turn. One way to start is to take a ferry from the westward tip of Lolland to Langeland. Langeland is a long stick of an island, fifty miles from north to south, nowhere more than twelve miles wide. It is noted today for its beaches, a few old houses and churches, and, out of season at least, for a sense of away-from-it-all. You could reasonably believe that nothing very noteworthy has ever happened there.

However, 190 years ago it was the scene of a remarkable Baltic happening. After the British bombardment of Copenhagen, Denmark, on the rebound from Britain's bloody wooing and in the hope of recovering something of her position, accepted Napoleon's embrace. A French army supported by Spanish auxiliaries marched into Jutland and on to Fyn on its way to invade Sweden. When it came to the belt of water separating Fyn from Sjaelland, ships of the Royal Navy blocked its way.

On 2 March 1808, the revolt in Spain against the French began. The British government set themselves to persuade the Spanish troops in Fyn that they were in the wrong place, preparing to fight on the wrong side: the Royal Navy stood ready to transport them back to Bilbao, there to go to war against Napoleon. One James

Robertson – a Scotsman who had been a priest in Aberdeenshire and a Benedictine monk in Bavaria before he turned his hand to secret service, and who might well have served as a model for Patrick O'Brian's Stephen Maturin – was employed to get the message through. His mission succeeded, and the Spanish commanders concentrated their troops in Langeland. In late August British ships picked up 9,000 of them and transported them to sunnier, bloodier climes.

A bridge now joins Langeland to Fyn and so to Jutland and the continent, but there is more magic in another route, the ferry to Aerø, a Danish island facing Germany across Kiel Bay. Aerø consists of no more than three villages and two towns, but one of them is Aerøskøbing, an urban jewel untouched – a few concessions to tourism apart – by time.

Denmark has fought as many battles as Britain for special treatment within the European Union. One of them is for the right to debar non-Danes – which here means Germans – from owning holiday homes in Denmark. It sounds a petty thing to fight for, but Aerø helps explain the passion the Danes bring to the issue. It lies within weekending distance from Hamburg, even closer to Kiel and Flensburg; and even the most passionate believer in integration and individual liberties can see the damage an unchecked influx of foreign property-buyers would cause in Aerø. It is hard to believe that Denmark can keep the place for ever protected in amber. But for the time being at least, Aerøskøbing offers gas-lit eighteenth-century streets, old sea captains' houses, a celebrated doll's-house, and the world's largest collection of ships in bottles.

Another ferry takes us to Als, and a bridge across Als Sound to Dybbøl, renowned for resistance to a different kind of German invasion. We are on the very edge of Denmark here, with Flensburg only thirty miles away across the fiord. But for most of recorded history the rule of the Danish throne, if not of Denmark, stretched into the duchies of Schleswig and Holstein, to the gates of Hamburg and Lübeck. The Schleswig-Holstein issue exercised and confused the chancelleries of Europe for the first half of the nineteenth century; in 1849 Denmark emerged victorious from a messy war over the duchies; in 1864, in the first of his wars to impose Germany on Europe, Bismarck set about uniting them with Germany. By February 1864 Prussian and Austrian armies were in Holstein; by the early spring they were entering Jutland. The outnumbered Danes withdrew into the Dybbøl peninsula, with their backs to Als Sound and with the navy doing its best to support their flanks.

Dybbøl marks the last memorable Danish feat of arms. The Danes dug into fortifications across the peninsula around Dybbøl mill; the Germans brought up heavy artillery to pound them. Some shells fell across the sound in Sønderborg, but the principal targets were military ones. It was a clean little siege of the weak by the strong, and on 18 April the Germans had a victory to celebrate. For the Prussians it was the first of a series that was to lead by way of Sadowa and Sedan to the power of a greater Germany united around Berlin. For the Austrians it was a last and unsatisfactory victory, followed within two years by their defeat at the hands of the Prussians. As for the Danes, Dybbøl taught them a lesson they did not forget: Denmark could not hope to fight her enemies successfully and must instead turn her attention to economic recovery and to the wiles of diplomacy.

Jutland is large by Danish standards, 200 miles long from the German border to its tip at Skagen. Its length, aided and abetted by the Danish islands, almost closes the mouth of the Baltic.

The voyage round Jutland frightened early travellers, who often transported their goods across its narrow neck in Schleswig instead. By the thirteenth century Flemish and Dutch merchants knew their way round Jutland, though they still feared its coasts. Its north-west face in particular remained a maritime graveyard well into modern times, and in 1801 European history came close to taking a different turn when Hyde Parker's squadron nearly ran onto its long wild coast on its way to Copenhagen. But the west coast and the interior of Jutland are only indirectly relevant to the Baltic, and in going north from Dybbøl we cling to Jutland's eastern, deeply indented shore.

Åbenrå is the first stop, a generally unremarkable town on its own small fiord. Å – the letter A topped by a circle – is the last letter in the Danish alphabet; but the townspeople tell you that if you spell the name foreign style – Aabenraa – it enjoys first place in most gazetteers. That fact, with its organ factory and the way it accommodates its German-speaking minority, is Åbenrå's main claim to fame. Haderslev further north has its own fiord, a thirteenth-century cathedral and an old main street which is precipitous by Danish standards. Kolding, again north, and again on a fiord, has the remains of a castle: remains only, because in the winter of 1807–8 the Spaniards burnt it down before their epic voyage back to Bilbao – whether by accident, out of malice, or in an attempt to kindle some Mediterranean warmth in chilly Denmark no one knows for sure.

Just west of Kolding is one of the most surprising buildings in Scandinavia. Its story starts as a wood-preservatives plant. It is, appropriately, built of wood, and is the largest wooden building in Denmark. The company's logo is adapted from the Chinese ideogram for wood. Its owners, GORI, practise a complex management philosophy, with elaborate arrangements for all employees to participate. Equality goes without saying: the building has one entrance, one canteen, and one cloakroom.

GORI's entrance opens into a vast and integrated single space under a curving roof. To the right, on the ground floor and on a broad open terrace at first-floor height, is the open-plan administrative area. In the middle is reception, with a canteen beneath a huge window beyond. To the left are ping-pong tables, with a dramatic display of modern art behind them, a vivid concoction of shapes and colours. Examined, the modern art reveals itself as machinery, each drum or pipe picked out in vividly contrasting colours. Around it, as functional as the machinery but as unstated as it is highlighted, stretch laboratories, warehousing, library, files. More confidently than Maersk, more dramatically than Denmark's hospitals or old people's homes, GORI demonstrates the particular Danish skill of reflecting in architecture and design the laid-back, egalitarian competence of the best aspects of Danish life.

All the fiords we have passed between Dybbøl and Kolding open into the Little Belt that separates Fyn from Jutland, and provides, with the Sound and the Great Belt, a third entrance into the Baltic. But unlike them, the Little Belt has had its bridges for decades. They span the narrows between Middelfart and Fredericia, and to all intents and purposes they make Fyn a part of Jutland. But it is worth turning aside and taking the motorway over the bridge because Fyn, the garden of Denmark, plays its part in the story of the Baltic.

Fyn is what many Danes would like all Denmark to be. To some, Jutland is go-ahead but aggressive, successful but bleak, and disrespectful of the intimacy which the Danes value so highly. To others, Sjaelland is overwhelmed by Copenhagen, itself overwhelmed by government, the public sector and welfare layabouts; they despise Sjaelland as the place that spends what Jutland earns. To all Danes the small islands are precious, an epitome of old-fashioned Danishness; but they are impractical, too – Aerø, Anholt, Samsø offer refreshment of the spirit but cannot provide a living. But Fyn, bang in the middle of Denmark, provides a golden mean. Thousand-year-old Odense is Hans Andersen's birth place and a centre of efficient ship-building. Svendborg is the birthplace not only of that most Danish of companies, Maersk, but of Elvira Madigan. Horne has a church-cum-fortress, like the round churches of Bornholm. Careful agriculture and quiet corners and manor houses abound. Fyn, like the Baltic Sea, is worth examination.

We double back to Jutland, and its succession of towns and vistas across fiords. Fredericia looks out at Fyn across the narrows of the Little Belt; it has a planned, slightly Latin air about it. Close to Vejle, old and beautifully situated, you can find the epitome of modern Denmark in the model city of Legoland, and the essence of old Denmark in King Gorm's runic stone outside the church at Jelling, which marks the very moment of transition from the old Viking world to Christianity, 1,000 years before Legoland came to delight today's children up the road.

By comparison, Århus is a big city, the second in Denmark. The guidebooks direct you to the cathedral, the collection of historic houses brought together from all over Jutland in the Old Town, and the remains of a 2,000-year-old man from a bog. In its way, the City Hall is more remarkable than any of these antiquities, its quality recalling the City Hall in Stockholm, its design the work of Erik Møller and Arne Jacobsen. To an outsider, its date of completion is remarkable too. In 1942, as the Russians and Germans tore each other apart and the British and Americans planned a second front, as the RAF rained bombs on Berlin, and Danish resistance to the Germans gathered strength, the burghers of Århus completed, in all its splendour of brick and glass and murals, their City Hall. For better and for worse, the story says much about the Danes.

Ålborg thinks of itself as Århus's rival for the affections of Jutland. To me it seems, despite its old streets, its castle and its aquavit, a bleak place, exposed to all the winds that blow. Ålborg stands beside the Limfiord which, unlike the other fiords of Jutland, cuts right across the peninsula to the North Sea, a conduit for winds from the west and winds from the east to chill Ålborgers to the bone. Technically, everything north of the Limfiord is an island. The Vendsyssel, the northernmost part of Jutland from which the Vandals are said to have set out on the long marches that eventually led them to Rome, has all the grim provincialism of Denmark's more pessimistic films. It also has the superb beaches of its north-western coast, 120 miles of sand and wind; Frederikshavn, ferry port and naval base; and the old fishing village of Skagen.

We started our excursions at the beginning of this book at the Skaw, where the Skaggerak and the Kattegat, the North Sea and the Baltic meet. Skagen lies five miles back from the tip of the Skaw. Fishermen know it for its fishing port, the second busiest in Denmark. Its beaches attract tourists: although Skagen is the most northerly place in Denmark it enjoys more sunshine than anywhere else in the country. To build a holiday home among its dunes is a sign that you have arrived. But above all it attracts painters, as it has done for more than a century.

From the first, Skagen offered its artists cheap living, seclusion from the world in the cheerful company of their peers, and an extraordinary light. You can find wonderful light all over the Baltic: clear as gin in Bornholm, grey with foreboding over the mouth of the Vistula, ice cold and harsh in the Gulf of Bothnia. No words can describe Skagen's light and only a few painters have captured it. Some attribute it to the ubiquitous sea, which laps at Skagen's back door as much as its front, the more dominant because the land here scarcely rises above sea level. Others talk more ambitiously of a microclimate created by the mountains of Scandinavia which curve invisibly but protectively round Skagen. Whatever its cause, the Skagen painters set up their easels, put the light to work, and so put Skagen on the map.

The first painter to have worked at Skagen was Martin Rørbye. Alone among the painters of Denmark's Golden Age, he tried to capture that special quality of Jutland to be found in its bleak wilderness of heath, sand and sea. His contemporaries criticised him for this preoccupation with naked nature, and at the end of his life he too seems to have hankered after something tamer, more populated. His last letter to his wife, written on his way home from Skagen in 1848, complains that there are not many people to be found in northern Jutland to set beside the splendour of the sea.

The painters who formed the Skagen school began to make their way there thirty years later, tentatively at first, by boat from Ålborg or Copenhagen, or by horse and cart across the sandy heath from

Hjørring. You can still find painters at work around Skagen today, and the school persisted into the 1930s. But the finest Skagen vintages were laid down in the years before and around the turn of the century, by artists such as Michael Ancher and his Skagen-born wife, Anna Brøndum, who taught herself to paint and became Denmark's finest woman painter, Carl Locher and Karl Madsen, Christian Krohg and Laurits Tuxen. Perhaps the greatest of them was P. S. Krøyer, whose wife, too, made something of an artistic name for herself. They painted seascapes, fishermen on the beach, weddings and christenings, and domestic interiors lit by sunlight or candlelight.

Ancher and Krøyer each made memorable paintings of their wives upon the beach, which you find in every compilation of Scandinavian art. Ancher painted the two women strolling together, their white dresses trailing on the grey-blue sand, against the pallor of the sea. Krøyer painted his wife in the same white dress, with a pale yellow sash and a yellow-trimmed hat. He included himself in the picture, artistically modish in white hat, white shirt and white jacket, and plus-fours. He holds her arm, as if to engage her attention, but there is a sense of distance between them; he seems closer to his dog, which sniffs around his feet.

In all his work, Krøyer shows technical facility and an enormous capacity to charm, perhaps most completely in his picture of a sun-dappled outdoor lunch party, *Hip, Hip, Hurrah*. Women and a child are seated round the table in the foreground; behind them the men are standing, glasses raised, exalted. But there is something deeply poignant about his vast painting of the bonfire party on Skagen beach on Midsummer's Eve in 1906. It depicts forty people, a good cross-section of the artistic community of Skagen, gathered round a bonfire. A semicircle of children face the blaze in the foreground; a patriarchal figure tends the flames and another faces him across the fire; Krøyer himself stands sketching on the right. Between the bonfire and the sea are another couple, absorbed less in the occasion than in each other. One is Krøyer's wife, Marie, the other a Swedish admirer with whom she eloped a year later, scandalising the Skagen community and all Denmark in the process.

Here ends our tour of Denmark. By most measures hers is perhaps the Baltic's most successful society, at ease with herself and with her neighbours, prosperous yet caring, efficient yet easy-going, with a talent for laughing at herself. But it has to be said that, by comparison with the rest of the Baltic, she lacks mystery. If it were not for the sea around her, you could even call her dull.

Almost everywhere you go in Denmark the sea brings movement and life to offset torpor and tranquillity. Nowhere in the whole country is more than forty miles from one marine indentation or another. Hundreds of thousands of Danes have summer cottages by the sea, or on favourite, hide-away islands. Tens of thousands more have yachts or motor-boats or fishing dinghies. For two months in the summer the sea dominates their lives. It is equally part of everyday life. You cannot travel far in Denmark without crossing water: a sales convention, a business meeting, a trip home to grandmother, all these are as likely to involve a ferry trip as a flight.

Danes everywhere look out to sea from their homes and offices. In the suburbs on the coast road north of Copenhagen, for example, thousands of houses and apartments have views over the Sound: of the sea itself, blue, grey or ice-bound by the season; of ships constantly passing on their way to and from the Kronborg narrows; of Tycho Brahe's island of Ven in the middle of the fairway; of the coast of Sweden beyond, often detached from the surface of the sea by a belt of fine mist, with the nuclear power station at Barsebäck levitating above it. Århus is the same, with long views across the bay towards Ebeltoft. So are innumerable lesser towns and villages all over Denmark. It was the struggle to control the entrance to the Baltic that made Denmark a nation, and the sea pervades every aspect of Danish life.

15
Schleswig-Holstein

The end of our journey has brought us back to the country in which we began. By her size and importance Germany, like Russia, earns her two chapters. She matters to the Baltic. For better or for worse, Germany and Russia are likely to dominate the region's politics, and more than any of the other countries we have visited they are likely to shape its future. And the Baltic matters to Germany, though not with the intense importance it has for some of her neighbours, for whom it is all in all.

But just as St Petersburg and Kaliningrad are both Russian yet totally different from one another, so in a way Schleswig-Holstein represents another country than the one we left behind when we crossed the Polish frontier. It may be one of the poorest of the *Länder* of the old Federal Republic, and the making of a unified Germany is well in hand in Mecklenburg and Pomerania. But Schleswig-Holstein still has a huge lead over Mecklenburg, and there is at least a decade to go before the two Germanies feel like one Germany again. In a sense there are still two states within the German nation.

Although Schleswig-Holstein has been a *Land* of the Federal Republic since its formation, it is not entirely typical of it. It has a semi-detached air about it: indisputably German, yet something else too, and German with a difference. A respectable motorway runs most of the length of Danish Jutland, and at the German border it develops all the virtues and vices of a full-blown autobahn. This change of style and of pace is the first sign of transition from Scandinavian to continental Europe. But in other respects change comes more gradually. It is over 100 miles from the border to Hamburg, and it is only there, as you approach the Elbe, that you fully encounter the German giant that sprawls so powerfully across central Europe. Until you reach Hamburg, you are in country that has been German since 1864 yet is still redolent of the north, of Scandinavia and the Baltic and of connections with the Danish monarchy going back 1,000 years.

If Schleswig-Holstein is different from the rest of Germany, it is different too from the rest of the Baltic. It is richer and more complex than Danish Jutland. Manifestly different from the eastern Baltic, it embraces a variety of characteristics of its own. Its North Sea coast is an empty desolation of wind, huge skies and salt marsh, which the painter Emil Nolde celebrated in ecstatic explosions of colour and light. Along its southern border the Elbe rolls majestically from Lauenburg to the sea. The Baltic coast is pierced by long and kindly fiords whose mouths face north towards Denmark, and punctuated by brassy bathing resorts facing south across Lübeck Bay. Schleswig-Holstein is a land of cattle pastures and woods, surprising lakes and sudden hills, and scattered outcrops of industry around quiet country towns. The countryside seems to offer pastoral simplicity, removed from change and economics and politics alike.

And yet Schleswig-Holstein used to be notorious for its Question, which puzzled all Europe during the nineteenth century and became a synonym for the incomprehensible and the insoluble. Its essentials, however, were simple. Throughout most of recorded history, Danes and Germans lived together in the area which we now call Schleswig and south Jutland, the proportions between them varying over time and by districts. Holstein by contrast, south and east of Schleswig, was almost exclusively German. Gradually the medieval nobility of Holstein fought and bought their way into property and power in Schleswig, which came to be regarded as dependent on Holstein. So far, so simple. Then, in the fifteenth century, the German nobility of Schleswig-Holstein agreed to subordinate themselves to the king of Denmark. Their condition was that German Holstein and predominantly Danish Schleswig should be linked in indissoluble union.

It was an arrangement that endured for more than 300 years, until Napoleon kindled throughout Europe a new sense of national identity. Nineteenth-century passion drove out eighteenth-century balance. The Germans of Holstein demanded a political expression of their German identity. So did the German minority in Schleswig. Their dukes, however, were kings of Denmark, and the Danes of Schleswig looked to Denmark for protection. Partition should have been the answer, dissolving Schleswig-Holstein and its Question, but the old commitment to union stood in its way.

The parties took up arms. The war of 1848–50 raged all over

Schleswig and as far north as Fredericia in Jutland. Eventually the Danes emerged victorious, and cocky in consequence. They over-reached themselves, and in 1864 Bismarck led the Prussians and Austrians into the brutal return match. The Danes were defeated. Denmark, licking her wounds, set herself to make good in Jutland what she had lost in Schleswig-Holstein, and the duchies of Schleswig, Holstein and Lauenburg joined the German Confederation. Bismarck had shown Europe how diplomacy and force could harness popular emotion to create a new European power.

We visited Dybbøl, where the Danes made their stand in 1864, in the last chapter, and you can find traces of old wars between Danes and Germans all over Jutland. But there are relics in Schleswig-Holstein also. The most important is the Danevirke, the fortified line which stretches across the isthmus from the head of Schleswig Fiord to the North Sea at Husum. Its origins are lost in early history, when pre-Viking Danish rulers established it to check the expansion northwards of the German tribes. Valdemar the Great, the twelfth-century Danish king who conquered Estonia, reinforced what had been an earthwork with brick fortresses. Over the centuries it marked some kind of division, if not always a defended line, between the Teutons and the Danes. As such it acquired a symbolic significance, increasingly at odds with its declining military importance.

When the nineteenth-century troubles over Schleswig-Holstein arose, the Danes pinned their hopes on the Danevirke. They lost it when the Schleswig-Holstein insurgents rose up in 1848. They captured it triumphantly when the Danish army marched south. They lost it again when the German Confederation came to the support of the insurgents. They were re-established in possession when, by the Treaty of Berlin in 1850, the European powers forced Prussia to withdraw from Schleswig-Holstein. And they thought they could hold it when Prussia and Austria came looking for a German revenge in January 1864.

But like the Maginot Line, the Danevirke was never securely anchored on the coast. German troops crossed frozen marshes and fiords on the flanks of the Danevirke and drove the Danish army north into Jutland. It was a campaign overshadowed by the infinitely greater campaigns of the Union armies as they moved into the American south. But it gave the Germans a taste for empire which in the end made perhaps as great an impact on the world as Lincoln's success in saving the American Union.

In a sense, the making of modern Germany started in Schleswig-Holstein. There Bismarck gave expression for the first time to a new sense of national identity and forged his own determination to create an imperial Germany with the kingdom of Prussia at its heart. He used diplomacy and arms to exploit sentiment and emotion; and his diplomatic and military success fed that sentiment and emotion. Victory over the Danes pointed the way ineluctably to victory over the Austrians and then the French. Three wars in six years created the German Empire. They created also a German dynamism in Bismarck's image which led eventually to self-destruction.

So the seeds of German defeat in 1918, just as much as of German victory in 1866 and 1870, were planted in the war over Schleswig-Holstein. It also marked the birth of a new brutality. In 1864, few of Europe's statesmen sympathised with the Prince of Wales's Danish wife, Alexandra, when she turned her back on Germany for good, and at least half Europe thought the Prussians were in the right when they later fought the Austrians and the French. But with hindsight one can see in photographs of victorious Germans posturing among the wreckage round the mill at Dybbøl a first illustration of a German frightfulness that stamps its way through European history for nearly a century thereafter. Schleswig-Holstein was the birthplace not only of German might but of Europe's wariness of it.

The Danes limped wearily home after their defeat and as we have seen they turned away from arms to other means of national fulfilment. They had learned the wisdom of the weak. They devoted themselves to economic progress, domestic issues, the concern for education and social well-being which still permeates their society. After 1864 Germany imposed conditions on the Danish minority in Schleswig which seemed harsh by the standards of the time and place. Policy required that Danish-speakers should be turned into dutiful German citizens; and their German neighbours were high-handed in the intoxication of victory. There was discrimination against the Danish language, against trade with Denmark, against anything that detracted from the German identity of the two duchies; and for young men who still thought of themselves as Danes there was the indignity of service as German soldiers in German wars.

Half a century later, Germany's defeat in 1918 led inevitably to a review of her frontiers in the north, as in the east and in Alsace-Lorraine. The result, after a plebiscite, was an adjustment in

Denmark's favour. On 10 July 1920 King Christian X rode his white horse across the old border, and north Schleswig (or south Jutland depending on your terminological preference) was incorporated into Denmark. The Danes could have asked for more. The 1920 adjustment transferred from Germany to Denmark only a belt of land between the North Sea and the Baltic in which Danes predominated. The great bulk of Schleswig-Holstein was by now manifestly German, but the Danish kings could have laid some colourable claim to it. Instead, Denmark wisely let it be.

The Danes faced the same temptation in 1945. This time they had suffered under the Germans as they had not in 1914-18, and there was talk of taking compensation in the old Danish possessions of Schleswig-Holstein. Again wisdom prevailed. The Danes left Schleswig unquestioned, to become with Holstein a German *Land* within the Federal Republic. Now Danish-speakers are accommodated within Schleswig-Holstein, just as German-speakers are accommodated across the border in southern Jutland. If there are resentments about language or nationhood on either side of the frontier today, they are no more than the quirks of individuals. The most the people of Jutland and Schleswig can find to quarrel about are those Danish pensioners who go frontier-hopping in search of cheaper groceries, or the German supermarkets near the border which exploit the Danish appetite for lower rates of VAT.

This domestication of old differences is commonplace in western Europe, as a day's shopping trip to Calais will testify. It is not yet so around the Baltic. We have seen Russian troops stranded in what was once German Königsberg; the tensions between Poland and Lithuania; problems over Russians in Estonia and Latvia; enduring resentment of Swedes in Finland. The Germans of Schleswig-Holstein could do worse than to get together with the Danes to show their Baltic neighbours how time and good sense have changed a Question without an answer into an Answer to other people's questions.

Flensburg is the most northerly city in Germany, and the border with Denmark runs down the middle of its fiord, a great sweep of water leading towards the southern Danish islands. Like so many Baltic waters it is an enchanting sailing area, as much so today as when the crew of Erskine Childers's *Dulcinella* started their cruise here, exploring northwards from Flensburg Fiord and up into the Sound of Als, before duty called them through the Kiel Canal to the wilder seas of the Heligoland Bight, eventually to arrive at the solution of the riddle of the sands.

Schleswig is the next town south from Flensburg. It stands at the head of the Schlei, a fiord twenty miles long which cuts almost half way across the Schleswig isthmus. The Vikings developed Hedeby, or Haithabu, at the head of the Schlei, as an entrepôt on the Baltic for goods shipped overland from the North Sea coast. But at Gottorf Castle, just outside Schleswig, you can see a seventy-foot merchantman half a millennium earlier than the Viking Age, testimony to the trade the Schlei has seen since before recorded history. The fact is that, at this narrowest point of the isthmus, the city of Schleswig stands at a natural centre of east-west and north-south movement, which the Danevirke, stretching away to the west, attempted to control.

Ten miles overland south-east from Schleswig, and four times that distance round the coast, lies Eckernförde, where at the end of the Danish-German war in 1850 an inventive corporal of German coastal artillery put Leonardo da Vinci's idea of a submersible warship to tentative military use. And ten miles beyond Eckernförde is Kiel, where the Kiel Canal empties into the Baltic. It is a matter of record that the canal is the world's busiest shipping lane, but when I was there constant observation of the watercourse during an idle two-hour picnic revealed only one tramp steamer, one coaster and six pleasure boats passing by.

The construction of the Kiel Canal was, all the same, a significant event in the history and geography of the Baltic. Man has always sought to sail from the North Sea to the Baltic, but he used to be deterred by the dangers of the voyage round the Skaw. Hence the overland route to Hedeby, and hence early attempts to link rivers and estuaries across the Schleswig isthmus. Gradually, more confident navigation and seamanship led to fuller use of the route round the Skaw, but dreams of a short cut persisted, and indeed, in the eighteenth century a modest canal was dug across the isthmus from the Eider river to Kiel Fiord.

Nineteenth-century commerce demanded something bigger, and the rise of imperial Germany brought political and naval considerations into play. Germany had interests in the North Sea – the German Ocean. She also had interests in the Baltic. Her growing navy was split in two by the Danish narrows, which might well be closed to the German fleet in wartime. A canal would give Germany flexibility, break the Danish stranglehold on the Baltic approaches, and further strengthen German pre-eminence in the Baltic.

So the great canal was carved across Schleswig, not on the shortest line, due west from Kiel, but south-west, to the mouth of the Elbe at Brunsbüttel, where canal traffic out of the Baltic meets river traffic from eastern Germany and Bohemia. It was first opened in the summer of 1895, when Gladstone was shocked by the naval pomp attached to what he had been assured would be a purely commercial undertaking. The canal created a fourth and purely German entrance to the Baltic to put beside the Danish Belts and the Sound between Denmark and Sweden. Traffic, and the size of the ships of the Imperial Navy, grew rapidly. A broader artery was needed, and in June 1914 an enlarged Kiel Canal was opened to shipping. The Kaiser was present and the Imperial Navy dominated the celebrations, but ships from all Europe's navies gathered for what was the last international naval occasion of the long peace.

Perhaps completion of the enlargement of the canal marked the final stage in Germany's preparations for hostilities. War broke out within six weeks, and with it came a renewed strategic significance for the Baltic. At the Admiralty, Churchill played with ideas of seizing a German North Sea island and using it as a base from which to force an entry through Danish waters into the Baltic. Established there, he imagined, the Royal Navy could link hands with Russia and land the tsar's armies on the north German coast within 100 miles of Berlin. These ideas remained fantasies, and only a few submarines of the Royal Navy slipped into the Baltic to harry German shipping, dangerously rebounding off the bottom if they dived too swiftly. For the Germans, the Kiel Canal served its intended purpose of strengthening Germany's naval grip upon the Baltic and her own north-west coast alike.

There is no pomp or warlike circumstance manifest about the canal today, but it still runs for sixty miles through the Schleswig countryside, perhaps at its most dramatic at Rendsburg in the middle of the isthmus. It is a great engineering achievement, an artery of commerce and a monument to German imperial and economic ambition; but, in my observation at least, strangely bereft of shipping.

The city of Kiel has none of the charms of Flensburg and Schleswig. It is a bustling modern town, and wartime bombing destroyed any last traces of its Hansa origins. But in this century it has had its moments of drama and significance. It was one of the last German cities to fall to the allies after Hitler's suicide. The sailors' mutiny there twenty-seven years earlier led to Germany's November revolution. Now it is a major Baltic port, the terminus of the canal, a ferry terminal, a ship-building city, the seat of a university and an economic institute, a naval base and a haunt of German yachtsmen.

Beyond Kiel a north-facing coast runs away to the east towards Fehmarn. Inland lie the little lakes and dark woods of an area the Germans call Holstein's Switzerland. These are places for quiet, away-from-it-all holidays, quite unlike the resorts a few miles further east that face onto Lübeck bay. They march north from Travemünde, where elegant hotels and bathing beauties compete for attention with yachts and windsurfers and ferries, all the way to Timmendorfer Strand and Gromitz. Each of these places in its different way offers value to its visitors: groomed beaches and sunshine in season, hotels and restaurants and holiday apartments. In summer they overflow with evidence of German prosperity. These holidaymakers could be in Spain or on the Croatian Adriatic. They choose the Baltic instead and, in the right season and with a little bit of luck, it delivers them the joys they seek.

All round the Baltic we have seen holidaymakers seeking similar pleasures. Some of the islands – Fehmarn, Gotland, Bornholm – are packed with them. So are the beaches east of Swinoujisce and at Sopot. Other places offer quieter, less crowded amusement. But growing prosperity is bound to bring them more visitors, looking for more sophisticated pleasures, turning Warnemünde and Sopot into new, glossy, fashionable Travemündes. Perhaps in the end it will be holidaymakers who unite the Baltic, something that the politicians have so far failed to achieve. But they will overwhelm what is left of its intimate charm and the various characters of the countries which surround it. If on a July morning you stand on Timmendorfer Strand, admirable as it is in its own way, you know why the Danes so persistently seek to check the tide of foreigners who threaten to inundate their beaches and fishing villages.

Schleswig-Holstein is not just a land of bathing beaches and rumina-tive cows. It links western Europe to northern Europe, and it controls overland access to Denmark. At the beginning of our journey we saw Churchill send British troops racing to capture Lübeck ahead of the

Red Army to secure the 'land-gate of Denmark'. For almost half a century thereafter it remained the key to the control of the mouth of the Baltic. During all those years, until the threat from the East gradually vanished into the morass of Soviet collapse, NATO nurtured painstaking plans to ensure that Denmark's land-gate would remain firmly closed.

Three major units were to hold it in the event of Armageddon. The Sixth Panzer Grenadier Division, one of the German army's most formidable formations, was to guard Hamburg. The main strength of the Danish army, the Jutland Division, was to march south and block the road into Denmark. But it is forty miles from the Elbe to the Baltic, a forty-mile front to be held against an attack from the east. More troops were needed, and for more than twenty years a third unit, the United Kingdom Mobile Force, exercised in Holstein against the possibility of a Soviet assault.

The Mobile Force was a paradoxical organisation. It was structured round an infantry brigade, but it had almost the fighting strength of a division. It was called mobile, but its role was a static one: to hold land and block an attack by mobile aggressors. It was a fire-fighting force, but seventy-five per cent of the men of its essential support units were reservists. It was based in Wiltshire, to give Britain a home-based capacity to deploy troops to meet varied emergencies, and yet it was a key element in NATO's plans to defend the Baltic approaches.

Yet to the end NATO was uncertain where it would deploy the Mobile Force if it came to war: here in Holstein, or in Danish Sjaelland in defence of Copenhagen. All the same, every four years the Mobile Force, with its 15,000 troops and innumerable vehicles, its squadron of tanks and artillery batteries and its ubiquitous helicopters, hunkered down in the Holstein woods and meadows south of Lübeck and practised war. The incongruities were striking, as these strange fighting men descended on unfamiliar country so far from home and from the rest of the British Army in Lower Saxony. But only a few miles away stood the line of East German watchtowers to emphasise the threat. Now they are gone, and it is hard to conceive of circumstances that might ever again bring British soldiers yomping through Holstein.

The Mobile Force used to practise its deployment between the lines of two canals. We have seen the Kiel Canal already, a formidable defensive line if the Mobile Force and its allies were driven out of Holstein. The other is the Elbe-Baltic Canal, an insignificant waterway with a famous history, that potters its way from Lauenburg on the Elbe to Lübeck on the Trave. In its time it has carried salt from Lüneburg to cure Scandinavian herring, and goods from Saxony for the Hansa to sell all over the Baltic. Now it caters only for tourist trips on narrow-boats, offering coffee and cake on gentle Sunday afternoon outings through the Holstein countryside.

The Elbe-Baltic Canal runs roughly parallel with the old East German border. In places, indeed, it formed the border itself. But south of Lübeck the line of the border swerved eastwards, where the old Duchy of Lauenburg was grafted onto Schleswig-Holstein. In it lie a few square miles of woods and pasture and the picturesque little towns of Ratzeburg and Mölln. What was always a tranquil corner became even quieter when the Iron Curtain shut it off from everything to the east.

Ratzeburg stands proudly on an island in a lake, dominated by a twelfth-century cathedral. An exhibition of the work of Ernst Barlach, sculptor and draughtsman of tranquil expressionist figures, provides a cultural interlude in this quiet little haven. Mölln down the road has a less spectacular setting, but it has its brick medieval church, and the tombstone of that quintessentially benevolent German hero, Till Eugenspiegel.

In 1992 Mölln erupted into political prominence as the idyllic little town in which neo-Nazi terrorists torched a Turkish family to death. The incident frightened all Germany and set alarm bells ringing throughout Europe. It made a much greater impact than the anti-foreigner riots in Rostock earlier in the year. For Rostock was an industrial ruin of the old East Germany, where desperation seemed understandable and violence almost to be expected. Murder in a prosperous little country town of the old Federal Republic seemed something else, and much more to be feared, a reminder of the old Teutonic Adam who too readily turned on strangers when times were bad, finding psychic reassurance in violence.

The commentators made too much of an isolated act of mindlessness, but they also made too much of the guileless innocence to be expected of a simple country town like Mölln. For Schleswig-Holstein has its shadow side, inseparable from its pastoral background and its honest Protestantism. It was Schleswig-Holstein and the rural north which swung most decisively towards the Nazis in the

1930 elections, giving Hitler the breakthrough he had been seeking in vain for ten years. Two years later, in the July 1932 elections, Schleswig-Holstein gave the Nazi Party more than fifty per cent of its votes. And it was not just ordinary farmers who put their faith in Hitler: Schleswig-Holstein's most famous artist, Emil Nolde, who was later persecuted by the Nazis when they decided that his art was decadent, was initially a National Socialist, impressed by the party's commitment to Nordic values and ethnic purity.

The fact is that rural communities as much as city-dwellers can cherish frightening political ideas; and in times of crisis it is not just the troubled, tempestuous cities but idyllic rural places like Mölln – blinkered and suspicious of outsiders – that seek simple answers to complicated questions and take refuge from doubt in racial pride and xenophobia. Schleswig-Holstein's response to Hitler, so different from that of nearby Hamburg, illustrates the point. And you do not have to be a foreigner to encounter hatreds in such places. When Hitler's chickens came home to roost and Holstein was inundated with German refugees from the east, the Holsteiners once again showed their limitations. I asked a woman who grew up in Holstein how they treated fellow Germans in their time of trouble. 'Like enemies,' she replied.

Such limitations have nothing specifically German about them. You can find their like elsewhere around the Baltic and for that matter anywhere around the globe. The difference is that, fifty years after the end of the Second World War, Germany's Baltic neighbours still look askance at the Germans.

Most Germans perceive no justice in such attitudes. Few share Günter Grass's suspicions of their country. They have worked their passage back to respectability, established their democratic credentials, done right by their western neighbours in the European Union. Now they are doing right by their neighbours to the east, pouring wealth far beyond others' contributions into efforts to help the former Communist countries build free and prosperous societies. In any case, why look only at Germany's record of wrongdoing ? What about Russia's? Quite as bad in the bad times, and sustained for so much longer.

Of course the Baltic countries remember Russia's record, and fear the Russians with an intensity that no one feels towards Germany today. Poland, the Baltic states and the Scandinavian countries have a deep dread of Russia and the dark forces that could emerge there. They seek safety in the European Union and western connections, and see Germany as central to that salvation. If alongside this fear of Russia there also lies a residual animus towards Germany, it is no more than a reflection of the particular horrors of Germany's modern history and of her massive strength today.

Now that Germany is reunited, no other country around the Baltic except troubled and distracted Russia can bring to the region more than a fraction of Germany's political and economic weight. Nowhere else can promise as much as the eastern *Länder*, as German resources flow into them and the Germans of the east begin to recover the Teutonic dynamism which is their heritage. More than any other Baltic people, the Germans shaped its medieval history. Throughout the modern period they have been among the most powerful influences there, and in the twentieth century they have twice dominated the Baltic in war. The record, like all historical records, is a mixed one: if Germans brought trade and Christianity and civilisation to the Baltic in the Middle Ages, they also brought exploitation, slavery, war and genocide. Now, with Russia temporarily broken, Germany has a freedom of action around the Baltic which eclipses that of any of her neighbours.

For the time being she is using that freedom benevolently. Schleswig-Holstein's lead in promoting a new awareness of the Baltic world has the weight of the German Government behind it. With Denmark, Germany proposed and helped to create the Council of Baltic Sea States, to give the emancipated countries of the Baltic a common forum. Nordic membership of the European Union serves German interests. So will Polish membership and eventually that of the three Baltic states. The Partnership for Peace extends at least part of NATO's protection eastward and northward. And Germany lavishes bilateral assistance and investment on her eastern neighbours. At the same time, Germany recognises the need to calm Russian fears: over Kaliningrad, over Russia's exclusion from the European Union, and over the advance of NATO up the Baltic towards St Petersburg. All over the Baltic German ministers and diplomats and businessmen spread the balm of reasonableness and reassurance.

Yet doubts persist. Her Baltic neighbours' fear of Germany arises not only from the enormity of historic German crimes but from an acute awareness of disproportion. Throughout the north, the

German giant is flanked by relative pygmies. This disproportion is political and economic; military and diplomatic. Germany's neighbours need her far more than Germany needs them. Only Russia has a potential to compare with hers. But for a decade at least Russia will be weak, more eager to engage Germany's interest and assistance than to keep her in check.

In these dilemmas Germany holds most of the cards: economic strength, a central position in the European Union and NATO, and a hard-earned reputation for political rectitude. Other countries may be suspicious of her, but they hold her in genuine respect and need her help. Germany can bring benefits to Scandinavia, to Poland, to the eastern Baltic and to Russia herself. United Germany turns a 250-mile face to the Baltic. She looks north towards a friendship of equals in Scandinavia, and east, rather more patronisingly, towards Poland, the Baltic states and Russia. Her interest lies in helping to build a prosperous, peaceful and co-operative Baltic world. Her problem is to do so without seeming to overwhelm her neighbours.

16

Prospects

Most of the people of the Baltic look to the future with more confidence today than at any time in the last sixty years. They acknowledge the region's economic woes, political uncertainties and environmental problems. But in most Baltic cities, optimists outnumber pes-
simists. Kaliningrad is the great exception, and with good reason. St
Petersburg is another, though even here you can find, amid all its
crime, corruption and poverty, citizens who cherish touching hopes
of a glad, confident morning again. Elsewhere, optimism prevails in
varying degrees, from the cautious to the euphoric. The peoples of
the Baltic acknowledge that the basic political and social facts that
shape their lives have changed spectacularly for the better in the
last decade. Change has brought problems with it, but beneath their
everyday complaints runs a current of rejoicing at the chance to be
themselves and to express themselves as free citizens. They welcome
the opportunity to deal with one another as fellow Baltic peoples,
their region no longer cut in two by the stern demands of security and
ideology.

We have seen how geography and history have shaped the present
political and economic life of the Baltic. They may also help define its
prospects. Neither pessimism nor euphoria can ignore the facts that
will shape the future of the Baltic; the weightiest among them are
Russia and the European Union.

As this book goes to press, the Russian people go to the polls.
They have had a bruising recent experience of democracy, and not a
single candidate on their ballot papers brings ready reassurance. But
whomever the Russians elect as their leader, whether they vote for
chaotic freedom or the old communist familiarity, for the market or
socialist allocation of resources, there will remain two fundamental
questions about their country's future.

The first concerns Russia's political, economic and social
prospects. On the one hand, if her people have the will to put them to
use, they have the courage, skills and patriotism to make her a free,

proud, prosperous nation. She has the continental space, raw materials, science and education to achieve in the twenty-first century what the United States achieved in the twentieth. Russia could be the world's next great economic miracle. On the other hand, she is sunk in sloth, crime, corruption and despair. She could go the way so much of the Third World went at independence, to depths from which countries like Bangladesh and the Philippines are only now beginning to emerge.

The second question concerns the face that Russia will present to her neighbours and the world. It is an important question even if Russia remains weak, and a critical one if, by whatever route, she finds her way back to effective international power. She may continue on the course of international co-operation on which Gorbachev set her and which Boris Yeltsin has followed. This would engage her in good-neighbourly relations with all her Baltic partners. Or she may seek solace for the humiliations of recent years, using self-assertion to recover psychic reassurance. On this route, she would put new pressures on Latvia and Estonia over their Russian minorities and on Lithuania and Poland over access to Kaliningrad; renew the old demands that Finland should match her step to her giant neighbour's; and make even more resolute attempts to block the advance of NATO up the Baltic.

I have no sure answers to either of these questions, but on both I come down, on balance and in time, among the optimists. Russia is not about to put the travails of transition behind her. Her people may well vote for the reassurance which they think a leader of the old Communist school can bring them. But between the clouds of bad news about Russia there are glimpses of good news. In the last five years Russians have repeatedly shown the will and the courage to resist reaction. Young people in particular cherish their new-found democracy and economic freedom. My forecast is that the next ten years, filled with misery as they will undoubtedly be, will be years of modest progress and increasing if cautious optimism. Russia's democracy will remain fragile but it will survive. Her economy will continue to respond to market forces and western opportunities, and it will begin to deliver the goods. Russian pensioners will still starve in attics, Russia's leaders will remain the heavy-handed bullies her tsars and commissars have always been, and her rich will continue to flaunt their wealth and their brassy molls. But other qualities will assert themselves: the courage that tackled the Chernobyl disaster, the scientific pre-eminence that took Russia into space, and the ordinary Russian's sheer capacity for everyday endurance.

As to the face that Russia presents to the world, I believe that in fighting her way towards this relative well-being she will recognise her need for others' goodwill, and accept that the price of international help is moderation in her attitudes towards the rest of the world. Over the next twenty years Russia will face enormous problems at home. She may be seeing not the end but the beginning of trouble in the southern republics. The Moslem world has the capacity to start new fires among Russia's Moslem millions. And a rich and assertive China cannot be anything other than a parlous neighbour. All this argues for Russia's good behaviour, and should restrain her from any attempt to revenge herself on her European neighbours for the humiliations of the last decade. If so, Russia will accept a cautious expansion of NATO into Poland, if not into the Baltic states. She will resolve her difficulties with Lithuania, Latvia and Estonia in ways that do not set the west's alarm bells ringing. She will continue, in short, on a course of co-operation rather than collision in the Baltic.

Besides Russia, there is a second great force at work around the Baltic. Four Baltic countries are members of the European Union. Germany was present at its creation. Denmark has been a member for over twenty years and Sweden and Finland since 1995. Poland is prominent among the leading central European candidates for membership, and Lithuania, Latvia and Estonia are eager to follow her. Within perhaps ten years, all the Baltic countries except Russia are likely to be members, committed to the Treaty of Rome's 'ever closer union', whatever that seductively tautologous or brilliantly ambiguous phrase may mean. The European Union will have as great an impact on the Baltic as did Sweden, Prussia, Russia and Germany in their earlier periods of predominance. It will be an effective counterweight to Russia in the region.

Today, Germany predominates in the north within the European Union even more decisively than she does in Europe as a whole. But the European Union is not just a cloak for her power in the Baltic. We saw in the previous chapter that she still summons up mixed emotions throughout the area. For her neighbours, as for Helmut Kohl and perhaps in moments of reflection for most Germans, the

European Union is a way of making Germany safe, harnessing her best qualities and holding the dubious ones at bay. This is the second reason why the Baltic nations welcome Brussels as a partner.

But the Baltic countries are no more agreed than those around the North Sea or the Mediterranean on the shape they want the European Union to take. For each of them brings different historical, political and economic baggage to the Union's affairs. For Germany, it is still an article of faith. Denmark still sees it more a matter of cold calculation. The same is true of Sweden and Finland, who also bring to the Union the realisation that it offers the nearest thing to a strategic guarantee that neutral nations can hope for. As for Poland and the Baltic states, they may not have fully digested all the implications of membership, but the European idea is an integral part of their hopes of a better world. It offers them a way to prosperity, an endorsement of their democracies and some guarantee of their security.

So Germany, for all her concern that the strengths of the Deutschmark should not be lost in a European currency, wants to see the Union continue on its measured way. When economic and monetary union comes, she will be a founder member. She wants a Union answerable to the European Parliament and pursuing a common foreign policy. Her leaders may not say so, but they would be happy to find a United States of Europe at the end of the rainbow. The Scandinavians lack the Germans' idealism; or perhaps they have more common sense. As for the Baltic candidates, their idealism about Europe is tempered by their idealism about their own recovered nationhood. The future shape and sense of the European Union is still to play for, in the Baltic as everywhere else in Europe.

Nevertheless, the European Union seems capable, however it develops, of acting as a pole of attraction for every country around the Baltic except Russia. It draws them closer to the European heartland and, simultaneously, to one another. It sets German pre-eminence in the north in a European context. And with American support it can counterbalance any Russian self-assertion in the eastern Baltic that might threaten to get out of hand. But it is not going to create, at least not at all easily or at all quickly, a single entity that submerges national identity and nation states.

For the Baltic countries, there remains another question. They prize their individuality and nationhood. They want the benefits of

European Union membership. Can they also develop an identity as a community of nations around the Baltic Sea, a distinct entity within the European family?

They have a common experience to draw on, a history of familiarity with one another that goes back centuries. The Scandinavians' sense of belonging together remains strong. The Baltic states reach across the sea towards Scandinavia; and Sweden, Finland, Norway and Denmark reciprocate. East German cities recall their Hansa origins, and Schleswig-Holstein sees the advantages that the growth of a Baltic identity can bring to it. The Finns maintain their symbiotic relationship with St Petersburg. Sweden and Poland talk incessantly to one another: about trade and transport; about politics and security; and about the pollution of the sea that lies between them.

Theorists propound elaborate ways of building on these affinities. They talk of Corona Baltica, a coming-together of all the members of the Council of Baltic Sea States. It offers a market potentially as significant as that of France or Italy, with 50 million consumers, some of them already rich, others with a well-nigh insatiable appetite for good things when they can afford them. Municipalities and chambers of commerce, think-tanks and cultural institutes cast around for ways of turning abstract theory into concrete substance, whether through a Hanseatic revival, exhibitions of Baltic art, town-twinnings across the sea, coalitions to fight pollution or the realisation of a distinct Baltic region within the European Union.

In May 1996 the presidents and prime ministers of all the countries around the Baltic held a summit conference in Gotland to discuss what more they can do together. They met in Visby, that quintessential Baltic city, and the political, economic and geographical realities which faced them were much the same as those which faced the merchants of the Hanseatic League 700 years ago. They decided on a series of initiatives to draw business, money and attention to the region. Some will sink and some will swim, but they rest on a conviction that the Baltic countries have interests and problems in common, as they had when the Vikings helped to found the first Russian state, when German salt was first used to cure Scandinavian herring, when Hansa merchants bought furs in Novgorod, and when the Knights brought civilisation and oppression, cruelty and the Cross to the pagan Prussians.

A Baltic identity is a prize worth having. It will not exclude a sense of belonging to Europe. It will not take the place of national identity

and love of country. But it expresses the simple truth that there is
something special about the Baltic. It is a reality that has survived
through bad times and good. Its persistence is yet another reason for
confidence about the future of the Baltic world.

Bibliographical Note

There are countless books that touch upon the Baltic. Each of the countries around it has its own story, and has attracted the attention of writers in English as well as its own language. So have the great Baltic themes, such as the Vikings, the Hanseatic League and the Teutonic Knights. But there are comparatively few books of substance that deal with the area as a whole. Outstanding among them in English is David Kirby's two-volume study, *The Baltic World 1492–1772* and *The Baltic World 1772–1993* (Longman, 1990 and 1995). An infinitely slighter book which nevertheless covers the whole area is Oliver Warner's *The Sea and the Sword* (Jonathan Cape, 1965). I found useful *The Struggle for Supremacy in the Baltic 1600–1725* (University of London Press, 1967), a textbook for sixth-formers. And Hilaire Belloc's *Return to the Baltic* (Constable, 1938) makes good sense of the physical characteristics of the Baltic Sea, even if most of the author's opinions are infuriatingly bombastic.

The range is vastly greater when attention shifts to individual countries or issues within the Baltic area. This is not a work of scholarship, but there is an *embarras de choix* among those that are. I particularly enjoyed Norman Davies's history of Poland, *God's Playground: a History of Poland* (Oxford University Press, 1981). Shorter and lighter treatments of Poland are to be found in his *Heart of Europe: a Short History of Poland* (Oxford University Press, 1984) and in Neal Ascherson's *The Struggles for Poland* (Michael Joseph, 1987). Ingvar Andersson's *A History of Sweden* (Weidenfeld & Nicolson, 1956) helped me make sense of Sweden's complex history and Stewart Oakley did the same for a country I know better in *The Story of Denmark* (Faber and Faber, 1972). Walter Bacon's *Finland* (Robert Hale, 1970) is a good general account of that surprisingly passionate country. Phillippe Dollinger's *The German Hansa* (Macmillan, 1970) describes the rise and fall of that astonishing medieval organisation, and Eric Christiansen's *The Northern Crusades: the*

Baltic and the Catholic Frontier 1100–1525 (Macmillan, 1980) explains the Teutonic Knights to English readers who know so little of them. John Hiden and Patrick Salmon are good on the twentieth-century history of the Baltic states in *The Baltic Nations and Europe* (Longman, 1991) and Anatol Lieven provides an extensive account of their recovery of independence in *The Baltic Revolution* (Yale University Press, 1993).

Wars play a large part in the story of the Baltic. C. V. Wedgwood's *The Thirty Years War* (Jonathan Cape, 1938) seems to my inexpert eye to have worn surprisingly well, as does Carola Oman's *Nelson* (Hodder & Stoughton, 1950). *The History of the Baltic Campaign of 1854* edited by Butler Earp (Bentley,1854) is a real curiosity, readier to recount Sir Charles Napier's disagreements with the Admiralty than his campaign against the Russians. Barbara Tuchman's *The Guns of August* (Dell, 1963) is very good on the 1914 Tannenberg campaign. Geoffrey Bennett's *Cowan's War* (Collins, 1964) describes the activities of the Royal Navy in the eastern Baltic in 1918–20 and Adam Zamoyski's *The Battle for the Marchlands* (Boulder, 1981) does the same for the Russo-Polish war of 1919–20. Anthony Upton is good on Finland's Winter and Continuation Wars (*Finland 1939–40* and *Finland in Crisis 1940-41*, Davis-Poynter, 1974 and Faber and Faber, 1964 respectively); and a newly-revised book, H. M. Tillotson's *Finland at Peace & War* (Michael Russell, 1996), also deals with the original War of Independence. Finally, Harrison Salisbury's *The Siege of Leningrad* (Secker & Warburg, 1969) is a vast and overblown but comprehensive story of the city's terrible 900 days.

Fiction and memoirs with a Baltic background offer something for all tastes. Thomas Mann's *Buddenbrooks* (Penguin, 1957) captures the claustrophobic life of Lübeck in decline, and Theodor Fontane's *Effi Briest* (Penguin, 1967) is as good on a Baltic port further east. The action of Erskine Childers's *The Riddle of the Sands* (Penguin, 1995) takes place mostly in the North Sea but it opens with some splendid sailing in the Baltic. Arthur Ransome's *Racundra's First Cruise* (Allen & Unwin, 1923) is another rousing sailing story by a man who, like Erskine Childers, had political depths to him. *Pelle the Conqueror* by Martin Anderson Nexø (Peter Smith, 1930) is a good book (which made a better film) about the life of contract labour in Bornholm in the late nineteenth century, and Czeslaw Milosz gives a lyrical account of life in rural Lithuania between the wars in *The Issa Valley* (Sidgwick & Jackson, 1981). He covers some of the same ground in his autobiography *Native Realm* (Sidgwick & Jackson, 1981) which is also excellent on life in Vilnius under Polish occupation and in Warsaw under German occupation. Tolstoy and Dostoevsky are both brilliant on St Petersburg. In *Coup de Grâce* (Aidan Ellis, 1983) Marguerite Yourcenar provides an exquisite insight into the tangled fighting in the Baltic states at the end of the First World War. In his second novel *Venusberg* (Duckworth, 1932) Anthony Powell captures many of the contradictions that suffused life in the Baltic states between the wars. Finally, William Palmer in his first novel *The Good Republic* (Secker & Warburg, 1990) gives a masterly impression of the practical and moral difficulties of everyday life in the Baltic states under German occupation.

Guidebooks are a matter of taste, but I found the *Rough Guides* consistently helpful. The *Insight Guide* to the Baltic states is also good, and superbly illustrated.

P.W.U.

Index

In a book about the Baltic, you may not expect to find index entries under 'Baltic, The', 'Baltic Sea', 'Baltic states', etc. You will find them here, with their sub-headings, in order that you may focus on Baltic essentials. Similarly, in a book about the Baltic and its countries, you may expect to find index entries under Denmark, Estonia, St Petersburg, Sweden, etc. You will find such entries here; and moreover you will find that these, being broken down as to national characteristics, historical events, and interplay with other nations and peoples etc., are virtually self-contained, especially when their 'see also' references are followed up. Proper names of artists, writers, monarchs, bishops, presidents, cities, towns, rivers, lakes etc., are indexed separately. Certain continuing themes, such as architecture, amber, cathedrals and churches, brick buildings characteristic of the Baltic, religions, wars, and lines of communication such as ferries and roads, are indexed as such – inviting the reader to explore further. Maps listed on page 6 are not indexed, neither are passing references or mere comparisons.

Note: In general, the term 'Baltic provinces' refers to the Baltic states under tsarist rule; the term 'Baltic republics' refers to the Baltic states under Soviet rule; and the term 'Baltic states' refers to them as independent nations.

106-7, 126, 174; landowners in, 109, 114; Baltic
states, Second World War occupation of, 116;
coastline, 15, 21, 31; Denmark, invasion of
(1940), 168; Denmark, relations and wars with,
227-30; East German economy, 43; Empire, 27,
79, 80, 229; Federal Republic of, 14, 31; German
Democratic Republic (GDR), 39, 42; Imperial
Navy, 232; Kaliningrad, visitors to, 74, 83;
Lithuania, invasion of (1941), 98; Middle Ages,
25-6; Norway, occupation of, 190, 202-3;
Poland, expulsion from (1945), 58; – influence
on, 70; – invasion of (1939), 64; – visitors to,
57-8; policy within European Union, 241-2;
post-Second World War division of, 30;
refugees, post-Second World War, 236;
reunification, 15, 31, 38, 43, 237; Treuhand, 42,
46; Roman times, 24-5; Russia defeated
(Tannenberg, 1914), 29; Russia, struggle with
for domination in Baltic, 29-30; trade, 26, 35-6,
61-2, 106, 174-5, 195; tribes, 24-5; troops against
Bolsheviks, 113; Stone Age, 23; Vilnius,
immigrants in, 99; see also Bismarck, Hanseatic
League, Hitler, Holstein, Mecklenburg-
Vorpommern, Pomerania, Prussia, Schleswig-
Holstein, Schleswig, Teutonic Adam, etc.,
Teutonic Knights
Goebbels, Joseph (1897-1945), 60-1
Goltz, Rüdiger von der, German commander on
eastern front (1917), 113
Gorbachev, Mikhail Sergeevitch (b.1931),
former President of Soviet Union, 41, 65, 95,
159, 240
GORI, Danish company, 221
Gorm the Old (c.885-950), King of Denmark, 211,
222
Gota Canal, between Gothenburg and E. Baltic,
193, 195
Gothenburg, Swedish port, 193
Gothenburg-America Line, 194
Goths, The, 24-5
Gotland, Swedish island, 14, 17, 165, 172, 173,
174-6, 211, 233, 243
Gottorf Castle, Schleswig, 231
Grass, Günter Wilhelm (b.1927), *The Tin Drum*,
59, 64; *The Call of the Toad*, 83-4; 217, 236
Great Belt, 19, 221
Great Northern War, 129
Greenland, 197; Danish possession, 210
Greifswald, German Hanseatic city, 47
Gustavus Adolfus II (1594- 1632), King of Sweden,
'Lion of the North', 11, 23, 48, 187, 188, 189,
194

Habsburgs, 23, 27, 29, 48, 99
Haderslev, Danish town, 220
Håkon VII (1872-1957), King of Norway, 198, 202
Halland, Sweden (former Danish province), 190,
191, 193
Hamburg, 21, 44, 165, 194, 209, 219, 226, 234, 236
Hamina, Finnish town, 150
Hammershus Castle, Bornholm, 168
Hangø, Finland, Soviet base, 157
Hanseatic League, Hansa, 10, 26, 36, 62, 68, 79,
121, 175, 176, 243; characteristics, 87, 88; cities
34, 41, 47, 62, 105, 124, 147; origins 243;

seafarers, seamen, 107, 125; trade, 25, 70, 106,
179, 198
Harald 'Bluetooth' (Gormsson) (910-85), King of
Denmark, 211
Hedeby (Haithabu), Viking port in Schleswig, 10,
231
Heiligendamm, German resort, 46
Hel, Polish resort, 64, 67
Heligoland Bight, 126
Helmstedt, German frontier post, 39
Helsingør, Danish port, 10, 20, 191, 205-6
Helsinki, 103, 142, 152-5, 160, 164, 172, 173, 183;
ancestry, 155; 'Athens of the North', fishing
settlement, Swedes' fortress of Sveaborg, 152;
Lutheran cathedral, Mannerheimintie, Uspenski
cathedral, 153; 'process' conferences, 154;
Saarinen's railway station, 153; see also
Finlandia Hall
Henry of Uppsala, patron saint of Finland (12th
century), 12, 161
Henry of Derby (1367-1413), later Henry IV, King
of England, 12; member of Teutonic Order, 79
Herbart, Johann Friedrich (1776-1841), 80
Herder, Johann Gottfried (1744-1803), 80, 126
Hertha, goddess, Rügen lake, 166, 167
Heyerdahl, Thor (b.1914), 202
Hiiumaa, Estonian island, 176, 177
Hill of Crosses, Lithuania, 92-3
Hindenburg, General Paul von Beneckendorff und
von (1847-1934), 29, 71, 97
Hitler, Adolf (1889-1945), 11, 29, 36, 48, 54, 64, 65,
69, 72, 81, 90, 98, 115, 116, 144-5, 157, 158, 188,
201, 202, 233, 236
Hudiksvall, Swedish town, 183
Hohenzollern, Albrecht von (Albert of
Brandenburg) (1490-1568), last Grand Master,
Teutonic Knights, 79
Hohenzollerns, 28, 28, 80, 112
Holstein, 210, 227; becomes, with Schleswig,
German *Land* (1945), 230; holidaymaking in,
233; NATO exercises in, 234; E. German
refugees in, 236; see also Schleswig-Holstein
Holy Roman Empire, 23, 26, 35, 174
Horne, Danish town, 222
Hughes, Reverend Edgar, *Two Summer Cruises
with the Baltic Fleet*, 172-3
Hungary, Hungarians, 65, 66

ice, 20, 22-3
Iceland, 85, 197, 210
Innocent III (1160-1216), Pope, 76
International Monetary Fund, 94
Iron Curtain, 37, 39, 235
islands, 10, 13, 14, 19, 47, 164-77, 178, 218, 233
Ivan IV (1530-84), 'the Terrible', Tsar of Russia,
141

Jelgava (Mitau), Latvian town, 110, 111
Jesuits, 80, 100, 129
Jews, Jewish, 116; exterminations of, 97-8, 100; in
Trakai, 99; in Vilnius, 99, 100; in Riga, 115;
Danish, 211
John Paul II, Pope (b.1920), 101
Juel, Niels (1629-97), Danish naval hero, 216
Jurmala, Latvian resort, 110